P9-BXW-894

KARAMZIN'S MEMOIR
ON
ANCIENT AND MODERN
RUSSIA

A TRANSLATION AND ANALYSIS

WITHDRAWN

N. M. Karamzin in 1815. *From a painting by V. A. Tropinin*

Richard Pipes

KARAMZIN'S MEMOIR

ON

ANCIENT AND MODERN

RUSSIA

A TRANSLATION AND ANALYSIS

ORIGINALLY PUBLISHED BY HARVARD UNIVERSITY PRESS AS
RUSSIAN RESEARCH CENTER STUDIES, NUMBER 33

ATHENEUM 1981 NEW YORK

141861

The Russian Research Center of Harvard University is supported by a grant from the Carnegie Corporation. The Center carries out interdisciplinary study of Russian institutions and behavior and related subjects.

This volume was prepared under a grant from the Carnegie Corporation of New York. That Corporation is not, however, the author, owner, publisher, or proprietor of this publication and is not to be understood as approving by virtue of its grant any of the statements made or views expressed therein.

Published by Atheneum
Reprinted by arrangement with Harvard University Press

Copyright © 1959 by the President and Fellows of Harvard College
All rights reserved
Library of Congress catalog card number 59-6484
ISBN 0-689-70157-8
Manufactured in the United States of America by
The Murray Printing Company, Forge Village, Massachusetts
Published in Canada by McClelland & Stewart Ltd.

First Atheneum Printing January 1966
Second Printing September 1969
Third Printing July 1872
Fourth Printing May 1974
Fifth Printing January 1981

TO IRENE

אֵשֶׁת חַיִל מִי יִמְצָא
וְרָחֹק מִפְּנִינִים מִכְרָהּ:

FOREWORD

In writing this book I wished to throw some light on a little-known yet very important aspect of Russian history, namely its conservative tradition. The core of the book is the political *chef d'œuvre* of an outstanding conservative thinker of the early nineteenth century, Nicholas Karamzin, the *Memoir on Ancient and Modern Russia*[1] (*Zapiska o drevnei i novoi Rossii*) in my own translation. I have supplied this work with explanatory notes, commentaries, and bibliographies, as well as with an introductory historical essay in which I try to provide the background of Karamzin's political thought in terms of both his environment and personal growth. The Harvard University Press is publishing simultaneously with this book a companion volume containing the original Russian text of the *Memoir*.

My interest in Russian conservatism has its origin in a feeling that the available interpretations of modern Russian history fail to explain, in intellectually and psychologically acceptable terms, the motivation of the rulers of Russia in the nineteenth and early twentieth centuries. Why did these men pursue a course of policy which in retrospect appears to have been so hopelessly unrealistic, and which, to boot, aroused the enmity of all that was best in Russian society? Above all: what accounts for their loyalty to the institution of autocracy? These questions are usually dismissed with off-hand references to historical blindness and bad intentions, or (in the case of Marxist and Stalinist historians) with assertions that the tsars and their associates had to act as they did because they were committed to defend certain class interests. Neither of these explanations seems satisfactory. Common sense compels us to reject the suggestion that a country of Russia's size and complexity could have been ruled by an unin-

[1] Often referred to as *Memorandum on Ancient and Modern Russia.*

terrupted succession of incompetents and hypocrites, and in this case common sense is buttressed by solid historical evidence: it can be shown that these same rulers administered their domain with sufficient skill to withstand repeated internal and external challenges to their authority; and that, furthermore, the system they represented enjoyed the support of many of Russia's outstanding national minds, men whose intelligence and knowledge of their country is beyond doubt. The class-interpretation is equally unacceptable, although for other reasons: above all because it is not possible to ascribe any definite class-complexion to the Russian monarchy. When all is said and done, the behavior of Russia's ruling groups in the century preceding the Revolution of 1917 remains a mystery. Something is clearly missing, and that something is a dispassionate explanation of the rational and emotional motivation of the men in power, that is, of those men who tried to conserve rather than to change.

The reason for this lacuna in Russian historiography is not far to seek. The writing of modern Russian history has been largely the preserve of Russian scholars whose own political views were either liberal or socialist, that is, of persons who were in varying degrees hostile to the old regime. The history of tsarism in the nineteenth and twentieth centuries was for them not an object of mere intellectual curiosity, but a political weapon which they used in their struggle for reform or revolution. However good their intentions, they could not approach the subject with the detachment and with the empathy which history requires. Most of these scholars, particularly the liberals who were very numerous among academic people (e.g. Pypin, Miliukov, Kornilov), were firmly convinced that the tsarist order was a hopeless anachronism from which there was nothing to learn, and which sooner or later would have to give way to a Western-type parliamentary democracy.

The course of Russian history since 1917 has demonstrated that their prognostications were wrong, and thereby thrown some doubt on the premises from which these prognostications had been derived. Thus a revision was in order. But since 1917 Russian historiography both within and without the Soviet

Union has been subject to political influences of a different kind, influences which in their own way also have hampered the judgment of scholars. The revolutionary events of 1917 produced an irresistible temptation to treat the entire development of modern Russian history as a grand prelude to the debacle of 1917. Hence, the post-1917 tendency of Russian historians has been to emphasize the shortcomings, crises, and failures of the old regime, rather than its positive achievements, in order to explain how the revolution came about. This approach, too, makes it difficult to reach a just appraisal of the men and ideas who had dominated the *ancien régime*.[2]

Only today, perhaps, has it become possible to approach this subject with the requisite detachment: the quarrels and political conflicts which perturbed prerevolutionary Russian scholarship have died down, acquiring a purely academic interest, while the revolution itself has settled, and it is easier now to determine in what respects the Soviet state follows and in what respects it departs from the practices of its predecessor.

The greatest single remaining obstacle in the investigation of Russian conservatism (including in this concept all movements dedicated to the preservation of absolute monarchy in Russia) is the scarcity of secondary studies dealing with its individual phases and aspects. Compared with the plethora of books and articles on Russian revolutionaries, the shortage of studies of the men who identified themselves with the regime, and, in many cases, shouldered the main burdens of administrative responsibility, is indeed appalling. There are no full-scale biographies of such influential statesmen and thinkers as Uvarov, Dmitrii Tolstoy, Katkov, or Stolypin; the others are rarely better served.[3]

[2] These words are not meant as strictures. The problem of treating an historical epoch as a self-contained unit which is not influenced by what ensues and yet leads up to it, is most difficult to solve under the best conditions. The author once tried, in the course of lectures dealing with nineteenth- and early twentieth-century Russian history, to de-emphasize the "road to disaster" pattern, until, his narrative having reached the year 1900, he discovered to his dismay that in terms of what *he* had emphasized, there should have been no revolutions of 1905 or 1917.

[3] A shining exception to this rule is the brilliant biography of Samarin by Baron B. Nolde: *Iurii Samarin i ego vremiia* (Paris, 1926).

The study of Russian conservatism, therefore, entails, first of all, the preparation of a series of monographic studies.

The need for such spadework became vividly clear to me at the beginning of my research. I had tried to secure a copy of Karamzin's *Memoir on Ancient and Modern Russia,* a work mentioned in most of the histories of Russia in connection with the reign of Alexander I, and found to my surprise that there was neither a definitive edition of this document, nor a scholarly biography of its author. In view of the place which the *Memoir* occupies in the history of Russian political thought in general, and in that of conservatism in particular, I decided to begin my investigations by preparing an annotated edition of this work: an edition which may, at the same time, serve as something of an introduction to the conservative thought of the reign of Alexander I.

In conclusion, one more question calls for an answer: why (pragmatically speaking), concern oneself with a movement which had failed, and whose resuscitation, at least in its original form, seems less than likely? To this question there are two answers. In the first place, the Russian conservative movement, although ideologically and historically associated with the institution of absolute monarchy, has in fact a much broader scope than this association indicates. As further analysis will reveal, Russian conservatism (like conservatism everywhere) is not only a political philosophy but also an intellectual movement, whose connection with a given political system is to a large extent a historical accident. It reflects a side of Russian civilization which subsists independently of governmental forms, and as such has lasting interest.

The second argument has less to do with Russian factors than with general historiographic ones. It is a commonplace among historians to say that the writing of history represents an attempt to interpret the past in terms of the present, and that, consequently, each generation reappraises past events in the light of its own concerns. It is also generally recognized that the historian — no matter how conscientious — is compelled by the nature of his subject to select from the endless variety of past events only those which are germane to his theme, and, in so doing, to play down or ignore altogether events which he finds irrelevant. These, so to say, "non-objective" qualities are built into the discipline of history: they are not pitfalls, which one can strive to avoid, but attributes, without which the writing of history is possible perhaps in theory, but never in practice. These properties of the discipline do, however, entail certain grave professional dangers. The principal danger is that they may induce the historian to disregard important trends of the past because they momentarily seem to have run out. To do so is not only to pervert the picture of the past, but also to becloud our understanding of the present and the future. We have no right to assume that the present — our natural point of departure — constitutes a fixed, unalterable terminal point, rather than another phase in the endless process of historical change. What assurance have we, appearance notwithstanding, that our era and its ideals will not themselves become "lost causes," and, conversely, that the causes which we presently consider "lost" are not destined to triumph some day? We simply do not know (one need only recall the fate of that famous Russian who with such supreme confidence relegated his opponents to the "trashbin of history"!). And as long as we do not know we would be ill-advised to dismiss lost causes or to ignore those who, in Dr. Johnson's phrase, "have the hiss of the world against them."

The present edition of Karamzin's *Memoir on Ancient and Modern Russia,* is based on that published by V. V. Sipovskii (N. M. Karamzin, *Zapiska o drevnei i novoi Rossii,* St. Petersburg, 1914), collated with the editions of Pushkin, Einerling, Bartenev, and Pypin. All these editions are discussed in the section called "History of the Text." In order to keep the text as free of notes as possible no variants are noted in the translation.

The document around which this book is built presents many problems of translation. It must be remembered that the *Memoir on Ancient and Modern Russia* was written in haste, and that it was not intended for publication. This means that it not only lacks the polish, clarity, and consistency of more formal writing, but lapses into colloquialisms which are occasionally quite ob-

scure. These features help make it an unusually fine example of
early nineteenth-century Russian prose, and in some respects it is
the outstanding stylistic achievement of an author whose principal fault was a weakness for excessively flowery language.
But these features also obstruct the work of the translator who
at times finds himself confronted with passages which have no
apparent subject or ending. My first inclination was to produce
a translation which resembled the original as much as possible.
But the result of this effort was unintelligible, and I replaced
it with one which was somewhat freer; whenever the thought was
in conflict with the actual wording, or was confused by it, I
favored the thought. And although I am still not certain that
I have translated correctly all of the more obscure passages, I do
feel fairly confident that my translation represents a faithful
rendition of the letter and spirit of the original.

In preparing this book I was fortunate to have the help of
the following persons, whose kindness I would like to acknowledge with gratitude: Professors Michael Karpovich, William L.
Langer and Robert L. Wolff who read the manuscript and gave
me many useful suggestions; Dr. David Perkins and Professor
Klaus Epstein who advised me on various aspects of the book;
Mrs. V. Weintraub and Mr. T. Sadowski who helped with the
collations; and Mrs. Lee Ambrose who did the editorial work.
I am also obliged to the Institute of History of the Soviet Academy of Sciences, and in particular to its director, Professor A. L.
Sidorov, for enabling me to gain access to Soviet historical archives. Finally, I want to thank two institutions: the Russian
Research Center which has shown me great understanding and
generosity when I was engaged in the basic research for this book,
and the J. S. Guggenheim Memorial Foundation, whose un-
restricted grant made it possible for me to write it in the pleasant
environment of Paris.

                                              Richard Pipes

October 1958

CONTENTS

N. M. KARAMZIN

A MEMOIR ON ANCIENT AND MODERN RUSSIA

*(Karamzin did not divide his MEMOIR ON ANCIENT
AND MODERN RUSSIA into parts, nor did he supply it
with a table of contents. The table which follows has been
prepared by the editor.)*

KARAMZIN'S MEMOIR

ON

ANCIENT AND MODERN

RUSSIA

A TRANSLATION AND ANALYSIS

"To live is not to write history, not to write tragedies or comedies, but to think as well as one can, to feel and to act, to love goodness, to strive with one's soul toward its source. Everything else, my dear friend, is a shell, including my own eight or nine volumes. The longer we live, the more clearly do we understand the purpose and ideal of life. Passions ought not to bring happiness, but to cultivate the soul. . . . There is little difference between trivial occupations and so-called important ones: all that matters is the inner motive and the feeling. Do the best you can, only love goodness, and what goodness is your conscience will tell you."

Karamzin to A. I. Turgenev (1815).

THE BACKGROUND AND GROWTH
OF KARAMZIN'S POLITICAL IDEAS
DOWN TO 1810

The French Revolution compelled every European society which had ever felt the breath of the Enlightenment to re-examine the foundations of its national life. It did not take contemporaries long to realize that the events taking place in France after 1789 were much more fundamental in their effects than would have been the case with a mere succession of political readjustments: it soon became clear that they marked something of a breaking point in the history of modern civilization, and that they challenged the very premises which had underlay European development for generations. As soon as the revolution had evolved beyond its early phases, there emerged a significant body of public opinion which upheld the proposition that the revolution was a logical consequence of the injuries inflicted on the ancient stabilizing forces of society by the corrosive actions of philosophic criticism. Even those opponents of the revolution who were not prepared to go along with this thesis on the whole agreed that there was some causal connection between the revolution and the antitraditionalist movements of the eighteenth century.

The reaction to the French Revolution throughout Europe expressed itself first and foremost in a desire to revert to tradition, to those habits and institutions whose weakening, it was widely believed, had led directly to the revolutionary upheavals. But before this could be done, the tradition had to be defined. This was no easy task, for the problem as posed was really unsound, a *Scheinproblem*, a "pseudo-problem," as Max Planck would have called it: there was, in fact, no clear dichotomy between "tradition" and "innovation." Europe had never stood still, it had always grown and changed, and the Enlightenment, the very force of change, was itself an intrinsic part of the European tradition. But the answers to this artificial problem were needed, and they were found.

To furnish the solution, or solutions, was the task of conservative movements. The conservatives took it upon themselves to reveal the hidden causes of the revolution, to define those factors which gave society strength and the capacity for peaceful development, and on the basis of this analysis to construct positive political programs. The conflict between traditionalists and innovators, of course, was nothing new in Europe, but it is only after 1789 that it assumed the form of a continuing public debate, a debate which divided every European society into two principal blocks, that of reformers, or liberals, and that of traditionalists, or conservatives.[1]

Conservatism was by its very nature more diversified than liberalism. The liberals, who espoused the ideals of the Enlightenment, wished to change society in accord with certain principles which all of them held in common; liberty, equality, fraternity meant much the same thing in Greece and Spain, Russia and Germany, at least programmatically. Liberalism was international, cosmopolitan, and its adherents regarded the triumph of liberal ideals anywhere in the world as a personal triumph. Not so the conservatives. The conservatives did have in common certain basic attitudes, for their movements developed in reaction to the same set of circumstances; but their attention was focused on local, particular factors. The search for traditions, for roots, naturally took a different course in every country, depending on its conditions. Thus, apart from the fact that people who are against something are less likely to agree than those who are for something, the conservatives lacked that sense of cohesion and of common interest which gives reform movements their vitality. Conservatism was heterogeneous, and the positive programs which its exponents advanced in various countries were

---

[1] Within this classification, the socialists belong with the liberals, as an offshoot, rather than to a separate, third, category.

often mutually incompatible. Paraphrasing Tolstoy, it may be said that while all liberals were alike, all conservatives were conservative in their own way.

For this reason conservatism is perhaps of greater interest to the historian of social and political institutions than it is to the historian of ideas. Ideas, we feel, must be true, and to be true they must be (or, at least, claim to be) universal. The variety and conflict of the conservative philosophies of various countries does not tend to inspire confidence in their soundness. They are obviously more pragmatic, more closely connected with the interests of those who espouse them, than are reform philosophies which, whatever their shortcomings, are at least in broad accord on fundamentals. How can one take seriously a political philosophy which in one country advocates monarchic absolutism, in another parliamentary monarchy, and in a third decentralization and republicanism? But, conversely, this very diversity indicates how useful a source of information conservative movements are for the historian of society: they reflect better than do reform movements the actual disposition of social forces, and the nature of the relationship between political institutions and social groups.

This holds true particularly of countries, such as Russia, where the social and political base of the forces striving for reform was generally weaker than it was among the forces striving for preservation. Both liberalism and its by-product, socialism, were in Russia imported forces which, even after they began to play a significant political role, lacked concrete social foundations. Interesting as these movements may be from the intellectual standpoint, they throw precious little light on the driving forces of Russian history. Conservatism, on the other hand, is in Russia native in inception as well as development. No other political movement offers such valuable insights into the inner processes of Russian politics.[2]

---

[2] Russia possesses another indigenous political movement, namely peasant anarchism; but though native in its origin, at the level of ideology it was always more heavily influenced by Western than by native examples. Bakunin and Kropotkin, the leaders of the Russian anarchist movement, are European figures *par excellence*.

In Russia, the conservative movement was born of a marriage between the gentry and the monarchy. To understand its genesis and its characteristics, it is necessary to make a brief excursion into the eighteenth-century background of these two institutions.

Of all the perennial problems facing the Russian monarchy none was more vexing than the inadequacy of the human and material resources available to rule the vast territories to which it claimed title, and to carry out its ambitious program of Westernization. Russia's geographic location, on the edge of an enormous continent, with a fluid frontier and restless neighbors, had induced her rulers since the fifteenth century to expand more rapidly than the country's internal resources warranted, with the result that the growth of the territory had usually outstripped the means available for its administration and defense. In consequence of this situation, in the sixteenth and seventeenth centuries the monarchy failed to secure a good grip on its far-flung possessions: the farther a province lay from the capital, the less subject it was to government control. Notwithstanding the monarchy's claim to absolute, autocratic authority, and the dismay with which some contemporary European observers contemplated the "tyrannical" nature of Russian governments, the fact remains that the effective authority of the Russian tsars over the mass of their subjects was considerably weaker than that exercised by their more enlightened Western counterparts. Compared to the France of Louis XIV, for example, seventeenth-century Russia was a veritable no man's land. In times of internal disorder, the power of the tsars hardly extended beyond the capital city itself.

To meet this problem, the Moscow government kept on recruiting at home and abroad large numbers of servitors for its civil and military establishments. Moscow was traditionally a place of refuge for soldiers of fortune, for disaffected individuals or groups, and for other elements who for one reason or another felt compelled to leave their homelands, and seek land and office abroad. This accounts for the unusually high proportion of families of foreign origin among the Russian nobility.[3] Despite intense efforts in this direction, the Moscow state never succeeded in enrolling in its service as many men as it required.

The monarchy's problems were compounded by the shortage of money. Russia lay outside the major trade routes of the modern world and hence did not participate in the commercial expansion which Western Europe underwent after the late Middle Ages. Her economy in the sixteenth and seventeenth centuries was still primarily a natural one: money was rarely seen in the cities, and hardly ever in the countryside. To reimburse its servitors, the government had to fall back on its resources in land which, thanks to its continuous expansion into sparsely populated or totally uninhabited areas, it had in relative abundance.

But the government not only had to administer and defend an enormous domain — it also wished to change it. One of the characteristic features of the Russian monarchical tradition was what Paul Miliukov had called its "critical" attitude. This attitude expressed itself in its dissatisfaction with things as they were and in its relentless efforts to transform Russia in accord with an essentially Western image. In Russia, the monarchy was traditionally a dynamic force, determined to reform and reshape society. In this striving it had to contend with social groups which resisted innovation and wished to preserve the *status quo:* the old aristocracy (composed of the descendants of princely and boyar families), the church establishment, and various other,

[3] One can form an idea of this proportion from the fact that in the middle of the nineteenth century, when Prince P. Dolgorukov undertook his great (but, unfortunately, uncompleted) genealogy of the Russian aristocracy, two thirds of Russia's sixty surviving families of counts were of foreign descent. They included defectors from the Golden Horde in the fourteenth and fifteenth centuries (Apraksins, Uvarovs), and the Crimea (Rostopchins); Germans who had migrated to Russia in the Middle Ages (Tolstoys, Buturlins, Golenishchev-Kutuzovs), and even more those who had entered Russian service in the eighteenth century from Germany proper as well as the Baltic provinces; Polish noblemen who had settled in Russia in the sixteenth and seventeenth centuries (e.g. Potemkins), and even occasional Frenchmen and Scotsmen. P. Dolgorukov, *Rossiiskaia rodoslovnaia kniga* (4 vols.; St. Petersburg, 1854–57), II, 111–277.

minor groups, all of which Miliukov classified as the "national opposition." [4] To carry on the fight against the reluctant forces of society, the monarchy needed a dependent, Westernized class which could serve it as a trusted weapon.

All three of these problems: the shortage of personnel, the lack of money, and the resistance of traditionalist elements, the monarchy tried to resolve by encouraging the development of a numerous servitor gentry. The process began with the very birth of the Moscow state, and reached its climax in the legislation of Peter I, which created a vast and (theoretically at least) homogeneous class of state servitors known first as *shliakhta* and later as *dvorianstvo*. This class in large measure set the tone of Russian history throughout the eighteenth century.

The modern Russian gentry came into being in consequence of a series of laws promulgated by Peter I, which received their final form in the Table of Ranks. The Table of Ranks merged the ancient nobility, the military gentry, and the various branches of state and court officialdom, into a single class of state servitors, required to render the monarchy permanent service. According to Petrine legislation, all male persons of gentle birth were required to enter one of the four branches of state service (court, civil service, army, or navy), and conversely, every state servitor, regardless of his social origin, was automatically admitted into the ranks of the gentry once he attained to a sufficiently high rank. The great innovation of the Petrine reform was that it gave the bureaucratic element precedence over the aristocratic: gentility was the product of service, and could neither be acquired nor retained without it. In this respect the Russian gentry differed fundamentally from what is normally understood by the term aristocracy, which is distinguished by the unconditional inheritance of titles. In an ideal aristocracy rank follows from social status; in the Petrine system, social status followed from rank.

The Russian gentry as conceived by Peter differed from an

---

[4] The conflict of these two tendencies constitutes the principal theme of Miliukov's masterpiece, the third volume of his *Ocherki po istorii russkoi kul'tury*.

aristocracy in still another respect: they were not a privileged estate. The Russian gentry were, of course, given important powers not extended to other classes, powers which could be construed as forms of privilege. The most important among these were extensive rights over proprietary serfs and exemption from the payment of taxes. But these powers were not so much privileges as obverse sides of obligations: the control which the gentry exercised over the peasants was intrinsically connected with their responsibilities for local administration which Peter had imposed on them; while the exemption from taxes resulted from the fact that of all the classes in Russia the gentry alone were required to render universal, continuous state service — they thus met state obligations with personal labor, rather than with money. Indeed, the obligations of the gentry to the state were so onerous, that the leading authority on the history of this class feels justified in speaking of the "bondage of the gentry to the crown," and in asserting that there was no vital difference between the degree of responsibility of the gentry to the state, and that of the peasantry to the gentry.[5]

The Petrine gentry were democratic, in the sense that their ranks were always open to commoners moving upward in the military or civil hierarchy. This feature, too, mitigated against the gentry considering themselves a nobility, or even a social estate in the proper sense of the word.

Under Peter the lot of the gentry was far from easy. Held in the iron grip of the state, they had to serve where and how the government wanted, and lacked occasion to enjoy the few amenities which their position afforded. Even the landed property which the state servitors held in hereditary possession by virtue of state service was not entirely at their disposal, since Peter, in an effort to prevent the break up and pauperization of gentry holdings, required them to leave their land to a single heir. What made the gentry's position particularly onerous was the discrepancy between their status and their education. In order to develop Russia's military and economic resources, Peter sub-

[5] A. Romanovich-Slavatinskii, *Dvorianstvo v Rossii ot nachala XVIII v. do otmeny krepostnogo prava* (2nd ed.; Kiev, 1912), pp. xvii and 151.

jected the entire gentry to a compulsory, Western-style education, which, although purely pragmatic in its intent, could not
fail to leave some imprint on the mind and the soul. Culturally
as well as materially the monarchy had given the gentry all that
was necessary to lead a pleasant existence; all that they wanted
were security and leisure. After the death of Peter I in 1725, the
gentry concentrated their efforts on the attainment of these two
objectives, striving to reduce their duties and to augment their
rights. In other words, they endeavored to consolidate the privileges granted them by the monarchy on the condition of service,
while doing away with the conditions themselves. The whole
history of the gentry for the next sixty years is the history of their
transformation from a class of dependent state servitors into a
full-fledged nobility.

This process began as early as the reigns of Peter's two immediate successors, Catherine I and Peter II, but it was only during
the brief interregnum which followed the death of Peter II
(1730) that it got underway in earnest. During this brief period
the crown, weakened by Peter I's abolition of the law of royal
primogeniture, found itself challenged by a small group of top
state administrators sitting in the Supreme Privy Council who
were attempting to take advantage of the crown's temporary impotence in order to impose on it permanent legal limitations.
The balance of power lay in the hands of the gentry. After some
hesitation the gentry sided with the monarchy, thereby assuring
the survival of absolute monarchy in Russia, and at the same
time initiating that long-lasting partnership between the gentry
and the crown which, within a generation, enabled them to
throw off altogether the yoke imposed on them by Peter I.

This decision was made in the course of a few eventful weeks
at the beginning of 1730. The sudden death of Peter II left
Russia without a legitimate heir to the throne, and confronted
the men actually responsible for the direction of state affairs —
the high state officials, the ecclesiastical leaders, and the military
commanders — with a set of unprecedented problems: Who
should succeed to the throne? By what legal procedure should
the choice be made? Was it advisable to take advantage of the

monarchy's predicament to impose conditions, or, at any rate, to exact rights and privileges from it? The natural instinct of all the parties involved was to settle on a weak monarch, preferably a woman, and to make use of their power to gain concrete benefits: this attitude characterized the *verkhovniki,* that is the members of the Supreme Privy Council, who had for five years ruled Russia and were quite loath to surrender their authority, the lower officialdom, as well as the disorganized, politically ineffective gentry, who wanted an easing of the conditions of state service and a firmer grip on their land and peasantry.[6] The first indications, therefore, were that Russia would emerge from the crisis of 1730 as a limited monarchy. But this did not occur, largely owing to the lack of political experience and the mutual distrust of the groups involved.

The movement favoring the imposition of formal limitations on the monarchy, initiated by the Supreme Privy Council, met at first, in its theoretical phase, with a sympathetic response from both the bureaucracy and the gentry. The *verkhovniki,* drawing on the experience of contemporary Sweden and intending to establish in Russia a system in which all the effective legislative power would be vested in the Council, compiled a set of "conditions" which they presented to Anne of Courland as a prerequisite to obtaining the throne. But when they did so they at once ran into resistance from other groups. Confronted with the prospect of concrete limitations on the monarchy, the high civil and military officials (known collectively as the *generalitet*) and the mass of the gentry had some second thoughts. What worried them was the absence of all assurance that the members of the Council would not use the authority acquired by virtue of the new arrangement for their own, private interests, which were publicly identified with the interests of the old aristocracy. Should this be the case, the power of the central government would be not diminished, but merely reapportioned. Lefort, the

[6] The best account of the events of 1730 is in D. A. Korsakov's *Votsarenie Imperatritsy Anny Ioannovny* (Kazan, 1880). Important additional data on the pro-autocratic tendencies and theories in the first half of the eighteenth century are to be found in Korsakov's *Iz zhizni russkikh deiatelei XVIII veka* (Kazan, 1891), especially the studies of Tatishchev and Volynskii.

Saxon-Polish legate residing in Moscow at the time, summarized
thus the misgivings of the gentry:

> Who will guarantee us that with time we shall not have instead of one
> sovereign as many tyrants as there are members sitting in the Council,
> and that their oppressive policies will not worsen our bondage? The
> Council has no firm laws to abide by: should its members take to issuing
> laws, then they shall also have the power to annul laws at will, where-
> upon Russia will fall prey to anarchy.[7]

Two other circumstances helped to consolidate the opposition
forces. One was the secrecy with which the Council carried on
negotiations with Anne, particularly its failure to take others
into confidence on the subject of the conditions. This behavior
confirmed latent suspicions that the Council was really interested
not in abolishing absolute power but in acquiring absolute
power for itself. The other had to do with the composition of
the Council. The leaders of the drive to impose limitations on
the monarchy, notably the Golitsyns and the Dolgorukis, represented the ancient Russian aristocratic families known to have
been opposed to many of Peter's reforms, and most particularly
to his degradation of the true aristocracy in favor of a mass-
produced, parvenu gentry. Here, too, the gentry had good cause
to suspect the motivation of the antiautocratic forces. What the
gentry wanted was not an undoing of Petrine reforms and a
return to the conditions prevailing in the seventeenth century,
but a consolidation of the privileges which these reforms had
granted them.

But what could the gentry, and the other groups which had
benefited from Peter's reforms, oppose to the aristocratic program of the *verkhovniki?* The trouble was that Russians had
never before had the opportunity of engaging in public discussions of fundamental political problems and therefore understood but dimly the alternatives to the existing system. Thus, as
the opposition to the Council crystallized, it tended more and
more to fall back on what was considered Russia's traditional
form of government, namely autocracy. Even this concept was
only vaguely defined. In studying the history of Russian political

[7] Korsakov, *Votsarenie Imperatritsy Anny,* p. 93.

thought between the fifteenth and the eighteenth centuries one is struck by the intellectual poverty of the whole autocratic tradition: Russia had neither Hobbeses nor Bossuets, nor even Filmers. Perhaps the absence of any serious opposition made it unnecessary to evolve a philosophical justification of absolutism; this was formulated only in the mid-nineteenth century, when the doctrine of autocracy was for the first time seriously challenged by liberal and socialist thinkers. In the 1730's the absolutist argument never went beyond simple *fiats,* such as those pronounced by the two leading apologists of the Petrine system, the preacher Feofan Prokopovich, and the historian Tatishchev, both of whom played prominent parts in the restoration of autocracy in 1730. "The nature of the Russian people is such," wrote Feofan, "that it can be safeguarded only by an autocratic power; should it adopt any other form of government, nothing will be able to keep it united and prosperous." [8] And Tatishchev: "The autocratic system of government is in Russia the most useful; all the others are dangerous." [9] Both thinkers fortified their argument with references to the divine origin of all authority, the immensity of the Russian realm, and the need for centralization of government (ideas partly borrowed from contemporary Western political thought), but these arguments never sank root in Russian consciousness.

Autocracy, of course, meant an unlimited, self-sufficient monarchy, in which there were no legal or institutional constraints on the tsar's authority. But one must bear in mind that the vastness of the Russian territory, coupled with the inadequacy of the means at the government's disposal, imposed on the tsar's power natural limits far more effective than any constitutions or consultative bodies might have done. One suspects, therefore, that when the gentry spoke of the autocrat they had in mind a fairly remote figure residing in St. Petersburg, one who did not exercise any direct control over the life of the country at large. The choice between an autocratic tsar and an aristocratic council was to them not so much a choice between different systems of gov-

[8] N. I. Popov, *V. N. Tatishchev i ego vremia* (Moscow, 1861), p. 104.
[9] *Ibid.,* p. 118.

ernment as a choice between the same autocratic system em-
bodied in one person and in a collective of eight persons. That
the government could be subject to direct control from below
did not enter into consideration at all in these confused days of
1730, when Russians for the first time in their history were able
to debate openly their country's political system.

Ambiguous as the concept of monarchical autocracy was from
the theoretical viewpoint, it had the immense virtue of being
readily understood; it was far easier for politically untutored
minds to conceive of a single, concrete individual vested with
full executive, legislative, and judiciary power, than of a vast
and complex system of legal and institutional safeguards necessary to carry on the business of constitutional government. This
simple solution appealed the more in that it also satisfied self-
interest. The autocrat was in many ways dependent on the
gentry, which formed the backbone of his military and civil
establishment. A strong monarch like Peter I could compel the
gentry to do his bidding, and this was a risk one had to take
with the autocratic system; but the chances of another Peter
appearing were remote, especially since Peter, by doing away
with the law of primogeniture, had made it possible to select
only malleable monarchs. Anne herself certainly gave no cause
for fear on this score.

Impelled by self-interest and armed with such arguments, the
gentry and the *generalitet,* backed by the high clergy, neutralized
the efforts of the Council and helped the monarchy to reassert
unlimited authority. This event marked the beginning of a lasting alliance between the crown and the gentry: the former depending on the latter for the services which it could not perform
with its own resources; the latter depending on the former for
help in acquiring the status of a privileged estate of the realm.

There is no need here to recount the steps by means of which
the gentry emancipated themselves from the Petrine bondage.
Beginning with the law of 1731, which permitted the gentry to
distribute landed estates freely among their heirs, through the
laws limiting the length of compulsory state service to twenty-
five years and granting the right to retain one son at home, the

monarchy progressively lightened the gentry's obligations and increased their rights, until, in 1762, it brought this process to its logical conclusion by freeing the gentry from the duty of bearing state service. Altogether, it is difficult to exaggerate the importance of the edict of 1762 for Russia's social and cultural history. With this single act the monarchy created a large, privileged, Westernized leisure class, such as Russia had never known before.

By the time this edict was passed, the gentry had already forgotten the inferior status from which they had originally emerged, and evolved a whole myth based upon the contention that they were historically descended from an ancient feudal nobility. By virtue of this myth some spokesmen for the nobility, outstanding among whom was Prince Shcherbatov, demanded that the monarchy grant the gentry corporate status, and deny access to that estate to all commoners, who were still able to enter it through promotion in state service. The absence of reliable historical studies prevented the exposure of this myth. It partly explains why Catherine II bestowed upon the gentry in 1785 a charter legally affirming all the rights which they had acquired in the preceding sixty years, supplemented by rights of her own making, which transformed the gentry into a privileged corporate estate. This charter granted them permanent exemption from the payment of taxes and gave them the exclusive right to own populated estates, as well as the rights of assembly, free speech, trial by peers, and many other important privileges and rights which never before had been granted as a body to any group in Russia. The 1785 Charter to the Nobility marked the culminating point in the history of the Russian gentry, the embodiment of all its historic ambitions, and also the beginning of its gradual decline.

Little wonder that the gentry made no attempt to translate their recent social and economic gains into terms of political power, being content to leave the reins of government in the hands of the monarchy. The gentry were a thoroughly satisfied class, which stood to gain nothing and to lose much from any change in the political regime: the iniquity of a system in which one class had all the privileges and the remaining classes all the duties mitigated against the privileged class's displaying great political ambitions. In fact, the gentry's distaste for politics went so far that they were recalcitrant to take advantage of the right to corporate self-rule granted them in the 1785 charter, or to participate in the organs of local government established by the state, because all political responsibility, even that freely exercised, smacked to them of the detested compulsory state service from which they had only a short time before freed themselves. At the legislative commission which Catherine II assembled in 1767 to prepare a new code of laws, the gentry displayed little interest in central government; they were almost exclusively concerned with their estate rights, and they wished above all to secure complete freedom from all government interference in the running of their villages. The gentry's ideal was something in the nature of a dyarchy, in which the monarchy had charge of "high politics": diplomacy, finance, war, etc., and the gentry had charge of the countryside. Within its own sphere of competence each of these two authorities was to have full power. The gentry, therefore, remained faithful to the ideal of royal absolutism: it was the only way of maintaining in practice their own manorial absolutism. As long as there were in Russia no other major contenders for political power, such an arrangement was feasible as well as profitable.

At the time the only potential source of danger lay in the constant growth of a professional state bureaucracy. After 1762 the gentry tended to avoid the civil service, despite the preferential treatment which was accorded to them, particularly in matters of promotion; office-clerking did not suit the lofty notions which the gentry had of their ancestry and function. The gentry preferred to serve in the army, not to speak, of course, of the diplomatic corps and the court, which were highly desirable but open only to the rich. For all but the highest posts, the government, therefore, had no choice but to draw the bulk of its civil service from the nonprivileged classes, especially the clergy and burghers. Although the gentry did not respond to the state's appeals that they enter the civil service, they were jealous of those who did, and resented profoundly the fact that another group was in a position to wedge itself between them and the throne. They liked to remind the monarchy of its duty to administer the country with the aid of the nobility, and they were particularly fond of quoting Montesquieu's dictum: "No monarchy, no nobility; no nobility, no monarchy." Hence, too, their insistence on a small, frugal government, and their scorn for the *liudi krapivnogo semeni* — the pettifoggers, the ink-stained scribes, who dared to usurp the functions which tradition (so they said) had reserved for the gentry. The hostility of the gentry toward the bureaucracy, which was not as yet very pronounced in the reign of Catherine II, in view of the relative smallness of the civil establishment, became in the subsequent century one of the hallmarks of the conservative movement in Russia.

During the second half of the eighteenth century the gentry consisted of three fairly distinguishable categories. The richest element, comprising those who through inheritance, favoritism, high state service, or other means (including commerce) had accumulated large fortunes, usually either settled down in St. Petersburg and Moscow, or went abroad. The life of the members of this category closely resembled that of contemporary Western titled nobility; they often had patrician aspirations, although very few of them could trace their titles or possessions further back than three or four generations. The rich gentry were especially eager to close ranks and to outlaw automatic ennoblement of the lower orders by means of service promotion.

The middle gentry, consisting of gentlemen affluent enough to live away from their estates but not quite enough to establish residence in the capital cities, tended to move into the provincial towns. As a consequence of the mass exodus of the gentry from the service which followed the Act of 1762, the Russian provinces underwent a noticeable upsurge of urban life, particularly in the rich agricultural lands of the south and east, along the Volga, where the prosperous gentry were numerous. Culturally, these gentry represented an intermediate class, halfway between the thoroughly Westernized court and rich aristocracy on the one hand, and the nonprivileged classes, the clergy, burghers, and peasants, who by and large continued to cling to the traditional pre-Petrine culture, on the other. They eagerly accepted Western languages, literatures, and many Western customs, but their intimate contact with the tradition-bound groups of the population, especially the peasantry, precluded thorough Westernization.[10] Their cultural development tended in the direction of a synthesis combining some Western and some native elements. Though their efforts failed to yield impressive fruits in the course of the eighteenth century, they did accomplish a historic mission of utmost importance: it is they, the middle gentry, who prepared the soil from which subsequently developed the great Russian culture of the nineteenth century.

The third component part of the gentry — and it included the majority (two thirds of the Russian gentry at that time owned less than twenty serfs) — lived in varying degrees of poverty. Their pauperization was due above all to the absence in Russia of outlets able to absorb the excess members of their class. Peter's efforts to preserve intact the landed properties by state-imposed entail failed, as it was bound to, because the younger sons of a nobleman had practically no opportunity of securing an income for their family except on the land or in state service: commercial possibilities were few, while the Russian clergy was held in too low esteem to attract the well-born, and the monastic establishments had been despoiled by Peter I himself. Hence the gentry either kept on dividing their estates among the heirs, until they no longer sufficed to support anyone, or else disposed of them for cash. The bulk of the gentry thus inherited merely enough landed property to eke out a bare existence. Most families belonging to this category lived on their estates, which, dull and primitive as they were, offered at least some amenities and a certain degree of local prestige; the remainder went of necessity into state service, usually the army.

If there was any disagreement between the crown and the gentry after 1762 it was over culture. This disagreement ex-

---

[10] "Westernization" is here used in a cultural, not in a geographic, sense. It entails a set of ideals, derived from rational, secular premises. In this sense, even the most advanced Western countries have never become thoroughly "Westernized." Westernization is in all cases a matter of degree.

pressed itself in a spirit of rivalry between the two capital cities, St. Petersburg and Moscow, which grew particularly acute in the closing decades of the eighteenth century. St. Petersburg was the residence of the court, which was Russia's leading patron of the arts. Thanks to the personal inclination of Catherine II, the prevailing influence here was French, and the life of the city modeled itself on that of the French court. The French example permeated manners, speech habits, social behavior, and to some extent even thought: for although Catherine did not allow the *philosophes* to influence her policies, their ideas nevertheless did color considerably the intellectual atmosphere of the city in which she resided. It was Voltairian, that is, above all, skeptical.

This entire French fashion, in manners as well as thought, was perceived by the rest of the country as something profoundly alien. The nonprivileged groups rejected it outright. But even the bulk of the gentry was unwilling to follow St. Petersburg's leadership in this matter. The headquarters of these culturally disaffected groups was Moscow. Here the prevailing foreign influence was German and English, that is sentimental rather than rational, mystic rather than skeptical, anti-Voltairian and anti-materialist. Of the French writers, the greatest influence was exercised by Rousseau and the mystic, Louis de Saint Martin. The cultural leadership, which in St. Petersburg was in the hands of the court, in Moscow resided in the university, where the dominant voice belonged to German and Germanophile professors.

The two cities engaged in a cultural competition which was not always benign, and in the mid-1780's assumed the form of outright persecution of the Moscow circles, especially the Moscow Free Masons (of whom more later) by the bureaucracy acting on orders from Catherine. In general, the gentry may be said to have been less satisfied with the monarchy culturally than either economically or politically.[11]

[11] The cultural cleavage between St. Petersburg and Moscow resembled in its principal features that which had existed a century earlier in France, between Versailles on the one hand, and Paris on the other. But whereas in France it was the salon which was skeptical and antitraditionalist, and the court which stood for the national tradition, in Russia their roles were reversed.

The condition and attitude of the Russian gentry on the eve of the French Revolution may be summarized as follows: 1) The gentry were a privileged order with extensive rights and virtually no duties; they were contented with the general structure of state and society. 2) The gentry were in favor of the autocratic system of government, in part because they had received all their benefits from the crown, and in part because any liberalization of the system could only have benefited the nonprivileged orders, or the bureaucracy; but their concept of autocracy carried with it connotations of a division of authority under which the monarchy was in absolute control of the central government, and they in absolute control of the countryside. 3) The gentry were Westernized, but they did retain strong native roots.

Until the outbreak of the French Revolution, the ideas of the Russian gentry played a secondary role in the development of Russian public life. The tone was set by the court, and the court paid lip service to the ideas of social equality, political liberalism, religious skepticism. None of the important recommendations of the *philosophes* were realized, not so much because of ill intent, but because they were inapplicable to Russian conditions of the time. But there was a formal adherence to these ideals, and the monarchy continued nominally to act in a critical spirit.

The French Revolution changed this situation. The monarchy was now confronted with a dilemma: should it keep on reforming Russia along Western lines, and remain loyal to ideals which in the West seemed to have led to civil upheavals and regicide, or should it revert to native tradition, and thus abandon the course to which it was committed by long precedent? And if it should adopt the second of these alternatives, as it was likely to do if only from the instinct of self-preservation, then precisely to which Russian tradition should it revert? A return to the Russia of pre-Petrine times was quite out of the question; the country had changed too much for that. What, then, was there left? Between 1792, when with the suppression of the Moscow Free Masons the government had served notice that it was prepared to defend itself. and 1815, when Alexander I, returning from Western Europe, handed over the administration of the country to the bureaucracy, the monarchy vacillated. It was loath to alter radically its traditional course, even though the dangers of this course seemed clear, because as yet it lacked an acceptable alternative. At this critical juncture in the history of the Russian monarchy, the second within a century, the gentry again came to the rescue; but whereas in 1730 they had acted in anticipation of favors, they now did so in defense of rights. The ideologists of gentry conservatism, of whom Karamzin was undoubtedly the outstanding figure, supplied the monarchy with a new set of aims to take the place of that liberal, pro-Western program which it had hitherto espoused. Basically, this program was the same as that with which the monarchy was to go to its grave a hundred years later.

KARAMZIN AS BELLETRIST AND POET
(UNTIL 1801)

Nikolai Mikhailovich Karamzin was born on December 1, 1766, on a country estate at Mikhailovka not far from Samara, on the middle Volga. Of his family background little is known. It has been conjectured that his ancestors were of Tatar origin, and that his name was derived from Kara Murza, or Black Prince. This suggestion is plausible because in the territories adjoining the middle and lower Volga, once parts of the Kazan and Astrakhan khanates, a considerable part of the local gentry descended from the Tatars who had lived there prior to Russian conquest in the sixteenth century and were later converted to Orthodoxy. All that is known for certain is that his father, Captain Mikhail Egorovich Karamzin, had served in the army and participated in the campaigns against the natives of the Urals and the Kazakh Steppe under the command of the then well-known governor of Orenburg, Nepliuev. When Karamzin was born, his father was already retired from the service. The family possessed two estates: one at Mikhailovka, Karamzin's birthplace, which his father had received from the government as reward for his services; the other in the village of Znamenskoe, not far from Simbirsk, a little farther up the Volga, where the family regularly resided, and where Nicholas spent nearly all of his childhood.[12] Judging by the father's military rank and property holdings, the Karamzins seem to have belonged to the class described above as the "middle" gentry; they were prosperous enough to enjoy the pleasures of gentry life and to give their sons a sound Western education, but not prosperous enough either to play a prominent part in society, or to assure their children of a good career.

In Karamzin's childhood the Simbirsk region was still practically a frontier area. Although nominally under Russian authority for over two hundred years, the lands of the middle and lower Volga were in fact quite free of government supervision which did not extend much beyond the chain of fortresses built in the middle of the seventeenth century to protect Russian possessions from the incursions of natives, Cossacks, and runaway serfs. The town of Simbirsk, founded in 1648, was originally one of these frontier fortresses, and in the 1760's, with a population under 10,000, resembled more a garrison outpost than an urban settlement in the usual sense of the word. How tenuously the government held this area, less than four hundred and fifty miles from Moscow, was clearly demonstrated in 1774–75, when the propertyless groups of the population, led by Pugachev, easily upset all established authority, and maintained themselves in power until suppressed by superior military forces dispatched from the center. In these disorders, Karamzin's father barely escaped capture and certain death.

It is indicative of the intensity with which Western European culture had penetrated Russia in the eighteenth century that in such a remote frontier area, which lacked most of the amenities of life, a young gentleman like Karamzin was from his earliest years exposed to Western culture. As a child he acquired the essentials of German from a local doctor. Later, at the age of eleven, the wife of a neighboring squire, a lonely young woman, took him as her page, and taught him the French language and French manners; the education progressed so well that his father,

[12] The Soviet government has renamed Samara Kuibyshev, and Simbirsk, Lenin's birthplace, Ulianovsk.

frightened by certain overtones of this relationship, decided to send the boy away to Simbirsk, there to learn French in a more conventional manner. Karamzin's mother had died while he was an infant and after his father remarried (in 1770) he grew up without strict guidance. His childhood was lonely but not disagreeable. In stories which he wrote later (especially "Frol Silyn," "The Knight of our Time," and "The Village"), he described nostalgically the years spent at the family estate: how he would steal into the attic to fight imaginary enemies with rusty swords left from his father's wars; how, reading on the banks overlooking the Volga, he was once caught by a sudden storm and while running to the house was charged by a bear, from whose clutches he was saved in the nick of time by a stroke of lightning; how the neighboring gentry used to gather in his father's home to argue and reminisce. In general, the milieu in which Karamzin spent the first ten years of his life exemplified a blending of native and Western cultures, very typical of the class to which he belonged.

Beyond that, it would be idle to seek for sources of Karamzin's spiritual and intellectual development in his native environment. Indeed, he lacked all the qualities which this environment demanded: robustness, gregariousness, a cheerful, superficial disposition. Throughout his life he was rather sickly and withdrawn, easily given to melancholy, more like the city-bred scholar than the frontiersman. As is often the case, the environment failed to influence deeply a character with which it was in basic discord.

In 1777, at the age of eleven, Karamzin was sent to Moscow to attend the private school of one Johann Matthias Schaden, a German-born professor at the University of Moscow. Schaden was a follower of the most recent Swiss educational methods and of the ideas propounded in Rousseau's *Emile*. His school concentrated on the emotional rather than intellectual side of the child's personality, and sought to secure obedience by appealing to the senses of generosity and kindness, instead of by severe discipline. At the core of the curriculum lay the reading of a literature, largely German and Swiss-German in origin, designed to stimulate and develop in the pupil a readiness to respond emotionally to a variety of experiences. Karamzin was exposed to a heavy dose of Gellert and other moralizing authors, the reading of whose works stimulated his innate tendencies toward tearfulness, and his intellectual eclecticism. He retained pleasant memories of the years spent at Schaden's pension, where, among other things, he acquired a good knowledge of German and French, as well as the rudiments of English — important tools in the pursuit of self-education which was to occupy him for the rest of his life.[13]

When he had completed his studies at Schaden's pension (in 1781 or early 1782) Karamzin wanted to go to Germany to continue his education at a university, but his hopes were frustrated. In conformance with contemporary fashion, his father had enrolled him at birth in the Preobrazhenskii Guard Regiment; in this way he could be regularly promoted while living at home, and join the active service with the rank of an officer. The guard regiments consisted of the cream of the Russian nobility, and service in them was not as contrary to Karamzin's temperament and interests as it might seem: the duties were light, and there was ample opportunity for social and literary diversion. In fact, it was while on active service that Karamzin published his first literary work, a translation from German of Salomon Gessner's *Das Holzerne Bein — eine Schweitzer-Idylle* (1783).[14] He also read much. With him there served I. I. Dmitriev, a nephew of his stepmother's, also a native of the Simbirsk region, who was later to acquire a reputation as a poet and high government official, and with whom Karamzin maintained ties of close friendship to the end of his life.

Karamzin stayed on active military duty for one year only. His father died in 1784, whereupon he resigned his commission, and returned home. A real military career was out of the question for someone of his frail health and limited financial resources. But

[13] On Schaden, see N. S. Tikhonravov, *Sochineniia*, III, Part 1 (Moscow, 1898), 44–59.

[14] This translation is reproduced, together with some other early writings of Karamzin, in L. Polivanov's *Izbrannye sochineniia N. M. Karamzina*, vol. I (Moscow, 1884).

what was he to do? He was a foot-loose gentleman of eighteen, with a smattering of an education, some literary ambitions, but lacking both the social connections and the financial means necessary for the kind of life for which his upbringing had prepared him. At first he spent some time on the family estate, but this apparently bored him and he soon moved to Simbirsk. That city was growing rapidly at this time: in 1780, during the reforms of Russia's provincial administration, it was designated the capital of a newly formed viceroyalty of Simbirsk, and now began to attract, in addition to the higher military and administrative personnel sent there in the line of duty, the well-to-do gentry from the neighboring countryside. It was, in fact, undergoing the transition from a garrison fortress into a provincial town. Karamzin was readily admitted into local society. He was bright, sympathetic, and already then gave evidence of the conversational talents testified to by all those who knew him in later years. Life in Simbirsk consisted of an endless round of parties and card games. He seems to have idled away the first year there, for although he joined a local Free Masonic lodge, called the "Golden Crown," there is no evidence that this circle, presided over by the deputy governor of the province and composed largely of officers and civil officials, was anything more than a social club.[15]

Karamzin might well have sunk without trace into the morass of provincialism, had it not been for the intervention of another Simbirsk nobleman, I. P. Turgenev. Turgenev resided at this time in Moscow, where he had close connections with the Free Masonic "enlighteners" gathered around Schwartz, Novikov, and Kheraskov. During one of his visits to Simbirsk, he persuaded Karamzin to move to Moscow to join the *Druzheskoe Uchenoe Obshchestvo* (The Friendly Learned Society) which had been founded two years earlier by Schwartz to spread religious knowledge and to promote learning in Russia. The Society operated something in the nature of a seminary for the training of young

---

[15] The only evidence of Karamzin's participation in the Golden Crown lodge is his signature on one of its documents; this document is reproduced in P. [I.] Bartenev ed. *Osemnadtsatyi vek* (Moscow, 1869), II, 369. The background of the members of this lodge is described in T. Bakounine, *Le répertoire biographique des francs-maçons russes* (Brussels, [1940]), *passim*.

writers and translators. Karamzin moved to Moscow in late 1784 or early 1785, and joined the Society in the capacity of translator and writer for Novikov's *Detskoe Chtenie* (Reading for Children), Russia's first children's magazine. This move was the first critical decision in his life: it marked the end of the aimless existence of a young squire, and the commencement of an important literary career. He was to make the second critical decision of his life nearly twenty years later when he abandoned *belles lettres* in favor of history.

By joining the company of men gathered around the University of Moscow and the Free Masonic lodges, Karamzin in a very real sense picked his intellectual credentials. In the cultural conflict between St. Petersburg and Moscow these two institutions, whose personnel overlapped considerably, were the central bastions of the anti-Voltairian forces, the headquarters of the national cause, of all those Russians who found life in the village and small town insufferable, and yet were repelled by the skepticism, immorality, and Gallomania which they associated with St. Petersburg.

In Russia's cultural evolution, and in the conflict between St. Petersburg and Moscow, the Free Masonic movement played a prominent role. The first Masonic lodges were established in Russia in the reign of Elizabeth, that is within a generation after the modern Free Masonic movement had come into being in England. In the reign of Catherine, the lodges, and particularly those in Moscow, exercised a powerful attraction on those Russians who sought to reconcile their moral and religious beliefs, shaken but not crushed by skepticism, with the Enlightenment — those who wanted to retain ties with native tradition without being compelled thereby to renounce belief in reason and universal progress.

Free Masonry (says Miliukov) was the most suitable solution for that entire young generation which hesitated in their choice between the old and the new faiths . . . Novikov was by no means the only person who "had found himself among the Free Masons because he was torn between Voltairianism and religion, and failed to find a foothold or a base on which to establish his spiritual tranquility." This was a common and typical experience of the more profound and sensitive natures of his generation . . . The intelligentsia saw in Free Masonry a *faith*, but a faith illuminated by reason. . . .[16]

The activities of the Moscow Free Masons had a twofold character: religious and educational. In common with Free Masons of other countries, they performed symbolic rites, and engaged in the reading and discussion of mystic literature, especially the works of Saint Martin (for which reason they were commonly known as Martinists). They also launched an ambitious publishing program, whose aim was to raise the moral and intellectual standards of the country by means of morally uplifting literature. The educational work was directed by Novikov, who in 1779 obtained a ten-year contract to do the printing for Moscow University.

The Free Masons lacked a concrete political philosophy, because their primary concern was with the moral and intellectual improvement of individuals, and not with society or state as such. But it is not difficult to perceive in their general outlook on life certain broad political attitudes. The Free Masons believed in the improvement of mankind primarily by means of *inner* moral regeneration; consequently, they denied the feasibility of achieving lasting reform through legislation or institutional manipulation. They were hostile to the political teachings of the *philosophes,* espoused, nominally at least, by St. Petersburg, being convinced that all social evils resulted from the imperfections of individuals, not from the inadequacy of laws or institutions. This denial of politics was, of course, in itself an expression of a certain political philosophy.

In 1785, when Karamzin arrived in Moscow, the Free Masons were already in trouble with the authorities. The governor general of Moscow, acting on instructions of Catherine herself, undertook an investigation of the Martinists, and ordered the dissolution of the Friendly Learned Society. Novikov's publishing activities, however, were permitted to continue for a few more years.

Karamzin was certainly much more attracted by the educational activities of the Free Masons than by their religious prac-

[16] P. Miliukov, *Ocherki,* III (Paris, 1930), 405–06.

tices or beliefs. His own religious feelings were superficial, confined to a vague faith in the existence of a "Providence," whose invisible hand guides human destinies, whether to save Russia from an enemy, or him from the clutches of a wild bear. Toward the mysticism of Novikov and his associates Karamzin maintained from the beginning an attitude of amused tolerance. He went to Moscow because the Moscow Free Masonic lodges succeeded in attracting the best, most active minds in Russia. He was not disappointed in his expectations. The four years which he spent in Moscow, from 1785 to 1789 (aged nineteen to twenty-three) were, from the point of view of intellectual development, the most important of his life. Those were his informal university years, devoted to self-education by means of reading, translating, and writing, in the course of which he acquired a sound grounding in Western literature.

The significance of Karamzin's move to Moscow from the point of view of his political evolution is this: that he had early in life identified himself with that city and with that intellectual environment which championed a fundamentally national and conservative cause. For this reason it is not correct to regard the young Karamzin as a "liberal." Insofar as this designation is at all applicable to those living in pre-1789 Europe, it surely applies to those who adopted the critical, philosophical doctrines of the French Encyclopedists, and not to those who followed the ideas of religious mystics and moralists. Radishchev, who was at this very time engrossed in Holbach and Helvetius, was a "liberal" in this sense; but Karamzin, whose reading consisted almost exclusively of English and German sentimentalists, Swiss "Natur"-philosophers, and Rousseau's novels, clearly associated himself with an antireform, and therefore an essentially "conservative," cause.[17]

During his four years in Moscow, Karamzin collaborated on

[17] Dostoevsky in his *Diary of a Writer* (New York, 1949), p. 723, probably projecting his own past, says that during his Free Masonic period Karamzin placed in his study a bust of Voltaire. This statement is incorrect. It is known from the description of an eyewitness, Dmitriev, that Karamzin's room had in it a crucifix and a bust of the Free Mason Schwartz. I. I. Dmitriev, *Sochineniia*, vol. II: *Vzgliad na moiu zhizn'* (St. Petersburg, 1895), p. 26.

the children's magazine, did some publishing (his translation of Shakespeare's *Julius Caesar* and Lessing's *Emilia Galotti*), but above all he read. He read mostly English poets (Thomson, Ramsay, Young, Macpherson) and novelists (Sterne, Richardson, Fielding), and German writers (Klopstock, Herder, Wieland, Gessner). He showed little interest in philosophy, satisfying a not too profound curiosity for "big questions" with the natural philosophy of Bonnet and Lavater. In politics he showed no interest at all. His closest friend of the time, and perhaps the only one who ever exercised a strong personal influence over him, was his collaborator on the *Reading for Children,* Petrov, "a sullen, taciturn, and occasionally sarcastic" young man, as Dmitriev described him in his memoirs.

In 1789 Karamzin decided that he had learned all there was to learn in Moscow. Reading had awakened in him an intense curiosity for Western Europe, and had stimulated dormant literary ambitions. Moreover, government persecution caused a progressive disintegration of the Free Masonic movement: Novikov's contract with the university was expiring, without there being any indication that it would be renewed, and he and his followers, frustrated in their educational work, veered ever more toward extremes of mysticism for which Karamzin had no taste. It was clearly time to leave. He now decided to undertake a journey to Western Europe, to meet some of the authors whose works he had admired, and to see with his own eyes some of the places which had inspired his favorite literary works. What he had in mind was a Grand Tour. This was something of a novelty in Russia. Young Russians, of course, had traveled west at least since the end of the sixteenth century, when Boris Godunov dispatched an expedition of Russian students to the West. In the eighteenth century the two leading German universities at Leipzig and Göttingen had sizable Russian contingents. But those Russians had gone west for formal studies, whereas Karamzin was going solely for pleasure and general enlightenment. To finance the trip, he sold to his brothers a share of the parental estate. He then took friendly leave of Novikov and his colleagues, and on May 18, 1789, departed by post-chaise for Riga on a sixteen-month journey which was to take him through Germany, Switzerland, France, and England.

The principal record of Karamzin's journey is to be found in his *Letters of a Russian Traveler,* which, next to the *History of the Russian State,* constitute his chief prose work. This book, written in a lively, conversational tone, is the most outstanding achievement of eighteenth-century Russian prose, displaying a charm and liveliness often difficult to find in Karamzin's later, more formal work. These qualities are most evident in the first half of the book, dealing with his sojourn in Germany and Switzerland, which has all the freshness of a real diary. The second half, as is known from careful textual analyses, is based not so much on personal observation as on secondary sources, and has less literary merit. This book remains one of the few products of Russian eighteenth-century literature which can still be read with pleasure.

The *Letters* contains enough observations on political subjects to furnish a good picture of Karamzin's political philosophy in 1789–90, but unfortunately it cannot be used as a source for this purpose except with the utmost caution. Though we know from contemporary sources that Karamzin actually kept a diary of his journey in the form of letters,[18] V. V. Sipovskii's researches demonstrated quite convincingly that a considerable part of that book was composed after the author's return to Russia on the basis of extensive reading in Western descriptive literature. Moreover, the publication of the *Letters* actually extended over a period of ten years, in the course of which it was subjected to considerable alterations and emendations. The first part of the *Letters* appeared serially in the *Moscow Journal* in 1791 and 1792; the second part came out in 1794–95 in the two volumes of a collection called *Aglaia;* then in 1797 part one, somewhat revised, was republished in book form in four volumes. The fourth volume of this book edition stopped with Karamzin's arrival in Paris. All the important observations on the French Revolution and on English politics are contained in the fifth

[18] Ia. L. Barskov, *Perepiska moskovskikh Masonov XVIII veka, 1780–1792* (Petrograd, 1915), p. 86.

volume, which did not appear until 1801. Thus, the *Letters,* and particularly its political reflections, depicts not the Karamzin of 1789–90, but the Karamzin of the late 1790's, when both European politics and his own political views were no longer the same.

The *Letters* is important not for what it says of Karamzin's politics in 1789–90, but for what it fails to say: for it demonstrates complete indifference to the vital political events of the time.

After visiting Königsberg, where he had a brief talk with Kant, Karamzin proceeded to Weimar. He failed to meet Goethe, and had to be content with a view of the poet through an open window, but he did have a long interview with Wieland. To Wieland's question: "What is your aim in life?" the twenty-three-year-old Russian gave a characteristic reply:

A tranquil existence. After I have finished my travels, which I have undertaken solely for the purpose of collecting a few agreeable impressions, and enriching my mind with new ideas, I will live in peace with nature, and good men. I will everywhere seek what is exquisite, and enjoy it.[19]

These words were uttered exactly one week after the fall of the Bastille.

From Weimar Karamzin continued his trip toward western Germany. The news of the Revolution first reached him at Frankfurt. But for the time being he seems to have been less interested in Paris than in the Frankfurt ghetto, to him a new and shocking sight; he expressed his indignation at the oppression and squalor which he saw there in a long passage which must rank as one of the earliest sympathetic treatments of the Jews in all Russian literature (and which, incidentally, was expurgated from the only Soviet edition of this work, published in 1950).[20] In Strasbourg, where he went next, he saw with his own eyes the arrival of the first victims of the Revolution: aristocratic French refugees, fleeing from their country estates menaced by peasants. The spectacle affected him, but it affected him emo-

[19] *Sochineniia Karamzina* (St. Petersburg, 1848), II, 149.
[20] *Russkaia proza XVIII veka* (Moscow-Leningrad 1950), II, 336–41.

tionally, not intellectually; he felt pity at the sight of suffering human beings, without making any effort to understand the causes of this suffering or to find remedies. Nor did the experience move him strongly enough to induce him to change his itinerary. Instead of proceeding to Paris, Karamzin made a short stop at Strasbourg and then calmly pursued his journey southward, to Switzerland. In 1797, in an article written for a foreign periodical, he had this to say of his first reaction to the French Revolution:

It is in Frankfort on Main that he [i.e. Karamzin himself] learned of the French Revolution; he was profoundly agitated; he went to Alsace, saw nothing but troubles, heard of nothing but robberies, murders, and he hastened to Switzerland, to breathe the air of peaceful liberty.[21]

This is the most significant item of evidence — negative evidence, to be sure — bearing on Karamzin's political ideas at the time of the outbreak of the French Revolution. He obviously was not interested in politics if at this particular time he could settle down in Geneva, visit Berne and Zurich, see Lavater, engage in long conversations on the nature of life with Bonnet, and undertake long excursions into the mountains. While the National Assembly was shaking the foundations of European society with its speeches and legislative measures, Karamzin walked through the Bernese Oberland, talking to shepherds, and admiring the waterfalls of Staubbach and Trümmelbach. His descriptions of Switzerland convey the impression that what he liked best in that country was the freedom from politics which it accorded to its citizens; a late worshiper of sensibility and fine feelings, he sought refuge in Switzerland from the mounting storm which threatened to rob him of his "tranquil existence."

Karamzin spent in Switzerland the entire winter of 1789-90, perhaps waiting for the turmoil in France to subside. In March 1790, he departed at long last for Paris. While crossing the frontier (he later wrote in the same foreign journal in which he told of his reaction to the French Revolution) he pinned to his hat a tricolor cockade: it was a sign of prudence, rather than of con-

[21] *Spectateur du Nord* (Hamburg), 1797, cited in Ia. Grot and P. Pekarskii, eds., *Pis'ma N. M. Karamzina k I. I. Dmitrievu* (St. Petersburg, 1866), p. 477.

viction, because three months later, embarking at Calais for Dover, he promptly disposed of it in the Channel.

In Paris he spent most of his time sight-seeing, and frequenting the theatre. Through letters of introduction he had entry to some French homes and enjoyed light conversation, but political talk bored him. In a passage in the fifth volume of the *Letters*, which, though published eleven years after the event, has an unmistakable ring of authenticity about it, he had this to say of a visit to one of the salons:

The host was the last to appear and he turned the conversation to the topic of parties, intrigues, decrees of the National Assembly etc. The French argued, praised, censured; while the young Englishmen yawned. I involuntarily joined the latter, and felt genuinely happy when dinner was announced.[22]

Karamzin stayed two full months in Paris before paying his first visit to the National Assembly. Yet the politically charged atmosphere of Paris had some impact on him, for it was here that he first began to show interest in politics: in Paris he read Mably and Delolme hoping to obtain from them an understanding of Western institutions, to be better prepared to participate in political discussions which, to his evident surprise, so strongly agitated the Western public.

From Paris he went to London. He liked England for much the same reasons as Switzerland: politics here were in the background; they did not intrude on the daily life of the citizen. The elections to the parliament (he witnessed a contest between Fox and Wilkes), the parliamentary debates (the trial of Hastings, the oratory of Burke) seemed to him side-shows, without real bearing on the life of society. England's public life ran smoothly, regularly, due to the excellence of her officials, and even more so, to the high moral standards of her citizens. "It is not so much the Constitution," he wrote later in his *Letters*, "as the enlightened condition of the public mind that is the true Palladium of the English."[23]

[22] *Sochineniia Karamzina* (1848), II, 453–54.
[23] *Ibid.*, p. 779.

He left England in August 1790, and arrived in St. Petersburg, by way of the Baltic Sea, later in the same month.[24]

The primary evidence at our disposal is thus insufficient to provide a clear picture of Karamzin's political views in 1789–90, but it is certainly sufficient to throw strong doubt on the persistent allegation that he sympathized with the French Revolution. The origin of these allegations very likely must be sought in the strange impression which Karamzin made on friends and strangers alike upon his return from abroad. He had departed a gentle, studious, and modest young man; he returned a fop, opinionated, contemptuous of everything Russian, and imbued with a burning ambition to make himself a name as a great writer. The contemporary correspondence of his friends reveals something of the shock they experienced from this transformation. The garrulous A. I. Pleshcheeva, one of Karamzin's closest friends of the time, could not find words strong enough to express her disappointment in the new Karamzin. She found him less kind than before, more self-assertive, and so "stubborn that he would do nothing at all for anyone, even in trifles." She quarreled with him all the time, and regretted the day when she had helped persuade him to go on his journey.[25] Another of his Masonic friends was quite explicit:

Lord Ramsay [Karamzin's Masonic nickname] has returned [to Moscow] before me. You won't recognize him, he is completely changed in body and soul. . . . He tells us thousands of things most amusingly. . . . He believes he can teach us things we never knew. Everything that concerns Russia he mentions with a contempt and unfairness that is truly appalling. Everything that concerns foreign countries he refers to in extasy . . . He calls himself Russia's first writer, he wants to teach us our mother tongue, which we rarely hear; he will unlock for us the hidden treasures. . . .[26]

The cause of this change is not difficult to find. In the course of his journey Karamzin had at last found himself: that is, he

---

[24] Most secondary sources date Karamzin's return in September or October 1790. However, the correspondence of the Moscow Free Masons published during the First World War reveals that he was back in August. See Barskov, *Perepiska moskovskikh Masonov*, p. 30.

[25] Barskov, *Perepiska moskovskikh Masonov*, pp. 28–29.

[26] *Ibid.*, p. 86.

found his vocation as a writer. The personal ambition and self-assurance which accompanied this discovery, however, were so contrary to all the virtues inculcated by the Free Masons that his old friends could not help but regard him as a thoroughly changed man, and in their political naïveté interpret his behavior as proof of his having succumbed to French "radicalism." Karamzin himself no doubt added to this impression by his loose talk. What could the old poet Derzhavin think of the young man introduced to him by Dmitriev who at dinner, in the presence of the deputy governor of St. Petersburg, spoke lightly of the French Revolution, the very name of which inspired the liveliest terror in those present? [27] It is quite obvious, however, that Karamzin, a youth less than twenty-four, was merely shocking and impressing his listeners, and that his behavior in Derzhavin's home was nothing more than an expression of the same exuberant self-confidence which struck his friends. Nevertheless, the impression which he created immediately upon his return from the West was so strong, that many years later the Decembrist Nicholas Turgenev could still believe that Karamzin had "venerated" Robespierre, and cried on learning of his death.[28]

Everything that is known of Karamzin's intellectual development suggests that he could not have sympathized with the French Revolution: his background, his literary interests, his ignorance of political literature, his behavior during the European journey. Karamzin was indifferent to the Revolution and to all that it entailed. The reasons for this indifference — so alien to the post-1789 mentality — must be sought in the character of politics in the century in which he had grown up, and in the psychological attributes of his vocation as a poet.

The first of these causes does not require extensive elaboration, for it has been touched upon at the beginning of the present essay. In eighteenth-century Russia public life and private life were confined to two distinct compartments and one rarely en-

[27] Bludov's account, cited in Ia. Grot, ed., *Sochineniia Derzhavina*, VIII, (St. Petersburg, 1880), 606–07.
[28] N. Tourgueneff, *La Russie et les Russes*, vol. I, appendix D.

croached upon the other. Politics were still essentially a technical enterprise entrusted to a relatively small class of professional civil servants, whose attention was concentrated on
administration and diplomacy.

In the case of a poet there were additional reasons for political
indifferentism. Belles-lettres, and poetry in particular, are in-
herently concerned with personal experiences; they are intro-
spective and individualistic. Psychologically, therefore, they
tend to conflict with politics, which operate with abstract, in-
tellectualized categories, not directly related to personal experience. This is not to say that poets, even excellent ones, do
not engage in politics, but rather that the spirit of literature
and the spirit of politics draw their inspirations from different
and to some extent incompatible sources. Though the poet may
be attracted to politics, may engage in them, and may even try
to consecrate himself to them, permanently he can do so only at
the sacrifice of his art and inner convictions. In the ultimate
scale of values, he cannot admit that someone else's "truths" are
more real or more valid than his own, that considerations which
lack an exact counterpart in the world of individual experience
may take precedence, and even less that the problems which
trouble him are capable of solution by legislative or diplomatic
action. He is committed to the view that his innermost thoughts
and reactions, no matter how trivial on the scale of world values,
constitute the ultimate reality. Since politics do not affect the
vital areas of a poet's consciousness, he is not inclined to consider
politics vital.

On the basis of his early poetry, correspondence, and prose
works, it is possible to reconstruct Karamzin's world outlook at
this period along the following general lines: The real problems
of human existence, such as uncertainty of the future, sickness,
death, are insoluble; hence, true happiness is nonexistent. Nevertheless, life can afford much pleasure to those who know where
and how to seek it. The trick is not to struggle against evil, but
to ignore it. The wise man follows his conscience and acts justly
in his personal dealings with others, expecting little in return.
The main delights within human reach are learning and art,

family and friends. A sound system of government makes it possible for the citizen to seek these harmless pleasures, and this means that it provides conditions of external and internal security. The condition of mankind can be improved only in consequence of enlightenment, the gradual spread of learning and good customs — never through direct legislative action of the state. Culture, therefore, is the key to such happiness as is available to man: for the individual it opens the door of escape from the dilemmas of human existence, while for society it unlocks the only gate to true progress. The essential feature of every good political system is that it grants freedom and security, the presence of which is indispensable to human self-improvement.

This cultural, Epicurean, approach to politics Karamzin retained throughout his life, and all his political ideas constitute essentially an elaboration of that theme, and an effort to adapt it to the specific requirements of Russia. He would have readily subscribed to Dr. Johnson's

> How small of all that human hearts endure,
> That part which kings or laws can cause or cure.

The staggering and lasting impact which the French Revolution made on world history was to establish the primacy of politics. In its successful bid for control of the instruments of government, society (first through its upper classes, and then the others which followed) greatly narrowed down the gap which had separated it previously from the state. With power came responsibility; with responsibility, involvement. Politics began to encroach upon every aspect of life, and the more state and society became identified, the less could individual members of society escape the pressures of the state. The price which mankind had to pay for liberation from arbitrary authority was, and continues to be, subjection to politics. How difficult it was to resist this product of the French Revolution can readily be seen from the example of so profoundly an apolitical man as Karamzin.

Upon his return to Moscow Karamzin found his friends in

very serious difficulty, political as well as financial. Government investigations and persecution, intensified after the French Revolution, had made further Free Masonic activity impossible; Novikov's contract with the Moscow University Press was not in fact renewed, and the company he headed, which Miliukov aptly described as "the first collective undertaking of the Russian intelligentsia," [29] dissolved, leaving behind a debt of 300,000 rubles. Karamzin, of course, had severed his connection with the Moscow Free Masons before leaving for Europe, and stood in no immediate personal danger; but he could not altogether escape involvement in the destiny of the men who had meant so much to him.

His main occupation at this time was editorial. In 1791 he founded his own periodical, the *Moscow Journal (Moskovskoi Zhurnal)*, in which, in addition to the first installment of the *Letters of a Russian Traveler*, he published also numerous original short stories, translations, and poems written by himself and many of the leading Russian writers of the day. He hoped that this journal would give him financial independence, and thus permit him to claim status as Russia's first professional man of letters. The journal was indeed well received. The short story *Poor Liza*, published there in 1792, brought him fame overnight. At the age of twenty-six he was acclaimed as the leader of a new "sentimentalist" movement, and moved to the forefront as one of Russia's outstanding literary figures.

But the pleasures of literary success were marred by the spreading maelstrom of government persecution. In April 1792, Catherine, having learned of the efforts of the Moscow Martinists to enlist for their cause her son Paul, decided to put an end once and for all to that movement. Novikov was arrested and sentenced to fifteen years in the Schlüsselburg fortress. His incarceration gave an enormous shock to Russian society in Moscow and the provinces. By suppressing the Moscow Free Masons the government suddenly reversed its traditional Westernizing, "critical" attitude, and took to interfering with society's cultural freedom; it violated, so to say, the dyarchy which society (at least its articulate members) had come to view as a normal and perma-

[29] Miliukov, *Ocherki*, III, 413.

nent condition. Novikov symbolized this division of spheres; in the words of Longinov, he had "succeeded in making himself a 'force' at a time when such status was acquired only through state service or court favors, he having risen without one or the other. Novikov expressed perhaps for the first time the power of *society*, independent of the court and the higher administration." [30]

In the investigations which accompanied Novikov's imprisonment, the authorities ran into the name of Karamzin. They became curious about Karamzin's connections with the Martinists, and particularly about his trip to Europe: they suspected that he might have gone abroad to establish contact with Western secret societies. Inquiries quickly revealed that Karamzin had severed all relations with the Free Masons before his departure, and that his journey had no connection with their activities. Still, a shadow had been cast; in Moscow there were even rumors that Karamzin was under house arrest. No one could tell how far the government would carry its repressive policies, and Karamzin had every reason to make himself as inconspicuous as possible.

But he was a man of strong convictions, and courage to match. He refused to stand by while the government violated what to him seemed the cardinal principle of good politics, namely the right of citizens to cultural freedoms. In May 1792 — one month after the arrest of Novikov — he published in the *Moscow Journal* a lengthy poem called "To Mercy" (*K milosti*), in which, addressing himself indirectly to Catherine, he stated what he considered the proper limits of tsarist authority:

So long as you are kindly, and respect the rights with which man is born; so long as your contented subjects can lay themselves to sleep without fear, and your children — free subjects — may dispose at will of their lives, everywhere enjoy nature, everywhere acquire knowledge, and sing praises to your glory: so long as malice, Typhon's brood, is committed to dark oblivion, far away from the golden throne; so long as truth is not feared, and those pure in heart can confess to you their wishes, to you, mistress of their souls; so long as you will grant freedom to all, and refrain from extinguishing the mind's inner light; so long

[30] M. N. Longinov, *Novikov i moskovskie martinisty* (Moscow, 1867), p. 330. Emphasis supplied.

as all your deeds are permeated with confidence in your people — so long you will be sacredly honored, worshipped by your subjects, and praised from age to age. . . . The throne will never tremble where it is guarded by love.[31]

The plea was for unfettered cultural freedom for all Russians; the justification, that such freedom gave stability to the state.[32]

His poem went unpunished. Even so it represented a magnificent act of courage. Of all his contemporaries Karamzin alone had the boldness to speak up publicly for intellectual liberties, and in the general panic which followed Novikov's arrest, to risk his future, and perhaps his very life, in defense of a man whose ideas he did not share.

Karamzin now began to watch with growing apprehension the developments occurring in France. He had no clearly formulated ideas as to the causes of the Revolution, or its issues; he preferred to make no choice between the warring parties, being convinced that each was ultimately motivated by selfish interests, and therefore emotionally insincere ("feeling" was to him then, as always, the touchstone of truth). Had the Revolution remained in its early phase, that is in the phase which so excited the admiration of enlightened public opinion in Europe, Karamzin would very likely have remained indifferent to it. But the Revolution soon evolved beyond this phase: the Terror, which had gotten underway in 1793, challenged the very foundations of civilized life, and it is from the viewpoint of its cultural effects that Karamzin found himself gradually drawn within its orbit.

[31] This prose translation has been made from the original version, reprinted in *Sochineniia Karamzina*, I (Petrograd, 1917), 61–63. In the nineteenth century the poem was known only in an expurgated version, which omitted mention of "rights with which man is born" and "free subjects"; the expurgated vision is reproduced in M. Pogodin, *Nikolai Mikhailovich Karamzin* (Moscow, 1866), I, 201–02.

[32] It must be remembered that in the second half of the eighteenth century, until the outbreak of the French Revolution, Russians enjoyed in many respects greater intellectual liberty than the French: works of French authors, prohibited in France itself, circulated freely in Russia both in their original form and in translation. Karamzin, therefore, was in a position to imply that the old regime in France collapsed because it had suppressed cultural freedoms, whereas the Russian monarchy stood firm because it had not done so.

"Will you believe me," he wrote to Dmitriev in August 1793, one month after Robespierre's rise to power, "that the dreadful European occurrences have thoroughly shaken me? Though I escape into the dark gloom of the forests, thoughts of ruined cities and slaughtered human beings everywhere oppress my heart." [33]

Apart from humanitarian considerations, what troubled him were the possible long-range effects of the French Revolution on the cause of enlightenment. He was afraid that the Revolution might be blamed on the spirit of free inquiry which had prevailed in France prior to the Revolution, and thus give rise to an obscurantist reaction, a rejection of all learning, or *misosophy*, as he referred to it. In 1794 he published "A Dialogue between Melodor and Philalet," in which he developed this theme at length.[34] Melodor speaks in tones of utter desperation; he compares mankind to Sisyphus, condemned forever to tumble to the lowest depths of barbarism as soon as the pinnacle of enlightenment is within reach, and he predicts the coming destruction of European culture. Philalet, on the other hand, is a moderate optimist. He admits disappointment with the turn which history had taken, but denies that learning and good manners can ever suffer permanent oblivion. Philalet finds comfort in the general condemnation of the terror in Europe, as well as in the fact that in the past all barbarians sooner or later succumbed to superior culture. Which of these two voices was Karamzin's? Novikov, upon his release from prison in 1797, read this Dialogue, and expressed the opinion that Melodor was Petrov, Karamzin's friend and collaborator of the Free Masonic period, and Philalet Karamzin himself.[35] Novikov knew well both Petrov and Karamzin, and his judgment must be respected. The literary historian, Galakhov, on the other hand, interprets this work as a dialogue within Karamzin himself.[36] In either event,

[33] *Pis'ma . . . k I. I. Dmitrievu*, p. 42.

[34] *Sochineniia Karamzina* (1848), III, 436–57.

[35] Rather than, as A. Pypin records in his *Russkoe Masonstvo* (Petrograd, 1916), p. 255, *vice versa*. Longinov, *Novikov*, p. 383.

[36] Quoted by K. Bestuzhev-Riumin in *Russkii biograficheskii slovar'*, Volume "Ibak-Kliucharev" (St. Petersburg, 1897), p. 505.

the differences between the two friends are differences of degree, not of kind: both reject the Revolution and the Terror, both express disappointment with the sudden break in the progress of enlightenment, both feel apprehension over the possible effects of the Revolution on manners and morals; but whereas Philalet believes the storm will eventually subside, and the cause of enlightenment triumph, Melodor looks upon the French upheavals as the end of a cycle of steady progress, and the beginning of a cycle of barbarism. It is worth noting that in the same year (1793) Karamzin published an essay in which he affirmed his faith in enlightenment, and rejected Rousseau's "paradox" that enlightenment causes decadence.[37] If Novikov was correct, then the oft-quoted exclamation of Melodor's: "Age of Enlightenment, I do not recognize thee — I do not recognize thee amid blood and flames, slaughter and ruin!" does not express the feelings of Karamzin, but of his misanthropic friend.[38]

After 1794 Karamzin went through difficult, bitter years of frustration and disappointment, the more painful because they contrasted so sharply with the happy period of great expectations which had followed his return from Europe. The intensified policy of repression enforced by the Russian government out of fear of sedition, and made even more unbearable by the aberrations of Paul, gradually choked off all creative activity in the country, driving Karamzin and most of his literary contemporaries to idleness and despondency. Karamzin suspended publication of the *Moscow Journal* at the end of 1792. In March 1793 Petrov died. Shortly afterwards Karamzin had a brush with censorship over a German version of his *Letters,* which had been scrutinized at the border, and in the spring of 1794 the authorities ordered that his translation of *Julius Caesar,* together with other books published by Novikov's press, be committed to the flames. His closest friends, the Pleshcheevs, with whom he resided at this time, ran into financial difficulties, and to help them out, he disposed of the remainder of his estate (1795). Two years

[37] *Sochineniia Karamzina* (1848), III, 373.
[38] Herzen was the first to give it currency in the introduction to his *From the Other Shore.*

later he stood to lose all his personal belongings to help pay Novikov's debts, which he had helped guarantee ten years before. When in July 1798 the censors stopped his translation of the speeches of Demosthenes, on the grounds that Demosthenes was "a republican," and further prohibited, for similar reasons, the publication of Russian versions of Cicero and Sallust, Karamzin practically gave up all literary activity. "I am dying *as an author,*" he wrote to Dmitriev in October 1798.[39] He took again to cards, and resumed an active social life. He spent much of the next two years in and out of bed, to which he was driven by recurrent spells of sickness and migraine, henceforth his constant companions.

It is in those dark days that Karamzin became for the first time seriously interested in history and politics. Unable to pursue his main delights, literature and good company, he spent much time in his cabinet, seeking in books explanations of the events of which he and his whole generation were the helpless victims.

KARAMZIN THE HISTORIAN
(1798 ff.)

"Nous avons une âme contournable en soi même; elle se peut faire compagnie," Karamzin wrote in his notebook in 1798.[40] The last years of the old century and the first years of the new were for him indeed periods of internal conflict: conflict between a sentimentalism, whose source was drying up, and the intellectual curiosity of a learned as well as pragmatic mind. Each failure of the emotions to respond to experience, each fit of boredom, drove him toward social studies; each subsequent disappointment with politics caused him regrets for the life of feelings which he was losing beyond recall. A melancholy renunciation of life and its pleasures became for him a habitual form of escape from this dilemma.

Karamzin greeted the accession of Alexander with a burst of enthusiasm. Overnight vanished the fears, the moods of depres-

<hr>

[39] *Pis'ma . . . k I. I. Dmitrievu,* p. 104.
[40] "We have a soul which winds around itself; it can keep itself company." Pogodin, *Karamzin,* I, 295.

sion, and, for a while, even the physical suffering which had seldom left him during the reign of Paul. Censorship was softened, policy rationalized, and the whole atmosphere of the country suffused with currents of new, fresh air such as it had not breathed since 1789. In the letters which he wrote in 1801 and 1802, Karamzin described as the greatest achievement of the new regime the reintroduction in Russia of the feeling of security. Abroad, too, there was improvement. The Treaty of Amiens terminated a long cycle of wars. Even the ascendancy of Napoleon seemed at this time to Karamzin a good augury: it indicated that France was reverting to a stable, semimonarchical form of government, and therefore was likely to abandon its policy of aggrandizement. Freedom at home, peace abroad — such were the delightful prospects. This was all that Karamzin ever asked of politics. In a poem composed on the accession of Alexander, he wrote of the new reign:

> Thus do spring's beauties and delights
> Cancel out terrors of dark winter nights;
> Hearts blossom forth like meadows green,
> And in their flower autumn's fruits are seen.[41]

In another poem, written on the occasion of Alexander's coronation, Karamzin renewed his plea for cultural liberty in terms not unlike those which he had used in the ode "To mercy" nine years previously:

Can slaves love? Are they capable of feeling gratitude? Love and fear are incompatible; free man alone possesses the capacity for feelings. Although the absence of all restraint is harmful, freedom is a precious thing, consistent with the monarch's interests; freedom was always the glory of kings. Liberty exists where decent men can live without fear; slavery exists where laws are absent, where the righteous and the wicked perish alike. Freedom is wise and sacred — while equality is nothing but a dream.[42]

The atmosphere of security and freedom which the new regime introduced, stimulated Karamzin to resume temporarily an active literary career. In 1802 he founded a new periodical, *Messenger*

[41] *Ibid.*, pp. 319-20.
[42] *Ibid.*, p. 322.

of Europe (Vestnik Evropy). This publication differed from the *Moscow Journal* largely in its emphasis, being less belletristic, and more political in its orientation. It was the prototype of the so-called "bulky journals" devoted to what the Russians call *obshchestvennye problemy* (the adjective *"obshchestvennyi"* itself was coined by Karamzin), that is, to all the subjects which have bearing on the life of society (as distinct from those that concern primarily the state or the individual), which afterwards became the Russian intelligentsia's principal medium of expression. The main purpose of the *Messenger* was to inform the Russian public, by means of news reports and translations, of current cultural and political developments in the West; its supplementary task was to publish original works of Russian writers and news items from within the country.

By its title, purpose, and content, the new journal accurately reflected Karamzin's cultural outlook: the belief that Western Europe was the fountainhead of all enlightenment. Although his view of the role of Western culture in the life of Russia was to change with time, Karamzin was never anti-European, not even at the end of his life when his nationalism became most pronounced.

Between 1801 and 1803 Karamzin made up for the silence of the late 1790's, by publishing a considerable number of works, some of which provide the first clear insight into his political philosophy. Among them are scattered essays and news reports printed in the *Messenger*, the last, and politically most informative, installment of the *Letters of a Russian Traveler*, dealing with his stay in Paris and London, and occasional pieces, the most important of which for the present inquiry is the *Historical Eulogy of Catherine II (Istoricheskoe pokhval'noe slovo Ekaterine II)*. To convey the flavor of Karamzin's political views of this time, one can do no better than cite two passages on the French Revolution, the first from the *Letters* (published in 1801, but probably written in the late 1790's), the second from the *Messenger of Europe* (1802):

You must not believe that the whole nation takes an active part in the tragedy, now performing in France. Scarcely one-hundredth part belongs to the real actors; the rest are spectators, and judge or dispute, cry or laugh, clap their hands or hiss, just as in the theatre. Those who have nothing to lose are keen, like ravenous wolves; but, on the other hand, those who may lose all are as timid as hares; the former would take all, while the latter seek to save something. But a merely defensive war against an impudent enemy is seldom successful. . . .

The multitude is a sharp-edged tool with which it is dangerous to play, and revolutions are often open graves which swallow up virtue as well as vice.

Every civil society, confirmed by centuries, is for good citizens a sanctuary; and in the most imperfect we may often admire a miraculous harmony, well-being, order. Utopia will ever remain a dream of good minds, or at least it can never be realized, but by the imperceptible effects of time, by means of the slow but certain and safe advances of the human mind, enlightenment, upbringing, and good manners. Then only, when men shall be persuaded that virtue is indispensable to their own happiness, then shall the golden age have arrived, and the peaceful enjoyments of life shall flourish under *every* form of government. But every violent upheaval is ruinous, and every rebel erects a scaffold for himself. Let us, my friends, trust in Providence: It surely has Its plan; in Its hands are the hearts of kings — that is enough.

Thoughtless men think everything easy; but the wise know the danger of all change, and live in peace.[43]

The Revolution clarified our ideas: we saw that the civil order is sacred even with its local and accidental imperfections; that its authority is not tyranny, but a safeguard from tyranny; that by shattering this beneficent shield, the people suffer dreadful calamities, infinitely worse than all the customary abuses of power; that even the Turkish government is to be preferred to the anarchy which invariably follows political upheavals; that all the bold theories of the mind, which wants from its cabinet to prescribe new laws to the world of morals and politics, can never come to life, any more than the remainder of the more or less curious constructions of human ingenuity; that the institutions of antiquity are endowed with a magic power, which no power of the intellect is capable of replacing; that the correction of the defects found in civil societies must be left to the force of time, and to the good will of legitimate governments; and that we, private citizens, confiding in this action of time and the wisdom of the authorities, must live peacefully, obey readily, and do all we can to spread goodness around us.

In other words, the French Revolution, by having threatened to topple all governments, actually helped to consolidate them. If mankind's tragedies can in any sense be called beneficial, then we certainly owe this benefit to the Revolution. Today, the civil authorities draw their strength not only from their military power, but also from the inner persuasion of the mind.[44]

The *Historical Eulogy of Catherine II* which Karamzin wrote in 1802 and published in 1803, was essentially a commentary on Catherine's *Instruction*. This work had been widely circulated by the government itself in the late 1760's and 1770's, but later, in the period of reaction, it was withdrawn, and by now had been virtually forgotten. In preparing the *Eulogy* Karamzin had an opportunity of deepening his knowledge of eighteenth-century political thought, particularly of Montesquieu, from whom he subsequently adopted the historical approach to politics, as well as much of the political terminology. As the title of this work indicates, it was a paean of praise for the Empress, of whom, in her lifetime, Karamzin was quite critical. Looking back at her reign, after the terrors of the French Revolution and of Paul, he saw nothing but excellence. Catherine's greatest achievement was to give Russians (read: "gentry") civil rights, and thus to transform subjects who previously had been mere slaves of the crown, into true citizens. She also deserved praise for the circumspection with which she made use of her authority, having exacted obedience not with terror, but with love.

In the political commentaries which he wrote for the *Messenger,* Karamzin touched upon a great variety of current political problems. He approved of most of the policies adopted by Alexander, such as his reforms of the central political apparatus, his educational measures, and his foreign policy; he only found cause to criticize the government's views on the peasant question, which to his mind were too radical.

Characteristic is Karamzin's attitude toward Napoleon, reflecting as it does his emphasis on the primacy of civil and cultural over constitutional factors. In the early issues of the *Messenger* he expressed a very favorable opinion of the First Consul, praising him for the restoration of authority in France: "[Napoleon] will certainly win the gratitude of the French if, having shattered

[44] *Ibid.,* III, 585–86.

the dream of *equality*, which had made all of them *equally* unhappy, and, having resuscitated religion, which in this world of flux is so necessary for the soul as well as for the integrity of states, he will use fatherly authority to wipe out the disastrous traces of the Revolution, provide the Republic with a wise system of civil laws, prove to be a sincere patron of the sciences, arts, and commerce, and upon these bases found the welfare of France, harmonizing peacefully the interests of his country with those of other countries." [45] Karamzin strongly favored peace with France; many numbers of his journal contained pleas for friendly Russo-French relations. But when Napoleon began to make increased use of authoritarian (i.e. arbitrary) methods, Karamzin turned against him: he definitely preferred a republic based on law, to a monarchy based on royal whim. In November 1802 he published a penetrating analysis of the new French Constitution of the Year X (issued three months before), in which he criticized the new regime on the ground that it vested in the First Consul arbitrary authority over French citizens, empowering him to deprive them of life and liberty without the due process of law. "In a word," he concluded sadly, "France, after long wanderings, returned once more to the starting point, with that difference that whereas the royal *'tel est notre bon plaisir'* used to be restrained by the Parliaments and the assemblies of the provincial estates, the will of the Consul calls for the silent submission of all.[46]

By 1803 Karamzin seems to have arrived at a fairly consistent political outlook. At its center lay the conviction that progress in all spheres of human endeavor was dependent on cultural progress; and that insofar as culture (understood to comprise morals, good manners, the arts, learning, and so on) could flourish only where people were assured of security and civil freedoms, the test of a good government was the degree to which it succeeded in assuring its citizens the maximum of legality and civic liberty consistent with its own security. The experience of the French Revolution had taught him that the main threat to

---

[45] *Ibid.,* I, 534–35.
[46] *Vestnik Evropy,* No. 21 (November 1802), p. 58.

legality and liberty came not from too much government, but from too little government, and above all from anarchy caused by human striving for perfection and equality. For this reason he henceforth tended to lean ever more toward strong, centralized governments, though in theory he continued to prefer authority which employed gentleness and persuasion. The choice between strong and weak government was to him a choice between evils, in which historical experience favored the former. The constitutional arrangement itself was a matter of little consequence. Hence, Karamzin thought it unwise to tamper with established institutions: the benefits which such tampering could bring were at best insignificant, while the dangers were always enormous, threatening as they did the collapse of the whole political structure, with ensuing chaos and reversion to barbarism.

--◀ ▶--

In 1803 Karamzin became involved in a controversy, which, while essentially linguistic in character, did have certain political overtones. The dispute involved the nature of the Russian literary language, which was at this time passing through its formative phase of development. The three styles formulated in the middle of the eighteenth century by Lomonosov, "high," "medium," and "low," distinguished from each other by a decreasing proportion of Church Slavonic words, and increasing proportion of words derived from the common Russian speech, no longer met the requirements of a rapidly growing secular literature. What Russia still lacked was an accepted standard of written prose, capable of rendering sublime as well as common thoughts and feelings in a language familiar to ordinary readers. Such a prose had been dispensed with for a long time, because cultivated Russian society spoke German or French; but toward the end of the eighteenth century the reading public, a public which normally spoke its native tongue, had increased to the point where the creation of a standard prose style could no longer be postponed.

The literary Russian in use when Karamzin had begun his career did not meet his requirements, and Karamzin, whose literary output was directed at what was then a mass-market, set out to refashion it. In common with most other good stylists he based his prose language as closely as possible on that used in cultivated conversation of his time; and since the speech of the Russian salon of the period was heavily suffused with Gallicisms (when it was not French altogether), Karamzin's prose naturally showed strong Gallic influences in syntax as well as vocabulary. This quality lent his early prose works, such as the *Letters of a Russian Traveler,* much of their novelty as well as popularity.

Karamzin's linguistic innovations did not pass unchallenged. Already in the 1790's several writers, among them Krylov, the future fabulist, ridiculed Karamzin's prose, and hinted that there was something un-Russian about it. But the controversy came to a head only in 1803 when Admiral Shishkov, self-appointed guardian-in-chief of the purity of the Russian language, published a scurrilous and ill-informed book called *An Enquiry into the Old and New Styles of the Russian Language (Rassuzhdenie o starom i novom sloge rossiiskogo iazyka).* Shishkov based his case on the contention that modern Russian grew out of Church Slavonic, and from this premise argued that both the structure and the vocabulary of all Russian prose should be modeled on Church Slavonic. In Shishkov's opinion Karamzin's efforts to modernize written Russian, as well as doing violence to the spirit of the language, corrupted the nation by undermining its moral foundations.

History has vindicated Karamzin. He not only stands absolved of the charge of Gallicising Russian, but his style, especially that which he used with such excellent results in the *Messenger of Europe,* was later adopted (with modifications) by Pushkin, and through him became the fountainhead of all modern Russian literary prose.[47]

[47] *Cf.* Ia. K. Grot, "Karamzin v istorii russkogo literaturnogo iazyka," *Trudy Ia. K. Grota,* II (St. Petersburg, 1899), 46–98. Contemporary historians of the Russian language like Vinogradov also side on the whole with Karamzin, and reject Shishkov's thesis of the derivation of modern Russian from Church Slavonic.

It is no doubt the fault of the historical criterion in literature, which weighs so heavily on the scales used to set apart "classics" from presumably

The political significance of the controversy between Shishkov and Karamzin lies in its bearing on the conception of Russian national culture upheld by two fairly distinct centers of right-wing public opinion, centers which with time evolved into reactionary and conservative political movements respectively. Both groups agreed that Russian culture should draw on its own resources, but whereas Shishkov and his adherents sought these resources in Russia's national-religious tradition of the pre-Petrine period, the Karamzinists saw it in the blending of contemporary secular Russian civilization with the best of Western. Shishkov wished to revert to a mythical past, when Russia had been allegedly unsullied by foreign contacts; Karamzin wished to move forward, to create a genuine Russian culture, which would retain its native roots, and yet take into account the achievements of the contemporary West. This difference was not without profound bearing on Russian politics, for which the attitude to the institutions and ideas of the West was always a touchstone; by it one can often distinguish in Russia conservatives proper from extreme reactionaries.

Karamzin was not a polemicist, and he refused to take up the challenge flung by Shishkov. At the urging of Dmitriev he composed a lengthy defense of his stylistic practices, but the public never saw it, because Karamzin committed the manuscript to the flames as soon as he had had a chance to read it to his friend. Anyway, by the time Shishkov's book appeared Karamzin had made up his mind to give up belles-lettres proper, and to devote himself completely to writing a grand history of Russia.

This was not an entirely new idea. His interest in this subject can be traced back to 1798, to the period of forced idleness. On June 12, 1798, he jotted down in his journal the following entry:

If Providence should protect me; if I should escape that which I dread worse than death itself . . . I shall occupy myself with history. I shall begin with Gillies, then read Ferguson, Gibbon, Robertson — I shall

lesser works, that the general reader knows Karamzin mainly from his cloying stories and uninspired poems of the sentimentalist period, particularly *Poor Liza*, rather than through his travels, dialogues, and political writings. The latter are interesting, intelligent, straightforward, and can still be read with profit as well as pleasure.

read them attentively, taking notes, and then turn to ancient authors, especially Plutarch.[48]

It will be readily seen that the authors whom Karamzin selected as his models were popular rather than technical historians, didactic writers who painted vast panoramas for the general instruction of the public.

This helps explain how Karamzin, who had no formal training in any branch of learning, dared to venture upon such an ambitious undertaking. The history he had in mind was not an academic but rather a literary creation. This genre of history did not pursue facts in the belief that precise knowledge of events is valuable in itself — this attitude was first established by the great German historians — but rather sought in the records of the past raw materials for an essentially imaginative undertaking, for a species of belles-lettres, as pleasing as a novel, and more useful, because "true." He lived in an age when history was still considered an integral branch of literature, which any imaginative dilettante might attempt. Consequently, his change of vocations was not as drastic as might appear, or as would have been the case were it to occur today.

The other striking feature of this earliest remark expressing his desire to study history, was that all his models were foreign. Karamzin deliberately ignored the accomplishments of Russian historiography, having found the existing literature excessively technical and entirely unreadable; he wished to recreate the picture of Russia's past directly from primary sources, using the most popular modern British historians as his guides. He certainly underestimated the magnitude of the task, and perhaps

[48] *Neizdannye sochineniia i perepiska N. M. Karamzina* (St. Petersburg, 1862), I, 203. John Gillies (1747–1836), Scottish historian, author of a *History of Ancient Greece, its colonies and conquests* (1786); Adam Ferguson (1723–1816), Scottish philosopher and historian, wrote the *History of the Progress and Termination of the Roman Republic* (1783); William Robertson (1721–1793), another Scot, wrote the immensely popular *History of Scotland* (1759) and *History of the Reign of the Emperor Charles V* (1769), the latter of which was translated into Russian in 1775.

What Karamzin dreaded worse than "death itself" cannot be determined with any certainty. It was most likely blindness.

even the achievement of his predecessors.[49] But his instinct was sound, and the métier he had chosen afforded great opportunities for creative achievement. Although modern Russian historiography could trace its origins to the reign of Peter I, by Karamzin's time it had not as yet succeeded in evolving much beyond the preliminary stages of gathering materials and establishing chronologies. The leading writers on Russian history in the eighteenth century, such as Tatishchev, Shcherbatov, and Schlözer, concentrated on editing or paraphrasing Russian medieval chronicles: their books were chaotic in form, and uncouth in style. Even the writings of Boltin, perhaps the most original Russian historian of the century, took the form of critical commentaries and polemics. What was missing was a general survey of Russian history capable of providing Russians, by means of a continuous and lucid narrative, with a coherent picture of their own past. This was the gap which Karamzin set himself to fill.

The curiosity in social and political problems which the events of the 1790's had engendered in his mind, undoubtedly played an important role in his decision to turn to history. It is more than likely that Karamzin's interest in history in general, and political history in particular, was a reaction to the abuses of monarchical authority under Paul, and that he sought in the past a definition of Russia's political system which the policies of Paul seemed to have thoroughly confused. But there was also a psychological element involved.

Ever since his childhood Karamzin had consciously cultivated his emotions; his entire world-outlook depended upon the ability of the heart to respond spontaneously to experience. Such was the teaching of the Western teachers he had chosen, as well as the natural inclination of his own temperament. But by now he had passed the thirtieth year of his life: experiences began to repeat, emotional responses to cool. He was passing through the typical crisis which the lyrical, romantic poet undergoes when he reaches

[49] P. Miliukov in his *Glavnye techeniia russkoi istoricheskoi mysli* (St. Petersburg, 1913) is very severe with Karamzin, and charges him with plagiarizing his predecessors. A. A. Kizevetter, in "N. M. Karamzin," *Russkii istoricheskii zhurnal*, Books 1–2 (1917), pp. 9–26, somewhat redresses the balance in favor of Karamzin.

middle age, the crisis which destroyed some of the greatest, including Pushkin. Karamzin, who was not a great poet, and whose sentimentalism disguised generous but superficial feelings, overcame it by gradually turning from poetry to scholarship, whose delights are immune to the corrosive actions of time.

This spiritual crisis and its resolution are mirrored in the letters and notes written between 1798 and 1803. "Late last year," he confided to Dmitriev in January 1798, "I had written a dialogue on happiness, and now, at the beginning of the new, I am thinking of writing on boredom! Philosophy can occasionally console us; but having lost its novelty for the heart, life flows slowly, languidly, contrary to all the beautiful theories of sages. My fate is in the hands of Providence, but I have no desire to live to old age." [50] In May 1800, he wrote:

Walking and enjoying myself, and conversing with Jean-Jacques ten times a day: o grand Être! o grand Être! I count the remaining hairs on my head, and sigh. Gone are the days when my heart expected indescribable joys; gone are the days of secret hopes and sweet dreams! Reason tells me that it is late to think of achievements; even those things which now afford me enjoyment must vanish little by little. Thus tired guests depart one after the other from the noisy ball room, the music dies down, the halls empty, the candles are extinguished, and the host goes to sleep — alone! Nature has arranged well so many things: but why does not the heart lose its desires when it loses hope? Why, for instance, being no longer lovable, do we still want to be loved? — Helàs!" [51]

And in 1803:

At a certain stage in our life, history occupies us much more than do novels; the mature mind finds in truth a peculiar charm, which invention lacks. In the saddest of all conditions, when the fruits of reason and imagination no longer afford us amusement, we may still with a certain melancholy pleasure devote ourselves to history; here everything speaks of what has been, and no longer is! . . .[52]

In May 1799 Karamzin reported to Dmitriev that he had purchased many books, all on philosophy and history, but no

[50] Pis'ma . . . k I. I. Dmitrievu, pp. 90–91.
[51] Ibid., p. 117.
[52] Sochineniia Karamzina (1848), I, 500–01.

novels.[53] A year later he signaled: "I am immersed in Russian history up to my very ears; I see Nikon and Nestor before my eyes day and night." [54]

Aware of his new interests, his friends persuaded him to apply for the post of the official Historiographer of the Russian Empire. He did, the request was approved, and he was granted by Alexander a pension of 2,000 rubles annually for life, together with the assurance that his History would be published at the crown's expense. This grant, together with the income from the estate of his first wife, and the large one brought by his second wife, gave him the financial security which he needed in order to venture on his long-range project.[55] He now resigned the editorship of the *Messenger of Europe*, which was doing extremely well: with over six hundred paid subscribers, it had earned for him 6,000 rubles annually;[56] it had also secured him a considerable following among young Russian authors, who had accepted his stylistic innovations and imitated his genre of writing.

From 1803 to his death in 1826 Karamzin devoted all his time and energy to the history of Russia, and nearly all his writings of this, the second half of his life, are on this subject.

This is not the place to analyze Karamzin's views on Russian history, which form a separate topic. In any event, the introductory section of the *Memoir on Ancient and Modern Russia* contains an excellent résumé of these views, superior in some respects even to the *History of the Russian State*, because in the latter the narrative stops in the year 1610, whereas the *Memoir* carries it forward for another two hundred years. What concerns us here is the influence of Karamzin's historical researches on his political views. It was seen that by 1803, when Karamzin turned to the study of history, his political ideas had been fairly clearly formulated. The study of Russian history now brought the de-

---

[53] *Pis'ma . . . k I. I. Dmitrievu*, p. 111.

[54] *Ibid.*, p. 116.

[55] Karamzin's first marriage ended after one year (1802) with the death of his wife. He remarried two years later. His second wife was the illegitimate daughter of Prince A. I. Viazemskii.

[56] Pogodin, *Karamzin*, II, 17.

velopment of his political thought to its conclusion. It accomplished two things: it deepened his appreciation of Russia's cultural heritage, and clarified his image of Russia's political tradition.

Until the late 1790's, when he turned to history, Karamzin was in many respects a typical eighteenth-century cosmopolite. He believed that all history moved toward the goal of enlightenment, and that if nations differed from one another in culture, it was because they stood at different stages on the common road to this goal; he also believed that the content of enlightenment was the same for all peoples. This attitude finds expression in his early opinions of Peter I. In the fifth volume of the *Letters of a Russian Traveler* Karamzin credited Peter with enlightening Russia, and defended him with much vigor from the charge that he had done violence to Russian national traditions:

Is not the way to improvement *one* and the same for all nations? All walk therein, one after another. . . . Is it rational to seek a thing already discovered? . . . Peter drove us with a mighty hand, so that now we only fall perhaps a few years short of these [Western] nations . . . We must be men above all, not Slavs. Whatever is good for men cannot be bad for Russians; and everything that the English or Germans have invented for the benefit and comfort of human society belongs to me too, for I am a man.[57]

In June 1798 he jotted down the following thoughts:

Thoughts for an eulogy of Peter I.

To appreciate the better the skill of Phidias, let us look at a shapeless block of marble: this is what went into the making of his Olympic Jupiter!

What was Russia?

The birth of the first idea.

The ever-present feeling for the exquisite, the source of greatness, the characteristic of all great men.

Lefort.

Zeal and patience. What does Buffon have to say of the latter?

Contempt for dangers. Faith in victory. "Fear not, you carry Caesar, and with him his fortune![58]

---

[57] *Sochineniia Karamzina* (1848), II, 513–15.

[58] "Caesarem vehis, Caesarisque fortunam"—said to be Caesar's words to a pilot during a storm.

Justification of his system. Silence, petty minds! The progress of nature is the same: one enlightenment, and one means of attaining perfection, happiness! (Levesque).[59] Should we have remained in this condition of spiritual and moral debasement? What is the meaning of this "national quality" (national character) of yours? The destiny of all nations is the same; he could not have driven us to this great goal with other methods. Justification of certain cruelties. A heart which is always gentle is incompatible with spiritual greatness. Les grandes hommes ne voyent que le tout. But occasionally sensibility won out, too.

Can I feel anything but burning love for the fatherland, thinking of Peter? — places where he walked, groves which he planted. . . .[60]

This cosmopolitanism was an early victim of Karamzin's historical studies. Between 1798 and 1803 he so to say "discovered" Russia. He learned, to his surprise, that Russia possessed her own, peculiar national tradition, which never was and never would be identical with that of France or England, and that Peter had not, as he had previously supposed, created civilization in Russia, but grafted one type of civilization upon another, equally worthy and viable. The change in his attitude, more pronounced in later years, is already visible in an article, significantly called "On the Love of the Fatherland and on National Pride," published in 1802:

I dare not believe that Russia lacks Patriots, but it does seem to me we are excessively *humble* toward our national values — and in politics humbleness is harmful. He who lacks respect for himself will surely not win it from others.

I do not maintain that love for the fatherland should blind us, and persuade us that we excel in all and over all; but a Russian should at any rate know his own worth. Let us grant that some nations surpass us altogether in enlightenment, having enjoyed more favorable conditions; but let us also not ignore all the blessings of fate when we consider the Russian nation; let us assume our place by the side of other nations; let us clearly pronounce our name, and repeat it with noble pride.

We shall never acquire wisdom from someone else's mind, nor glory from someone else's fame; French, English authors have no need of our acclaim; but Russian authors do need, to say the least, the attention of

[59] P. C. Levesque (1736–1812), French historian who published in 1782–83 a history of Russia; until the appearance of Karamzin's *magnum opus*, his was the best known history of Russia in Western Europe.
[60] *Neizdannye sochineniia*, p. 201–02.

Russians. My soul, thank heaven, is quite averse to the spirits of satire and censure; but I feel I must scold many of our readers who, being better acquainted with all the works of French literature than the Parisians themselves, do not even deign to look at a Russian book. Do they want foreigners to teach them about Russian talents? Let them read French and German critical journals which do justice to our abilities, basing themselves on some translations.[61] Who would care to repeat the experience of D'Alembert's nurse who, although she had been living with him, was astonished when told that he was a wise man? Some plead poor knowledge of Russian as an excuse; this excuse is worse even than the vice. Let us leave it to our dear society ladies to maintain that Russian is coarse and disagreeable, that it cannot render *charmant* and *séduisant, expansion* and *vapeurs,* in short, that it is not worth the bother to know it. Who dares to show the ladies they are mistaken? But men cannot claim this amiable privilege of erring. Our language is capable not only of lofty eloquence, sonorous, picturesque poetry, but also of tender simplicity, and sounds of feeling and sensibility. It is richer in harmonies than French; it lends itself better to effusions of the spirit; it has more synonyms, that is words according with the action expressed! . . . It is our loss that we all insist on speaking French instead of toiling over our own language; is it commendable that we are unable to express certain nuances in Russian conversation? . . . Language is important to the Patriot; and I like Englishmen for preferring to *whistle* and *hiss* in English when addressing their tender loves, rather than use a foreign tongue, with which nearly every one of them is familiar. Everything has a limit and a measure: man and nation alike begin always with imitation; but in time they must become *themselves,* in order to be able to say: *I exist morally!* We possess now so much knowledge and taste that we have no need to ask: how do they live in Paris and London? What do they wear there, what do they ride, and how do they furnish their homes? A Patriot hastens to adapt to his fatherland all that is beneficial and useful, but he rejects slavish imitation in trivialities, offensive to national pride. One needs and one ought to learn: but woe to both the nation and the man who remain eternal pupils![62]

From the views expressed here there was only a small step to a defense of the positive values of the Russian national tradition, and a condemnation of Peter's cultural policies. As Karamzin deepened his knowledge of Russian history, he came more and

---

[61] Karamzin alludes to some favorable reviews of the odes of Lomonosov and the plays of Sumarokov, which appeared at this time in the West.

[62] *Sochineniia Karamzina* (1848), III, 468–69, 473–75.

more to side with those critics of Peter whom as late as 1798 he had dismissed as "petty minds."

Karamzin's pro-autocratic views, which dominated the political writings of his latter periods, were also by-products of his historical studies. The espousal of autocracy entailed not so much an abandonment, as an amplification of the previous opinion that constitutional forms are not directly related to the social and political condition of a people. As long as the system was secondary, Karamzin felt, it was best not to tamper with it; the system at hand was as good as any, and enjoyed, in addition, the respect which men instinctively accord to all that is traditional. The study of Russian history revealed to him that autocracy was Russia's traditional form of government. This, of course, was by no means an original thought: in eighteenth-century Russian political and historical literature it was virtually axiomatic, and its roots went back to the official ideology of the Moscow monarchy of the fifteenth and sixteenth centuries. But Russia lacked as yet a continuous intellectual tradition, and what one generation took for granted, the next had to discover. Moreover, some of the most important Russian political works of the past were either forgotten or not yet published around 1800; the major political writings and speeches of Shcherbatov, for instance, became publicly known only in the second half of the nineteenth century.

What did Karamzin understand by the term "autocracy"? [63] In the historical literature Karamzin is usually represented as an advocate of unlimited tsarist authority, of state control over social classes, of blind obedience to government — in short, as an ideologist of the system of reaction practiced by Nicholas I in the last years of his reign, and later by Alexander III. In its extreme form this appraisal was expressed by Pokrovskii (writing, *nota bene,* before the revolution) when he said that "Karamzin accepted the system of Paul I with all its consequences," and

---

[63] This question is discussed at greater length in my article "Karamzin's Conception of the Monarchy," *Russian Thought and Politics — Harvard Slavic Studies,* IV (Cambridge, Mass., 1957), 35-58.

that he considered despotism "the last word of political wisdom." [64]

Such a judgment is entirely wrong. The political system which Karamzin advocated had as much as and no more in common with the reactionary policies of Nicholas I (1848–1855) or of his successors at the end of the century, than the ideals of prerevolutionary Russian socialists had in common with Stalinism. That is to say, there was a certain link between the thought and the subsequent practice, but this link was not a causal one: in both cases the practice resulted not from what theoreticians had said, but from what, out of ignorance or misunderstanding, they had failed to say. The distinction may make little difference as concerns the outcome, but makes all the difference as concerns the intention, and it is the intention of Karamzin that is so often misrepresented.

The main reason why so many critics misunderstood Karamzin was their failure to take into account the historical framework within which he had evolved his conception of autocracy. This framework rested on the eighteenth-century social foundation, and was constructed of categories derived from eighteenth-century political thought, mainly from that of Montesquieu. Once the social substructure disintegrated (as it did with the decline of the gentry, and the emancipation of the serfs in the middle of the nineteenth century), the theoretical superstructure lost its meaning and pertinence.

Following Montesquieu, Karamzin distinguishes four constitutional archetypes: republics, aristocracies, monarchies, and despotisms. The latter two types coincide insofar as both vest sovereignty in a single person, but in all other respects they differ. The distinguishing feature of monarchies is the rule of law, and the cooperation between the crown and the "intermediate and dependent orders," of which the most important is the nobility. In despotism (or tyranny) the whim of the monarch takes the place of law, and the rights of the estates are violated by a government which wishes to administer the whole country directly.

[64] M. N. Pokrovskii, in *Istoriia Rossii v XIX veke,* I (Moscow, [1907]), 57.

In the Russian context, Catherine II was a monarch, while Paul I was a despot.

Karamzin rejected despotism for reasons which require no elaboration; only anarchy, which entailed the absence of all government rather than a system of government, was worse. The choice of governments, therefore, narrowed itself down to three. The republican system was, theoretically, the best, but in practice it was feasible only in very small countries or in city-states. As for the aristocratic method of government, experience indicated that Russia, because of the vastness of its domain and diversity of its peoples, always fell apart when she tried to divide sovereignty, and in consequence came under foreign domination.[65] There remained, therefore, only the monarchic system: this was the system which best accorded with Russian traditions and interests; it was also the only legitimate one, having been formally ratified in 1613 by the Land Assembly which elected the Romanov dynasty.[66]

Karamzin uses for "monarchy" the Russian term *samoderzhavie*. This word is a literal translation of the Greek *autokrateia,* and originally signified a self-sustained government, one which was not a vassal or other dependent of any foreign power, and therefore capable of entering into direct diplomatic relations with other states. With time, as the authority of the Moscow princes and their successors grew, this term also acquired the connotation of unlimited power. The two meanings were never clearly differentiated, and it is illustrative of the confusion prevailing in Russian political terminology, that all three limited monarchs of Russian history: Shuiskii, Anne (between her acceptance of the "conditions" and assumption of full power), and Nicholas II (after 1906) continued to be referred to in official documents as *"samoderzhtsy"* — i.e. as autocrats. In general, the term *samoderzhavie* and its derivatives performed in the Russian political literature the same function that the term "sovereignty"

[65] Karamzin, like Tatishchev before him, believed that Kievan Russia had a centralized state system, and that its collapse was due to the weakening of the royal (or Grand Princely) authority.

[66] See below, pp. 213–14.

performed in the West,[67] and in the eighteenth century *samoderzhets,* or autocrat, meant the sovereign, the monarch. The
term autocracy in Russian usage of that time must not be confused with despotism or tyranny (often called *samovlastie*) from
which it was usually (though not always) distinguished.

Side by side with *samoderzhavie* Karamzin noted another quality of the Russian monarchical tradition which, like Tatishchev
before him, he called *edinoderzhavie.* This term was used to
describe the process of the "gathering of Russian lands" and the
struggle of Kiev as well as Moscow with the centrifugal tendencies displayed by the principalities. *Edinoderzhavie* referred to
the existence of a single supreme political authority over all the
peoples and lands of *Rus'; samoderzhavie,* on the other hand,
referred to the measure of power which this authority enjoyed.
The former concerned the geographic scope of monarchical authority, the latter its political scope. If *samoderzhavie* is rendered
by "autocracy," *edinoderzhavie,* for lack of any other equivalent,
may be rendered by "monocracy." Both these qualities were considered by Karamzin to be essential attributes of the Russian
monarchy.

To Karamzin the autocratic system was one in which the ruler
did not share sovereignty with any group or institution, and was
free of all formal constraints in his exercise of authority. In this
sense he was conceived as truly an unlimited ruler. But to be
properly understood this conception of monarchical power must
always be considered in conjunction with the concept of estate
rights, that is, of that dyarchy to which the Russian gentry
aspired, and which for a time it actually achieved. Applying
H. Maine's formula it may be said that for Karamzin autocracy rested on a contractual relationship between the crown and
its subjects, but that the contract was one unilaterally drawn
up by the monarchy; in despotism, on the other hand, the subjects had no contract at all, only status. An essential part of the
contract between the monarchy and the subjects were the rights
which the crown had granted the gentry in the course of the

[67] G. Gurvich, *"Pravda voli monarshei" Feofana Prokopovicha i ee
zapadnoevropeiskie istochniki* (Iurev, 1915), pp. 46–47.

eighteenth century, by virtue of which the gentry had practically unlimited authority over one third of the country's population bonded to them. In effect, therefore, autocracy entailed not so much unlimited authority (for it was unlimited only within a prescribed zone of "high politics"), as undivided authority. Such a conception of royal power presupposed firmly guaranteed estate rights, and a clear line separating the state from society.

It is worth noting that Karamzin nowhere advocated the autocratic system as best *per se*. He was for firm, stable government — but whether such a regime was attained by means of a republic, aristocracy, monarchy, or (if anarchy was the alternative) even despotism, depended entirely on local traditions and the prevailing circumstances.

This conception of autocracy matured in Karamzin's mind between 1803 and 1810, during the years devoted entirely to historical work. His life in this period passed uneventfully: he spent the summers at the Viazemskii estate at Ostafevo, the winters in Moscow, reading, searching for manuscripts, and writing drafts of his History, the first book of which was ready in 1806. He lost interest in society, so completely devoted was he to his researches. The only significant interruption of this period of calm study was the incident, or rather series of incidents, which led to the writing of the *Memoir on Ancient and Modern Russia*.

THE MEMOIR ON ANCIENT AND MODERN RUSSIA
(1810–1811)

The general circumstance which inspired the writing of the *Memoir on Ancient and Modern Russia* was the failure of Russian foreign and domestic policies in the first decade of the reign of Alexander I. This failure engendered among considerable segments of Russian public opinion first disappointment, then resentment, and finally fear for Russia's very survival. Karamzin's work echoes all these sentiments. The specific circumstance resulted from the efforts of the politically ambitious sister of Alexander I, the Grand Duchess Catherine Pavlovna, to substitute her own influence at the court for that of the "liberal" party, personified by Speranskii.

There is no need to recount in detail the policies of the Russian government between 1801 and 1810; they are analyzed thoroughly (if not always fairly) in the *Memoir,* and explained further in commentaries which here follow it. It may, however, be useful to recall briefly the history of the relationship between the monarchy and the gentry during this period, for it constitutes the essential background of the *Memoir.*

The gentry at first welcomed the accession of Alexander; they approved of his promise to revert to the policies of Catherine II, and to revoke the most obnoxious (from their point of view) of his father's laws. But the honeymoon was brief, and soon came rude shocks and disappointments.

The first shock was the revelation of the government's attitude toward serfdom. This attitude, though it was never fully spelled out, expressed itself in certain practical measures, most particularly in Alexander's pledge to put an end to the practice of distributing to nobles populated estates from crown properties, and also in the so-called Law of the Free Agriculturalists, which allowed the gentry to manumit bonded peasants with land. These few gentle taps at the institution of serfdom frightened the gentry out of all proportion to their practical consequences, because the gentry saw in them, and with good cause, harbingers of an eventual peasant emancipation. What made the gentry particularly sensitive to any tampering with serfdom was that institution's legally indeterminate status: serfdom as such had never been legally instituted in Russia; it was established in practice by a succession of individual acts, which restricted the rights of proprietary peasants, and vested them in their landlords. Firmly as serfdom was implanted on Russian soil *de facto, de jure* its position was vague. A condition which had come into existence by precedent could easily go out of existence in the same manner, and this was what the gentry feared.

The second shock to the gentry was the defeat dealt the Russian armies by Napoleon in the war of the Third Coalition. The gentry had not objected to war when it started in 1805, because they cordially detested Napoleon, and had full confidence in the ability of the Russian armies to handle the French. As Karamzin later wrote in his *Memoir,* under Catherine II the Russians had grown accustomed to considering themselves invincible. They felt, therefore, doubly keen disappointment over the debacle at Austerlitz, and the inability of the Russian armies to stop the subsequent French drive toward the Russian frontier. A war which had begun in 1805 as a safe venture on foreign soil, far from home, ended two years later with the establishment of French dominion over Warsaw, and the threat of an invasion of Russia herself.

Then came Tilsit, and perhaps the worst shock of all. The alliance with Napoleon, Russia's adherence to the continental blockade, the attack on Sweden: all these features of the Tilsit Treaty and its aftermath were extremely unpopular with the gentry. To make peace with the man who epitomized the illegitimate revolutionary regime was bad enough — to make common cause with him was unpardonable. The treaty exacerbated the wound which the military defeats had inflicted; it made people wonder whether the government really knew what it wanted, if it was willing one day to risk the country's fate on one cause, and the following day to wager it with equal determination on its opposite.

The psychological unpopularity of the Tilsit Treaty was compounded by economic difficulties which accompanied Alexander's foreign ventures. To finance the war, the government had taken to printing large quantities of inconvertible paper currency, thus driving out specie and causing serious inflation. The economic consequences of the treaty, especially the continental blockade, also affected adversely Russian trade, and further aggravated the currency situation.

It was at this psychologically very unpropitious moment for the regime that Speranskii appeared on the scene with his grandiose scheme of reforming Russia's institutions. Speranskii had nearly everything against him: his low social status (only ten years before he had eaten with the domestics in Prince Kurakin's household); his unfriendly personality; his disregard for public opinion; his association, in the public mind, with the unpopular pro-French turn in Russian policy; the immensity of his task, and the meagerness of the resources at his disposal. In addition to his genius, he had only one thing in his favor: the support of the tsar. Under the conditions then prevailing, court backing outweighed all the adverse factors, permitting him for three and one-half years to manipulate institutions almost at will; but it could not assure the successful completion of his plans. The immediate result of Speranskii's efforts was further to isolate the court from society.

Speranskii's plan[68] was to "legalize" the monarchy, that is to establish the relations between the crown and its subjects upon a regular constitutional foundation. This he hoped to achieve by two means: by eliminating overlapping competences in the administrative apparatus, and by establishing a closer relationship between authority and responsibility. Ultimately, he wished Russia to be transformed into a constitutional monarchy. Unfortunately for Speranskii's cause, Alexander, who approved of his project, decided to keep it secret, thinking to frighten public opinion less by piecemeal reform. Experience soon showed that secrecy had the opposite effect, for the public became extremely alarmed by a rapid succession of seemingly pointless constitutional changes, some of which bore striking resemblance to those carried out in republican and imperial France — changes whose ultimate purpose was obscure, but whose immediate effect was the disorganization of a viable system of government.

In 1810 the regime's prestige sank to its nadir. The alliance with Napoleon was crumbling, and Russia was diplomatically isolated, and yet she continued formally to adhere to the Tilsit policy. Internally, this year saw the greatest number of reforms: the establishment of the State Council, the beginning of the reorganization of the ministries, the appearance of the first parts of the projected Civil Code, and the fiscal reforms. Russian paper currency dropped to its lowest level, with assignats fetching less than one fifth of their face value.

Discontent with the government focused in three centers: the Senate, the literary circle dominated by Shishkov and Derzhavin,

[68] See below, pp. 228–32.

and the salon of Alexander's sister, the Grand Duchess Catherine at Tver.

The senatorial opposition arose at the very beginning of Alexander's reign, in 1801–1803, at the time when the new government was taking its first uncertain steps toward reform. Led by experienced and influential statesmen (Troshchinskii, Count Zavadovskii, Rumiantsev, Vorontsov and others), this group sought to prevent abuses of the autocratic system such as had been perpetrated under Paul, by strengthening the Senate. The Senate, in their view, was to regain control over the administration, which it had gradually lost in the second half of the preceding century, and to acquire in addition the "right of remonstrance" by virtue of which it could protest to the Emperor whenever an imperial decree violated the laws of the realm. In this way the Senators hoped to reconcile the principles of autocracy with those of government by law. Alexander and his liberal advisers of that time viewed with distrust the "oligarchic" tendencies of the Senators, and preferred to improve administration by centralizing it in new, streamlined bureaucratic institutions: the ministries and the Council of State. But the Senatorial group was influential and the first administrative reforms (1801–1803) were in effect a compromise between their desires and those of Alexander and his Unofficial Committee. By 1803, in consequence of a bold attempt of the Senate to protest to the tsar a law which violated the charter of the gentry, the Senate was completely deprived of its political power, and the movement quickly folded up. Its leaders were removed from key positions and replaced by new men, protégés of the Unofficial Committee, outstanding among whom was Speranskii. But the ideas initiated by the Senators lived on, and the movement left behind a residue of opposition inside the government itself.[69]

The St. Petersburg Grumbletonians, headed by Shishkov and

[69] This interesting subject is treated in greater detail by G. G. Tel'berg, *Pravitel'stvuiushchii Senat i samoderzhavnaia vlast' v nachale XIX veka* (Moscow, 1914), and A. N. Fateev, "Politicheskie napravleniia pervogo desiatiletiia XIX veka v bor'be za Senat," in *Sbornik Russkogo Instituta v Prage*, I (Prague, 1929), 205–60.

Derzhavin, had their headquarters in a literary society called "Gathering of the lovers of Russian literature" (*Beseda liubitelei rossiiskoi slovesnosti*). The formal membership of this society was very diverse, and it could boast of virtually every important personality in Russia, including its political and literary arch-enemies, Speranskii and Karamzin. But its driving force came from a few embittered men, who, having attained to some influence in the preceding two reigns resented Alexander's reliance on what they considered a coterie of upstarts, led by Speranskii and sponsored (so they suspected) by the Free Masons. These men arrogated for themselves the authority to act as guardians of the Russian national heritage, and to drive out from Russian life all foreign influences, especially the French. They were obscurantists, xenophobes, anti-Semites, whose nationalism thinly veiled powerful political ambitions. In them one can perceive the forerunners of the movement of Russian reaction whose influence made itself felt through much of the last century of the old regime.[70] The *Beseda* held formal public meetings at which its members recited their works, written in pure, un-Gallicized Shishkovian Russian, the hope being that this practice would have a salutary influence on the younger generation of writers corrupted by Karamzin and his school. As it turned out, the impact of this society on the development of Russian language and literature was virtually nil, because it rested on entirely unsound philological theories; but it did make, accidentally, one lasting contribution to Russian letters, namely the Fables of Krylov, one of its members, which were first read at the *Beseda's* public sessions.

The Tver circle (or salon) was much less formal and publicity-minded, but in the long run more important, because it was headed by no less a person than Grand Duchess Catherine, Alexander's younger sister. It is impossible to ascertain with any degree of certitude whether or not Catherine held any firm political views: in Russia she had the well-deserved reputation of

---

[70] Prince P. A. Shirinskii-Shikhmatov, who directed the Ministry of Education in the most reactionary period of the reign of Nicholas I (1850–1855), was among the active members of this society.

an out-and-out conservative, and an opponent of constitutionalism; yet later in her life, when, after the death of her first husband she married the King of Würtemberg, she worked energetically on behalf of liberal reforms in her adopted homeland.[71] Her interference in politics seems to have been inspired less by conviction than by ambition. She wanted to play an important role at the court and to secure an influence over her older brother, who, much as he loved her, showed no inclination to respect her advice on political matters. Catherine's unsavory meddling in affairs of state during Alexander's visit to London in 1814 indicates that she had a more than ordinary taste for intrigue.

Catherine was married in January 1809 to an insignificant German princeling, George of Oldenburg, after having declined, at her mother's request, a marriage proposal from Napoleon. After the wedding, her husband was appointed Director General of Bridges and Roads, as well as Governor of Tver, Novgorod, and Iaroslav, and in August 1809 the young couple left Moscow to establish residence at Tver, a hundred miles from Moscow. Although the provinces over which her husband was put in charge were considered highly desirable, Catherine chafed in her new environment. To disperse the boredom of provincial life, and to maintain contact with the outside world, she began in the winter of 1809–10 to invite to Tver leading personalities of Moscow society and high bureaucracy; among others, Theodore Rostopchin, then in forced retirement, known as an extreme nationalist, was a frequent visitor there. Before long she associated herself with the Muscovite nationalists, and made her salon the center of conservative resistance to the policies of the court, and particularly to Speranskii. Her circle, if one can call it that, included also the heir apparent, Grand Duke Constantine, and Prince Musin-Pushkin.[72]

[71] I. N. Bozherianov, *Velikaia Kniaginia Ekaterina Pavlovna* (St. Petersburg, 1888), p. 3.

[72] Prince Aleksei Ivanovich Musin-Pushkin (1741–1817) was a well-known book collector. His most celebrated find was the discovery of the manuscript of the *Lay of the Host of Igor*. Karamzin made much use of Musin-Pushkin's collection when working on his history.

It was through Rostopchin, a relative of his first wife's, that Karamzin first came in contact with the Tver group. Rostopchin introduced Karamzin to Catherine at a ball in Moscow in the autumn of 1809, and there he received an invitation to Tver. Karamzin's first visit to Tver took place in February 1810. It lasted six days, in the course of which he read long extracts from the manuscript of his as yet unpublished History. He was showered with compliments, and asked to come again soon. His second visit took place at the end of November or beginning of December, 1810. During this stay the discussion turned from history to current politics. Although there is no record of these discussions, it may be presumed that Karamzin spoke of the government in very critical terms, for Catherine then and there asked him to write an essay for her on the contemporary condition of Russia. From correspondence of a later date it is known that Catherine told Karamzin she meant to submit this memorandum to the Emperor himself.

It is highly unlikely that Karamzin undertook on his own initiative to write what became the *Memoir on Ancient and Modern Russia*. All his life he had shown a constitutional aversion to every kind of controversy, and only a few years earlier he had refused to defend himself against a vicious personal attack by Shishkov. What could he have gained from criticizing the tsar and his advisers? Exactly nothing. Political office, the only conceivable result of pamphleteering, he did not want, having turned down tempting offers both before and after 1810. But he did stand to lose much. Ever since his appointment as Historiographer of the Empire the lion's share of his income derived from the pension paid out of the private funds of Alexander. His two marriages had brought him a thousand serfs, but this was not enough, for, like many another landlord living away from the estate, he had difficulty collecting rent. He very likely could not have continued work on the history if his pension were cut off. In fact, even with the pension he was unable to afford private quarters, and had to live in Moscow with wealthy friends, the Mordvinovs. History was now his only passion; it is not likely that he would have lightheartedly jeopardized it for the sake of a political dispute.

One cannot, of course, hope to clinch the argument by reference to material self-interest alone. But the fact remains that there is no concrete motive of any sort to explain why Karamzin should have wished to engage in a personal polemic with Alexander. Lacking such a motive, and knowing what we do of the personality and political ambitions of Catherine, we must conclude that the original inspiration had come from her. To persuade Karamzin she may well have appealed to his sense of patriotism: Karamzin states in the *Memoir* that in his opinion patriotic duty alone gives the citizen the moral right to criticize his monarch.[73]

All the circumstances connected with the origins of the *Memoir* are shrouded in deep mystery. Catherine could want nothing less than to create the impression that she was forming at Tver an organized center of opposition against her brother's government. She imposed the strictest discretion on Karamzin, and requested that he make no copy of his memorandum.[74] Discretion was so well observed that for the next quarter of a century no more than six or seven persons in all Russia were even aware of the *Memoir*'s existence.[75]

Karamzin went to work on his commission as soon as he returned to Moscow. From Catherine he may have received some materials, including, one historian conjectures, confidential documents concerning Speranskii's projected reforms;[76] other mate-

---

[73] Karamzin's *Memoir* is not the only memorandum on current politics which Catherine elicited from her visitors. It is known, for instance, that in 1811 Rostopchin prepared at her request a paper on the Martinists ("Zapiska o Martinistakh predstavlennaia v 1811 g. grafom Rostopchinym Velikoi Kniagine Ekaterine Pavlovne," *Russkii Arkhiv*, III (1875), 75–81).

[74] "Mnenie grafa Bludova o dvukh zapiskakh Karamzina," in E. Kovalevskii, *Graf Bludov i ego vremia* (St. Petersburg, 1866), pp. 231–33.

[75] They were, in addition to the author: his wife, Alexander, Grand Duchess Catherine and her husband, Count Bludov, and, very likely, Arakcheev.

[76] V. I. Semevskii in *Otechestvennaia voina i russkoe obshchestvo*, II (Moscow, 1911), 225 n. Semevskii records erroneously the date of the pertinent Karamzin letter to Dmitriev as March 3, 1811, instead of 1810.

rials came from Dmitriev, who was at that time Minister of
Justice, and, *ex officio,* a member of the Council of State. These
nonpublic materials, however, were of minor importance for his
work. Karamzin almost certainly based his analysis on sources
publicly available, and with the exception of the Civil Code
Project of 1810, which, while not publicly distributed, was widely
known, he made no use of restricted documents. This fact partly
explains why his analysis frequently misconstrues the government's intentions.

Catherine urged Karamzin to hurry. On December 14, 1810,
she wrote him: "I await with impatience *A Social and Political
View of Russia*[77] (this was apparently the title originally agreed
upon); and she alluded to it again in a letter written on January
5, 1811.[78] These are the earliest known references to what was to
become Karamzin's political *chef d'oeuvre.* He worked on it in
December 1810 and January 1811, and on February 3 returned
to Tver, bearing a lengthy manuscript called *A Memoir on
Ancient and Modern Russia (Zapiska o drevnei i novoi Rossii).*
During this, his third visit, he remained at Tver for two weeks,
in the course of which he read it to Catherine either in part or
in its entirety. Before departing for home, he left the manuscript
with his hostess. (Years later he still recalled the clicking of the
lock in Catherine's drawer as she put it away.) "I can't speak for
the future," he wrote to Dmitriev the day after his return to
Moscow (February 19, 1811) "but right now the kindness which
this serene couple displays toward me is one of the greatest
delights of my life." [79]

Karamzin was probably eager to return to the history, which
the writing of the *Memoir* had disrupted for the better part of
three months.[80] But Catherine would not leave him in peace. A
day or two after he had gone back to work, the post brought an
urgent note from Catherine, dated February 18, in which she
informed him that her brother was shortly expected at Tver;

[77] *Neizdannye sochineniia,* pp. 88–89.
[78] *Ibid.,* p. 89.
[79] *Pis'ma . . . k. I. I. Dmitrievu,* p. 137.
[80] Cf. letter to brother, dated 28 February 1811 in Pogodin, *Karamzin,* II,
85.

she expressed the hope that this visit would afford Karamzin an opportunity of meeting the Emperor. On March 8 she wrote a second letter with news of Alexander's impending arrival. "Arrivez, Monsieur," she exhorted him in Caesarian verbs, "venez, voyez et rendez les armes." [81]

The meeting between Alexander and Karamzin at Tver in March 1811 was not entirely fortuitous. Alexander had known Karamzin only casually from one or two social functions. He was eager at this time to get to know him better and to see him in private because he wished to persuade him to enter state service, probably as Director of the Ministry of Education; for this reason he had only a short time before asked Dmitriev to arrange a meeting. He must have welcomed, therefore, Catherine's rendezvous, though it is unlikely that he anticipated the use to which Catherine actually put it.

Karamzin and his wife arrived at Tver on March 14. While waiting for Alexander's arrival, he had a talk with the Grand Duchess, in the course of which the subject of the *Memoir* came up. "You know," she said, "your *Memoir* is very strong." [82] Alexander arrived the next day. During the following four days (March 16–19) Karamzin dined four times in the company of the imperial family, and had one private conference with Alexander. At the private meeting Alexander offered him a high government post, the exact nature of which, however, is not known. Karamzin declined it. The most important meeting between Alexander and Karamzin took place in the evening of March 18. After dinner Karamzin recited long passages from the manuscript of his History, and then engaged in a heated discussion with Alexander on the general subject of "autocracy." "I did not have the good fortune to agree with some of his ideas," he cautiously wrote Dmitriev from Moscow a few days later, "but I did feel sincere admiration for his intellect and his modest eloquence." [83] A curious spectacle of a private citizen defending the institution of autocracy from the autocrat himself!

[81] "Come, Sir, come, see, and surrender." The allusion is to her brother's charms. *Neizdannye sochineniia*, p. 91.

[82] Pogodin, *Karamzin*, II, 78.

[83] *Pis'ma . . . k. I. I. Dmitrievu*, p. 140.

Alexander was scheduled to leave for St. Petersburg in the evening of the following day, March 19. Before his departure, he took Karamzin aside for another private talk. He again urged him to enter the service, and invited him to move permanently to St. Petersburg, where he assured him of an apartment in one of the imperial residences. Karamzin declined both offers.

The Tver meeting was superficially a great success. "My heart was always attracted to him," Karamzin confided to Dmitriev, "divining and feeling the goodness of this unusual monarch: now I love and respect him from an inner belief in the beauty of his soul." [84]

Before his own departure from Tver, Karamzin requested Catherine to return him the manuscript. What must have been his feelings when Catherine replied that it was now "in good hands"? Apparently the night before, after the debate between Alexander and Karamzin on autocracy, Catherine slipped the manuscript to her brother. On its title page she had written: "A mon frère seul." [85]

Did Alexander ever read the *Memoir*? No one knows, and there is no direct evidence to help answer this question either way. He certainly never made any public reference to it.[86] As for the manuscript itself, it disappeared on the evening of March 18, 1811, to be accidentally rediscovered a quarter of a

[84] *Ibid.*

[85] *Russkii Arkhiv* (1871), p. 1138 n. This version of March 19 is reconstructed from Karamzin's correspondence. There exists a slightly different version, supplied by Bludov and Serbinovich, two good friends of the historian. They told Pogodin that many years after these events Karamzin said that Alexander had shown him great coolness when departing from Tver; from which one may infer that Alexander had read the *Memoir*, or at least a part of it, between the evening of March 18 and the evening of March 19. *Cf.* Pogodin, *Karamzin*, II, 80–81, 85. Letters written by Karamzin during and immediately after the Tver encounter, however, do not convey this impression; nor is there any other corroboration of this version.

[86] Though Count Bludov, to whom we owe most of our information on the history of the manuscript of the *Memoir*, reported, in a testimony dated December 12, 1860, from Karamzin's own words, that in 1816, when Karamzin was decorated for his services, Alexander said the decoration was not for the *History* but for the *Memoir on Ancient and Modern Russia; Grot, Trudy*, III, 162.

century later, by which time all the principals in this incident were dead.

This third visit to Tver made a disagreeable impression on Karamzin. When Catherine again invited him two months later he refused. "I am a passionate homebody," he wrote to his brother, "and the prospect of traveling on highways to spend ten days in idleness worrying about the children does not appeal to me." [87] These words were written a mere two and a half months after he had described the visits to Tver "as one of the greatest delights" of his life. But the pressures did not relent, and Karamzin, whose position after the delivery of the *Memoir* into Alexander's hands was more precarious than ever, could hardly afford to alienate his powerful patroness. He went to Tver three more times in the course of the same year, more from a sense of duty than from a prospect of pleasure. He was finally relieved of this onerous social obligation in 1812, when the Tver household broke up following the outbreak of the war and the death of Prince George.

—◖ ◗—

The quality which first strikes the reader of the *Memoir on Ancient and Modern Russia* is the violence of its criticism. It is true that Karamzin concedes Alexander's good intentions, but in the exposition of the policies themselves it is difficult to find anything except charges of ignorance, stupidity, and uncontrollable vanity. Even the chance approval of some minor government actions actually reflects contempt: so insignificant are they compared to the failures. The whole work is filled with the spirit of anger and of scorn. In this respect it is a document without precedent in Russian history: never before had a Russian subject dared to address his monarch in similar terms. Karamzin spoke out not as a dispassionate observer, but as a living conscience of his nation, as a prophet.

This quality determined the style and to some extent even the content of his work. Written hastily, with a sense of urgency, it

[87] Pogodin, *Karamzin*, II, 85.

abounds in minor errors and inaccuracies. Though it opens with major stylistic chords, which resound with all the rich tones demanded by the age of weighty subjects, most of the narrative is composed in a conversational style, which in certain parts (e.g. the section dealing with finance) acquires an almost steno-graphic brevity.

The *Memoir* divides itself naturally into three principal parts: an historical introduction, an analysis of the policies of Alexander I, and a conclusion.

The main purpose of the historical introduction is to bolster the thesis, further developed in the second, principal part of the work, that the security, welfare, and very survival of Russia are indissolubly bound with the institution of a monocratic and autocratic royal power. Karamzin advances here views elaborated by the "statist" school of Russian historians, whose origins go back to the fifteenth and sixteenth centuries. This school stressed the continuity and extension of Russian monarchic authority from the time of Kiev to that of St. Petersburg, and interpreted the entire course of Russian history in terms of the centralization of power.[88] Karamzin, like his predecessors, pays little attention to the social factor. To him the social structure is a constant quantity, which functions like a machine, either well or badly, depending on the use to which it is put by those in political power. In other words, he views social and economic develop-ments as consequences of political action; for this reason he attaches extraordinary importance to the Russian monarchy, the monarchy being in Russia the source of all political initiative.

The novelty of this historical introduction is twofold. It is the first more or less coherent attempt to interpret the course of all Russian history in the light of autocratic principles. Right or wrong, this interpretation is important because it constitutes an essential ingredient of all Russian conservative thought both before and after Karamzin. Its second novelty lies in the un-precedented criticism which it levies at some Russian monarchs. When Karamzin was writing, Russian monarchs, past as well as present, were considered beyond the pale of criticism, and books

[88] Miliukov, *Glavnye techeniia,* I, 167–78.

on recent history still resembled more hagiography than history proper. Even Ivan IV was accepted by the literate public as a "good" tsar. Karamzin's condemnation of the vices of Russian rulers, particularly of the private lives of eighteenth-century empresses, was new and shocking. Especially audacious were his allusions to the death of Paul I; this subject was not publicly discussed, and Alexander was for understandable reasons most sensitive to it.

The major part of the *Memoir,* and nearly half its bulk, is devoted to a discussion of the foreign and internal policies of Alexander I. The brunt of the critique is directed against the "counselors" of the monarch, but they are nowhere mentioned by name. Even Speranskii, whose figure looms in the background of the entire essay, is never directly referred to.

The analysis begins with foreign policy. Karamzin assumes an isolationist position, and opposes all Russian intervention in European affairs, even when it results in expansion (e.g. Finland): Russia should mind her own business. War in his view is justifiable only in self-defense. In Karamzin's analysis of contemporary European diplomacy one can discern outlines of the thesis that the security of Russia lay in the maintenance of a strong Austria and Prussia as a buffer shielding her from the West: a thesis which in the 1830's became the cornerstone of Russia's foreign policy for the following half a century.

Karamzin next takes up the subject of political institutions. Here he voices a concern deeply felt by many of his contemporaries, including men with extensive administrative experience, that Speranskii's reforms instead of legitimizing Russian government, would merely increase the already extensive power of the bureaucracy. Psychologically speaking Karamzin was perhaps less concerned with the details of Alexander's institutional reforms, although he found much to criticize on this level too, than with the emergence, through the reforms, of a vast, centrally directed bureaucratic apparatus which would upset the equilibrium between state and society established in the preceding century. This fear focused on the institution of the ministries.

Parallels to Karamzin's arguments against the ministerial re-

forms can be found in memoranda submitted to Alexander I and
Nicholas I respectively by two professional administrators, D. P.
Troshchinskii and N. S. Mordvinov. D. P. Troshchinskii, a one-
time leader of the senatorial opposition, submitted in 1811 a
long note in which he developed a detailed case against the
proposal to replace all colleges with ministries. Insofar as Russia
was an autocratic state and lacked institutions capable of cur-
tailing supreme authority, Troshchinskii argued, the safeguards
for the protection of citizens from the arbitrary exercise of
power had to be built into the administrative structure itself.
In his opinion, such safeguards had been provided by the colleges. In the colleges all decisions had been subject to group
criticism and group approval, whereas in the ministries the
power and responsibility were vested in individuals.[89] The same
conclusion was drawn by Admiral Mordvinov in a memorandum
which he submitted to Nicholas I in 1827. Mordvinov stated
that the introduction in the ministries of bureaucratic procedures as a substitute for the traditional collegiate procedures,
accomplished in the early 1800's, resulted in the removal of the
most effective restraints on the executive branch of government,
and presented in the long run a serious danger for state and
society alike.[90] In his political discussion Karamzin takes a strong
stand against the bureaucratization of the government implicit
in the establishment of ministries and the State Council. He
advocates a system essentially identical with that proposed by
the senatorial opposition a decade earlier: a strong Senate, with
supreme administrative authority and, under it, colleges or
ministries.

After discussing briefly individual legislative acts dealing with
the raising of a national militia, education, and the civil service,

[89] "Zapiska Dmitriia Prokof'evicha Troshchinskogo ob uchrezhdenii ministerstv," *Sbornik russkogo istoricheskogo obshchestva*, III (St. Petersburg,
1868), 1–162. The complete text of this memorandum is in the Central State
Historical Archive in Leningrad (TsGIAL), Arkhiv Speranskogo, Fond 1251,
op. I, No. 11.

[90] "Mnenie Admirala Mordvinova o kollegial'nom i ministerskom upravlenii
v Rossii," *Chteniia v imperatorskom obshchestve istorii i drevnostei ros-
siiskikh*, III (Moscow, 1864), Part 5, 154–60.

Karamzin takes up the problem of serfdom. He is emphatically in favor of its preservation. In defense of this institution he cites an array of historical, moral, and political evidence. There can be little doubt that in so doing, Karamzin, like other conservatives of his time, defends the vital economic interests of his class, that is to say, he and they are motivated above all by self-interest; the historical and ethical arguments cited are nothing but flimsy attempts to rationalize this fact. In his historical argument Karamzin conveniently forgets that originally the enserfment of the peasantry occurred in conjunction with the rendering of state service by the gentry, and that, legally and morally, the gentry which gave no service had no claim on the services of the serfs. He also ignores the argument that as long as it is impossible to distinguish between the descendants of slaves and of serfs proper (as he himself points out) it can be equally well argued that all should be manumitted, as that all should be enserfed. Nor is it necessary to comment on his praise of the alleged blessings of serfdom for the peasants. Serfdom was essential for the gentry, and thus indirectly for the preservation of Russia as it was then known — this was sufficient to rouse a chorus of protests against all the government attempts to ameliorate or even to regulate the status of the serfs. Any tampering with serfdom the gentry construed as an act of unwarranted state interference in their private affairs. On no subject were the various right-wing groups in quite so complete accord as on this. Karamzin's views on this subject agree in most respects with those upheld by other prominent opponents of emancipation, including Rostopchin and Derzhavin.[91]

Two aspects of this otherwise transparent case of defense of class-interest, however, do require brief comment. One concerns the political argument with which Karamzin buttresses his case. Karamzin argues that with the abolition of serfdom the entire burden of administering the country would fall on the shoulders

[91] V. I. Semevskii, *Krestianskii vopros v Rossii v XVIII i pervoi polovine XIX veka*, I (St. Petersburg, 1888), 241, 254-59, 302-05 etc.; also M. I. Bogdanovich, *Istoriia tsarstvovaniia Imperatora Aleksandra I i Rossii v ego vremia*, I (St. Petersburg, 1869), 98.

of the monarchy. Can it manage to carry this burden, he asks, and hints gloomily at the catastrophe which must follow if it should turn out that it could not. This political argument was subsequently much used by proponents of serfdom both before and after the Emancipation of 1861. It was not entirely without merit: one may well contend that Russia's political disintegration in the second half of the nineteenth century was in no small measure due to the excessive administrative responsibility assumed by the monarchy when it abolished the gentry's authority over the bonded population.

The second point to note in connection with the serf problem is that, under the conditions then prevailing, the conservative argument was not without economic merit either. In the reign of Alexander I emancipation was conceived by those who were for as well as those who were against serfdom as an emancipation without land. Everybody recognized that the land itself was the property of the gentry; an emancipation with land was conceivable only in consequence of large-scale redemptions, the means for which were not to be found either in the state's treasury nor in the villages. Thus the serf-emancipation carried out in the Baltic provinces in 1816 deprived the peasants of their traditional land allotments. Had the government emancipated the serfs in Russia proper in the early 1800's, the net result, as far as the peasants were concerned, would have been mass-expropriation. It is the great merit of the conservative opponents of emancipation in the reign of Alexander I that by calling attention to the disastrous implications of a landless emancipation they cleared the ground for the landed emancipation which took place fifty years later — a contribution which is not vitiated by its admittedly selfish inspiration.

The longest part of the analysis of Alexander's reign is devoted to financial problems. Karamzin's economic views are derived from Western liberal economists, whose ideas had gained wide currency in Russia under Catherine II.[92] He favors free trade; he looks to natural resources and to labor rather than to precious

[92] V. V. Sviatlovskii, *Ocherki po istorii ekonomicheskikh vozzrenii na Zapade i v Rossii*, I (St. Petersburg, 1913).

metals as the basis of national wealth; and he advocates soft money, light taxes, and fiscal economy as the principal means of stimulating the productive forces of the country. His economic liberalism is in sharp contrast to his political conservatism. It re-emphasizes the fact that to him individual liberty was the ultimate goal of all statesmanship: in the sphere of politics he sought to secure it by means of strong, centralized government, and in the sphere of economics by means of *laissez-faire*.[93]

The brunt of Karamzin's financial criticism is directed against the theoretical premises of the government's fiscal reforms of 1810, and particularly against its stated preference for metallic currency over bank-notes. The relative merits of these two types of money were widely discussed in Europe in the second half of the eighteenth century, with the Mercantilists and other traditionalists sponsoring metal, and the liberal innovators, including the Physiocrats, sponsoring paper. Adam Smith, in *The Wealth of Nations,* compared metallic currency to a highway which, while useful to transport people and things, was of itself unproductive, and paper currency to an "aerial wagonway" which made it possible to transform these roads into fertile plowland and pasture. The proponents of paper argued that there exists an iron law regulating the relationship between money and goods; money symbolizes a definite quantity of produce, so that its value is determined by the amount of produce available: if the quantity of produce remains constant but the quantity of money rises, then prices rise too, and *vice versa.* Money of itself, therefore, can neither enrich nor impoverish a country, although a sudden change in the sum total of currency can injure trade by temporarily unsettling the accepted standards of exchange. Karamzin, looking at Russia's financial difficulties from the viewpoint of a private citizen, contended that paper money, judiciously handled, could be a great boon to the country by

[93] In this connection it may be noted that the French Physiocrats also advocated political absolutism, although for other reasons. They felt that only an all-powerful monarch was impartial enough to prevent any interest group from using the state for its own purposes, and thus able to assure the state a truly free, competitive economy. *Cf.* B. Güntzberg, *Die Gesellschafts- und Staatslehre der Physiokraten* (Altenburg, 1907), p. 75 ff.

supplementing the specie, of which Russia always had an inadequate supply. Speranskii, on the other hand, viewing these
difficulties as a statesman whose primary concern was with
budgetary stability, rejected paper notes on the ground that they
made proper planning of the state budget impossible. Both sides
were in a sense right; their difference was largely one of approach.[94]

The final section of the second part is devoted to codification.
This subject was of utmost importance to Karamzin, because in
his mind the monarchical system was indissolubly bound with
the legal order. In his conversations with Alexander, which
became frequent and very frank after he had moved to St.
Petersburg in 1816, Karamzin repeatedly insisted on the necessity of providing Russia with firm and lucid laws. The very last
conversation he had with Alexander in August 1825, four
months before the latter's death, was on this subject. Alexander
at this time solemnly promised him to give the country a code
of laws.[95]

Here, as in other parts of his discourse, Karamzin looks at the
subject from a pragmatic, historical viewpoint. A nation's laws
must be derived from its own experience, and designed to meet
its actual needs. The Civil Code Project of 1810 satisfied neither
of these two conditions. Karamzin's criticism of Speranskii's and
Rozenkampf's preposterous effort to transplant to Russia the
Code Napoléon was, of course, entirely justified. As for his suggestions on the best manner of compiling a code, all that need
be said about them is that the procedure eventually adopted by
Speranskii in the reign of Nicholas I in his successful attempt to
compile a code followed closely that which Karamzin had out-
lined in the *Memoir*. To what extent Speranskii was influenced
by Karamzin one cannot say. It is known, however, that shortly
after he had been put in charge of the Second Department of
the Imperial Chancery, in March 1826, he paid Karamzin a visit
to discuss this matter. Karamzin approved wholeheartedly of

---

[94] The dispute, of course, concerned only paper currency which lacked a
100 per cent metal backing.
[95] *Neizdannye sochineniia*, p. 12.

Speranskii's new plan: "This is what I have always been preaching," he told him.[96]

In the third, and concluding part, Karamzin outlines the most effective ways of improving the general condition of the country. Boiled down to its essentials, the program he proposes aims at producing certain psychological effects. It calls for the restoration of the government's prestige through a prudent use of rewards and punishments, that is, through an appeal to ambition and fear. The image of the tsar which he conveys is that of a patriarch who rules impartially and wisely like a paterfamilias over his brood, but displays particular affection for the gentry, whose help he needs to keep the household in line. The emphasis in this part of the *Memoir* is on the emotional bond between the monarch and the country; this is accomplished at the cost of political institutions whose importance for the welfare of Russia Karamzin deliberately minimizes.

To what extent was Karamzin's criticism sound? He certainly tended to underestimate the complexities of practical government, and dismissed as superfluous features of political life without which administration was inconceivable: a tendency particularly striking in his discussion of political institutions. In certain parts of his analysis he was handicapped by the secrecy with which the government surrounded some of its reforms; lacking knowledge of Speranskii's constitutional project, for instance, he could not justly appraise the reorganization of the State Council. He was at his best in the discussion of the financial and legal reforms; these sections are factually correct (save for some trivial inaccuracies) and original in conception. The sections dealing with foreign policy and political institutions suffer from the author's ignorance of the vital documents, and are less convincing, yet they too, broadly speaking, are justified. The least satisfactory part of the criticism is that devoted to the serf question; here Karamzin reveals a complete lack of social conscience, and twists the evidence to suit his arguments. But this part does at least have the merit of pointing out certain connotations of a landless emancipation of which the government was

[96] Pogodin, *Karamzin*, II, 475–76.

not fully cognizant. In the balance of things, his criticism thus comes out well.

Karamzin is far less convincing as a constructive than as a destructive critic. He has an extremely naive conception of administrative procedure, and rejects nearly all attempts to reform the governmental apparatus on the correct but irrelevant grounds that states are run by men and not by institutions. He is blind to the need of a soundly planned system of political institutions, and his positive suggestions are, for all practical purposes, quite useless.

In the debate between Karamzin and Speranskii — for this is what the *Memoir* really implied — we have an illustration of how heavy a price societies must pay for the suppression of free opinion. The disagreement between them actually rested on a misunderstanding. Ultimately, Karamzin and Speranskii wanted the same thing: a "true" monarchic system based on law and respectful of civil liberties. But they approached this ideal from different vantage points: Speranskii from that of a responsible, practical statesman, Karamzin, from that of a private citizen. The two approaches were really complementary. Speranskii had the knowledge of the techniques of government, Karamzin had the knowledge of Russia. In a free society their conflicting viewpoints would have clashed in the open, and, through confrontation, the area of disagreement would have narrowed down. In Russia, voiced in secrecy, obliquely as it were, and without the benefit of a direct encounter, the disagreements were magnified out of all proportion, and instead of leading to fruitful action, led to frustration and bitterness.

Karamzin is sometimes blamed for having caused by this *Memoir* the downfall of Speranskii in March 1812. This charge is not supported by the available facts. There is no evidence that Alexander paid attention to any of the recommendations contained in the *Memoir* (if, which is not even certain, he had ever read it at all), nor does the *Memoir* attack personally Speranskii: it criticizes rather the conception behind the government's whole political program, a conception which was as much Alexander's as it was Speranskii's. It must be remembered that Speranskii stayed in full power for one whole year after the *Memoir* had been placed in Alexander's hands. Speranskii was finally dismissed and exiled because Alexander resented the power which he had acquired through his control of the bureaucratic apparatus, and because by firing him Alexander hoped to regain the sympathies of the gentry which he vitally needed in view of the imminent resumption of hostilities against Napoleon. Karamzin and Speranskii never harbored any personal ill-feelings toward each other. As late as July 1810 Karamzin sent a friendly letter to Speranskii, seeking his protection against accusations lodged with the police by his archenemy, the follower of Shishkov, Golenishchev-Kutuzov, who accused him of "Jacobinism." [97] At the time of Speranskii's fall (1812) Karamzin is said to have remonstrated on his behalf with Alexander, and as soon as Speranskii returned from exile (March 1821) he sought Karamzin out.[98] They subsequently met a number of times. Of course, men of such different personalities and viewpoints could never reach a great degree of intimacy; yet the absence of rancor in their personal relationship is not compatible with the charge of Karamzin's complicity in the disgrace of Speranskii. For that he had neither the inclination nor the power.

It is only in a very general way the Karamzin's *Memoir* may be said to have played a part in the suspension of Alexander's reform policies, and that is insofar as it expressed the gentry discontent to which the government sooner or later had to pay heed. In that respect, however, Karamzin was not the cause, but the symptom of a cause. He spoke for no definite group, let alone organized party. The *Memoir* seems to have been composed free of any external influence, and there is no evidence that Karamzin had any personal contact with the leaders of the conservative opposition inside the government.[99] For that reason it cannot

[97] *Pis'ma . . . k I. I. Dmitrievu*, p. 128.

[98] *Ibid.*, p. 305; *cf.* p. 310; Grot, *Trudy*, III, 162.

[99] A. N. Fateev in his informative essay, based in part on unpublished materials from the Archive of the State Council, links Karamzin with the senatorial opposition. But while it is clear that Karamzin shared the principal views of this inchoate group (stress on the Senate as the administrative center, and hostility to the ministries) it is far less clear that he actually

be treated as a tract of an organized party. Rather, it was the voice of a man who, by virtue of his upbringing, social contacts, and intellectual affinities identified himself with what may be called a conservative gentry viewpoint — a viewpoint which had attained to a remarkable degree of consistency, considering that Russia at that time offered few opportunities for the development of public opinion. The views which Karamzin championed had no effect whatsoever on the policies of Alexander, who, even when he finally gave up all intention of reforming Russia, turned for assistance in governing the country not to the conservatives, but to the bureaucrats. But in the subsequent reign of Nicholas I these views became the monarchy's official state program. They continued to dominate Russian policies during much of the nineteenth century, long after the conditions which engendered them had ceased to exist.

CONCLUDING REMARKS

Viewed from the political vantage point, there are two clearly distinguishable types of conservatism. One type can be found in every society: it results from the effort on the part of the social organism to preserve itself, and represents as it were a counterpart of the instinct of self-preservation in individuals. Its most vociferous exponents are to be found among groups enjoying some measure of preponderance, economic or other, which it is in their interest to retain. It makes little difference whether these groups be landowning, commercial, bureaucratic or other; as long as a social group derives from the system more than its proportionate share of wealth and power, it is instinctively driven to its defense. This type of conservatism is a social rather than a

---

identified himself with it. There is no evidence that Karamzin was in contact with the leaders of the senatorial opposition (Troshchinskii, Vorontsov, Zavadovskii) or that he wrote under outside instructions. See Fateev, "Politicheskie napravleniia." The only likely external influence on Karamzin may have been that of Rostopchin (then still in retirement) with whom Karamzin was on very intimate terms, and whose views coincided in many respects with his own. *Cf.* Tikhonravov, "Graf F. V. Rostopchin i literatura v 1812-m godu," *Sochineniia*, III/1 (Moscow, 1898), 305–79, and A. Kizevetter, "Politicheskie i sotsial'nye vozzreniia gr. F. V. Rostopchina," *Russkaia Mysl'*, January 1913 (pp. 38–67), and February 1913 (pp. 1–31).

historical phenomenon for, although it assumes different shapes in different societies in conformity with the prevailing distribution of benefits, as a type it remains basically the same, representing everywhere and at all times a defense of vested interests for which ideas are little more than a smokescreen.

The other type of conservatism represents a specific phase in the history of European political thought. It is closely connected with the emergence of the modern dynamic, egalitarian state, and manifests itself, broadly speaking, in an individualistic reaction to that broad extension of the claims of society and state on the citizen which had its inception in enlightened absolutism, its greatest single triumph in the French Revolution, and its inglorious fulfillment in twentieth-century totalitarianism. Conservatism as a political idea (in contrast to conservatism as a social movement) expresses itself in a reaffirmation of the primacy of traditional social groupings over the all-embracing body politic, and in an opposition, variously inspired, to all forms of social engineering. Its rise was most spectacular after 1789, when the principle of social engineering suddenly acquired unprecedented strength from a fusion with the principles of democracy and egalitarianism, but its roots reach back several centuries, to a tradition of aristocratic resistance to royal absolutism of which Montesquieu was philosophically perhaps the outstanding proponent.

In Russia of the time of Karamzin both these types of conservatism were in existence, but the former was considerably stronger. That is to say, at the beginning of the nineteenth century, Russian conservatism was as yet more a defense of interest than an expression of a philosophy, more a social than an intellectual movement.

Socially, Russian conservatism of this period drew its strength from the aspirations of a single class, the gentry. Here was a contented class in the fullest sense of the word, endowed with every conceivable economic and social privilege for which it was not required to give society anything in return. Any change in the *status quo* could only work to the detriment of this class, and for this reason it staunchly defended the established order,

gladly forfeiting all claim to political power. The gentry supported the autocracy, and received in return the autocracy's protection. Between these two there existed a partnership resting
on a broad community of interest: the crown safeguarded the
privileges of the gentry, while the gentry helped the crown to
shoulder the responsibilities of governing an immense, under-
developed empire, responsibilities which were far beyond the
latter's capacity to bear alone. This partnership rested on an
unwritten understanding that each party possessed undisputed
mastery within its own sphere of competence: the monarchy over
affairs of state (at that time conceived quite narrowly by modern standards), the gentry over the manor. Russia owed much
of her stability as well as political ossification to this arrangement. Controlling between them as they did most of Russia's
wealth, namely her land and serfs, the crown and the gentry
could repel all challenges to their authority, but this entailed
excluding from participation in the running of the country all
of its truly productive elements.

The gentry's only source of dissatisfaction with the existing
order was cultural, but even this dissatisfaction was not very
keen. Though Westernized in thought, speech, and manners, the
gentry had a much more intimate contact with the masses of the
population than did the court. The monarchy favored a program
of Westernization to which the gentry did not fully subscribe,
and even if this program had little effect on these features of
Russian life which really mattered, there was always a certain
discrepancy between the critical outlook of the court, and the
national outlook of the gentry.

The French Revolution ended this disagreement once and for
all. The breakdown of that European society which the Russian
monarchy had adopted as a model for itself, and the seeming dissolution of the stabilizing forces of traditional civilization,
emphasized the dangers which faced any country treading the
path of Western Enlightenment. This danger was perhaps more
keenly felt in Russia than in the West, for here the contrast between the traditional and the modern was not only cultural, but
also national in character. Throughout the Napoleonic period

the Russian monarchy vacillated: habit was strong, and, more important, there was as yet no acceptable substitute for the old Westernizing policy. It was during this critical period in the history of the Russian monarchy that the gentry stepped into the breach, and supplied the monarchy with its own national ideology in place of the discredited Enlightenment and Francophilia.

Thus, Russian social conservatism between 1789 and approximately 1812 resulted from an exceptionally close interdependence between the monarchy and the gentry, originally established as a result of the overextension of the Russian state; this interdependence, brought into being in the eighteenth century, was firmly cemented by the challenge flung to the monarchy and nobility alike by the French Revolution.

When one turns to the ideological side of Russian conservatism at this period, the picture is far less coherent. None of the Russian conservative thinkers, not even Karamzin, made any serious attempt to construct a philosophic defense of the Russian political tradition. Their argumentation was either pragmatic or purely emotional, but in either event strikingly devoid of the philosophic content which distinguished the best of Western conservative thought of the time. Karamzin, for example, perhaps the most widely read Russian of his time, showed no interest either in Burke or in De Maistre, the latter of whom he knew personally; De Maistre's *Soirées de St. Pétersbourg* he described as "profound to the point of absurdity."[100] This intellectual poverty of Russian conservatism in the reign of Alexander I was due partly to the general immaturity of Russian political thought, and partly to the absence of any vocal opposition to the *status quo,* which would compel the conservatives to elevate their argument to higher levels; after all, in the first decade of the nineteenth century the center of discontent with the *status quo* was still to be found at the court itself.

It is always difficult to use concrete facts to illustrate broad historical generalizations. Karamzin naturally does not fit fully this image of Russian conservatism, for being a human being

[100] *Pis'ma . . . k I. I. Dmitrievu,* pp. 310–11.

and not an abstraction he had his personal peculiarities, contradictions, and inclinations. For one, it is not possible to pin on
his conservatism any label of material self-interest, since he derived his livelihood not from land and serf labor, but from his
writing and royal pension; he was a landed gentleman more in
the cultural than economic sense of the word. Indeed, in view
of the climate prevailing at the court, self-interest dictated that
he pursue a moderately liberal, rather than a conservative course.
Yet, by and large, he reflects well in microcosm the broad
tendencies of Russian conservatism of his time. His intellectual
eclecticism actually increases his value for the historian: in his
very unoriginality one finds added assurance that the ideas he
espoused were current rather than contrived.

In following the central thread of Karamzin's political development, one finds not a fundamental change, as has often
been claimed, but a steady, even logical, evolution. He began
with a rejection of politics, concentrating his attention entirely
on aesthetic and moral self-improvement; then, under the impact
of the French Revolution and its Russian repercussions, he
acquired an interest in politics, having come to realize that the
self-improvement which he desired was possible only in societies
capable of assuring the citizen of firm civil rights; and, finally,
his historical studies led him to the conclusion that in Russia
civil rights had to be attained at the cost of political rights, that
is, through the acceptance of an autocratic system of government. Self-improvement — civil rights — autocracy: such were the
principal stages in his political evolution. He retained to the
end a belief in republicanism, but he became gradually convinced that in Russia the conditions which the republicans desired could be brought about only by a strong, centralized, legally
unlimited monarchy. Similarly, he adhered throughout his life
to the belief that politics were incapable of solving any of the
fundamental problems of human existence.

Karamzin's defense of the autocratic system was little more
than an elaboration of ideas current in Russia in the eighteenth
century. The only new element which he contributed to the
autocratic ideology was an historical argument derived from

Montesquieu and bolstered with evidence from Russia's past. This strengthened, but did not appreciably deepen the case. The intellectual deepening of the Russian conservative movement occurred only in the following generations, first under the stimulus of German romantic philosophy, and then in reaction to radical excesses.

Karamzin's conception of the Russian political system agrees in all essentials with that espoused by the gentry in the eighteenth century, and by the crown under Catherine II. He wanted control over the country divided between the monarchy and the gentry, neither encroaching on the other's province; and he was consistent enough to demand that the gentry leave the crown undisputed authority in affairs of state, as a corollary of the crown's noninterference with their rights and freedoms. He wished the monarchy to rule lawfully, and to respect the estates, particularly the gentry.

The program which Karamzin and his class proposed was entirely utopian. It rested on a misunderstanding of the workings of government, and on a completely unrealistic conception of Russia's social structure. It ignored the fact that political power, subjected to no restraints, does not stay within self-defined limits, but inevitably expands as its human and material resources expand. It made no provisions for changes in the social structure, or for granting the other classes a more equitable share of the national wealth which, as was evident even then, they would sooner or later demand. The very image of a Russia divided into estates on a Western model — an image without which the conservative case could not subsist — was in stark contradiction to Russian realities as well as traditions.

But the significance of the argument advanced by Karamzin lay not so much in the specific criticism of state policies or in his recommendations, as in the peculiar ambivalence in the attitude toward the state characteristic of a certain kind of Russian conservatism which we find revealed in it.

Karamzin considered a substantial rise in the cultural level of the Russian population an indispensable prerequisite to all fundamental social and political reform. Such a rise, in his opinion, could be achieved only within the framework of a strong, centralized state, which alone had the means to give Russia the requisite stability, and to keep in check the predatory instincts of its diverse classes and races. He was a "statist," and in this respect differed sharply from most Russian conservative as well as radical political thinkers of the subsequent century, who were in varying degrees influenced by Populist sentiments. On the other hand, however, Karamzin rejected the modern bureaucratic state and the principle of equality which it carried with it. He saw in the rights of the gentry the single most important factor in the emergence in Russia of a civilized society. He was anti-liberal not because he disliked liberal ideals, but because he felt the "liberal" reforms carried out by Alexander meant, in effect, the abrogation of the powers of the gentry and the introduction of an enormous and potentially uncontrollable bureaucratic machinery.

This ambivalence, stemming from a distrust of both the masses and the omnipotent egalitarian state, explains the static quality of Karamzin's political philosophy, and indicates the main cause of the failure of the type of conservatism he espoused. For all his shortcomings, however, he was sounder in his appraisal of Russia's problem than those who in the developing conflict between state and society placed their hopes unreservedly on either one or the other.

THE HISTORY OF THE TEXT

The original manuscript of the *Memoirs on Ancient and Modern Russia* is lost, and all the extant versions of this work are descended from handwritten copies first taken down in 1834–35.

No one has ever been able satisfactorily to explain what has happened to the original manuscript after Grand Duchess Catherine had given it to Alexander during his visit to Tver in March 1811. There are, broadly speaking, two hypotheses. The first, suggested by K. S. Serbinovich, a close friend of the Karamzin family, and supported by the historian I. N. Grech, holds that Alexander left the manuscript in Tver, and that there it fell into the possession of I. M. Born, the private secretary of Catherine's husband, Prince George of Oldenburg.[1] This suggestion, however, is not plausible. Had Born really secured such an important document he would not have been likely to keep it secret for a quarter of a century. Moreover, it is known that when Karamzin had asked Catherine to return his work to him, following Alexander's departure from Tver in the evening of March 19, 1811, he was told that it was in "good hands," which could only mean that it was in the possession of Alexander.[2]

The second hypothesis, and the one generally accepted, holds that Alexander took the manuscript with him on his departure from Tver for St. Petersburg, and there entrusted it to Arakcheev for safekeeping. This theory is supported by the close coincidence between the death of Arakcheev (April 1834) and the reappearance of the *Memoir* (1834 or 1835) as well as the testimony of a reliable witness, Count Bludov.

[1] P. Pekarskii, *Istoricheskie bumagi sobrannye Konstantinom Ivanovichem Arsen'evym* (St. Petersburg, 1872), pp. 47–48.

[2] I. N. Bozherianov, *Velikaia kniaginia Ekaterina Pavlovna* (St. Petersburg, 1888), pp. 38–39.

It is certain that the manuscript was not found in the private archives of Alexander I, which were thoroughly examined after his death by Nicholas I and by several trusted persons, including Karamzin's friend, Count Bludov. Shortly after Alexander's death Karamzin requested Bludov to retrieve the *Memoir,* whose existence apparently continued to worry him, but Bludov was unable to find any trace of it. Nicholas I himself learned of the *Memoir* only in 1835 or later, when copies of it began to circulate in St. Petersburg. Sometime afterward he commissioned Bludov to investigate and report on the unpublished works of Karamzin, particularly on an allegedly seditious work called "Thoughts on Russia." In his report Bludov suggested that Nicholas apparently had in mind the *Memoir on Ancient and Modern Russia,* of which Karamzin had spoken to him in confidence, but which he had never given him to read because, complying with Catherine's request, he had made no transcriptions. After Alexander's death, Bludov continued, Karamzin had asked that it be returned to him, but it could not be found. He, Bludov, had first read it in 1834 or 1835, from a transcript, one of the many which suddenly appeared in St. Petersburg at that time.[3]

Bludov did not feel free to tell Nicholas about the circumstances under which he had first come into possession of a copy of the *Memoir,* but he fortunately confided many years later in Ia. K. Grot:

After the death of Emperor Alexander Pavlovich, I failed to locate this *Memoir* among his papers, but it was discovered shortly after the death of Arakcheev. One day K. I. Arsenev came to see me, and asked whether I was acquainted with Karamzin's *Memoir on Ancient and Modern Russia.* I told him yes, I had heard of it, but had not read it. "I can let you have a copy," he said, "but do not ask me to tell you where I had obtained it." Most likely (Count Bludov added), it was found

---

[3] "Mnenie grafa Bludova o dvukh zapiskakh Karamzina," in E. Kovalevskii, *Graf Bludov i ego vremia* (St. Petersburg, 1866), pp. 231–33; also A. Fateev, "Sud'ba Zapisok Karamzina o Rossii i Pol'she pri Imperatore Nikolae I," in *Zapiski Russkogo Istoricheskogo Obshchestva v Prage,* I (Prague, 1927), 114–19.

among the papers of Arakcheev: the Sovereign, who had received it from Catherine Pavlovna at Tver, went from there directly to [Arakcheev's estate at] Gruzino, and probably left it with his favorite.[4]

Konstantin Arsenev, historian and statistician, was, from 1832, member of the Council of the Ministry of the Interior, and tutor in the imperial household. In 1835 he was granted permission to work in the state archives, and it is probably in one of these capacities that he gained access to the papers of Arakcheev who, dying heirless, had left all his possessions to the tsar. Bludov's account is the only item of evidence we possess on the circumstances in which the *Memoir* was rediscovered; it leaves no doubt that credit for the rediscovery belongs to Arsenev. The copy (or copies) which Arsenev transcribed served as the source of the numerous manuscript versions which circulated in Russia after 1834, as well as of all the printed versions, with the possible exception of Sipovskii's, on which the present edition is based.

The earliest dated reference to the *Memoir* after its rediscovery is in the report which Prince Shirinskii-Shikhmatov made to the Russian Academy on January 18, 1836. In a statement called "Something about Karamzin," Shirinskii-Shikmatov reported that Karamzin had written an essay *On Ancient and Modern Russia,* "which is of importance for those who cherish his glorious memory, but is as yet unknown to the present-day public." [5] In fact, at the time of its rediscovery the very existence of the *Memoir* was probably known only to two persons: Karamzin's widow (to whom Karamzin had dictated the original) and Bludov, since all the actual participants in the Tver encounter (save for Karamzin's widow) were dead by now.

[4] *Otchet po Otdeleniiu russkogo iazyka i slovesnosti Akademii Nauk za 1865 god,* in *St. Petersburskie Vedomosti,* Nos. 36–37 (1866), quoted in Pekarskii, *Istoricheskie bumagi,* pp. 47–48. The only correction which must be made in Bludov's account concerns the circumstances in which Alexander might have given Arakcheev the manuscript. We know from Arakcheev's diary of Alexander's visits to Gruzino, that Alexander did not go to Gruzino from Tver in March 1811. Cf. *Russkii Arkhiv,* IV (1866), 925.

[5] *Sovremennik,* No. 2 (St. Petersburg, 1836), p. 13.

Once rediscovered, Karamzin's essay became quickly and widely known. At the beginning of 1836 a copy fell into the possession of Zhukovskii, who in March had a transcript made for the widow of Karamzin, and in December another one for Pushkin.[6] Pushkin, who had known Karamzin as a youth, had by this time arrived at a political position not far removed from Karamzin's own, and decided to publish the *Memoir* in the next issue of *Sovremennik,* of which he was the editor. He apparently submitted to the censors only the first part of the *Memoir,* containing the historical introduction, but even this was severely cut. When the text came back from the censor's, Pushkin appended to it a brief foreword:

In the Second Number of the *Sovremennik* (for 1836) we made reference to an unpublished work of the late Karamzin. We consider ourselves fortunate to be able to present to our readers at least an excerpt from the precious manuscript. In it they will hear, if not the whole speech of our great compatriot, then at least the sound of his silenced voice.

A. Pushkin.

He then gave instructions to have the *Memoir* printed in the next, that is, fifth issue of the journal, scheduled for early 1837. But Pushkin died in January, before this issue went to the printers, and the responsibility for seeing it through the press fell on Zhukovskii.[7]

Although the censors had approved the publication of the truncated version of the *Memoir* while Pushkin was still alive, they now began to make difficulties, and in the end refused Zhukovskii permission to proceed with the printing. This decision, handed down by the censor A. L. Krylov, Pushkin's *bête noire,* was allegedly motivated by the desire to respect the wishes of Karamzin: it was said that since he himself had not seen fit to publish the *Memoir* it was improper to do so after his death. Late in February or early in March 1837, Zhukovskii addressed

[6] A. S. Pushkin, *Polnoe sobranie sochinenii,* XVI (Moscow, 1949), 91 and 205.

[7] V. Modzalevskii, "K istorii 'Sovremennika'," *Pushkin in ego sovremenniki,* I, Vypusk IV (St. Petersburg, 1906), 85–89.

two letters to S. S. Uvarov, the Minister of Education in whose competence lay much of the censorship, requesting that the prohibition be rescinded. "This is merely a survey of Russia's condition up to the time of the death of Catherine, which has nothing in common with that lengthy *Memoir* it derives from and which is none of the readers' business." Karamzin himself had not published it for the simple reason that he had no copy.[8]

The difficulties with the censors were finally ironed out, and a severely pruned version of the first part of the *Memoir* appeared in No. 5 of the *Sovremennik* for 1837, bearing Pushkin's foreword. Pushkin thus was personally responsible for the first printing of Karamzin's chef-d'oeuvre. His version contained only the historical introduction, which for all practical purposes stopped at the time of Peter (pp. 103–27 of the present edition), from which all hostile or even mildly critical remarks had been expurgated. The general impression which it conveyed was quite different from that produced by the original text: instead of an impassioned critique of Russia's past and particularly Russia's present, the public read a paean in honor of all previous tsars, and a grand eulogy of the course of Russian history.[9] This text was reprinted in a slightly expanded version five years later in the fifth edition of Karamzin's *History*, published in St. Petersburg by P. Einerling.[10]

The public, however, was not dependent on these official versions, for those in the know had access to the integral version in the numerous handwritten copies which circulated in Moscow and St. Petersburg. One of these copies was taken abroad, where it fell into the hands of the Decembrist Nicholas Turgenev, who published long exerpts from it in a free French translation in his three-volume study of Russia, printed in Paris in 1847.[11] Others were used by M. N. Longinov and M. A. Korf in their studies of Speranskii, published respectively in 1859 and

[8] *Ibid.*, pp. 87–88.

[9] *Sovremennik*, No. 5 (St. Petersburg, 1837), pp. 89–112.

[10] N. M. Karamzin, *Istoriia Gosudarstva Rossiiskogo*, ed. P. Einerling (St. Petersburg, 1842–43), III, xxxix–xlvii.

[11] N. Tourgueneff, *La Russie et les Russes* (Paris, 1847), I, 469–509.

1861, each of which cited long passages from hitherto unpublished portions of the *Memoir*.[12]

The whole text of the *Memoir* was first published in Naumburg in 1861, by the publishing house of G. Pätz, under the false imprint "Ferdinand Schneider, Berlin." [13]

In the early 1860's, Michael Pogodin began work on a full-length biography of Karamzin, to coincide with the forthcoming one hundredth anniversary of the latter's birth. In this connection he sought to locate the original manuscript of the *Memoir*, but his searches proved fruitless, and in his book he printed only brief extracts transcribed from a copy.[14]

Inside Russia, the first full-length version of the *Memoir* (except for the brief section dealing with the assassination of Paul I) appeared in 1870, as a supplement to the journal *Russkii Arkhiv*, edited by P. Bartenev.[15] Bartenev unfortunately failed to indicate which text he used as the basis of his edition. A year later, in a footnote to Pogodin's article, he wrote: "The original, with the inscription of the Grand Duchess Catherine Pavlovna 'A mon frère seul' has now been located." [16] But this assertion was not confirmed subsequently, nor is there any reason to assume that his own edition was based on the original text. The *Russkii Arkhiv* version did not gain wide currency in Russia, because shortly after its appearance the censors removed the supplement with the *Memoir* from all the copies of the journal which fell into their hands; Ponomarev, Karamzin's bibliographer, found it missing from every issue of the *Russkii Arkhiv*

[12] *Russkii Vestnik*, Vol. 23 (1859), pp. 534–47; M. A. Korf, *Zhizn' grafa Speranskogo* (St. Petersburg, 1861), I, *passim*. A photographic reproduction of one such manuscript copy, taken down in 1851 by K. A. Polevoi, the brother of the historian of the same name, was kindly sent to me by Professor A. L. Sidorov, the Director of the Institute of History of the Soviet Academy of Sciences in Moscow.

[13] *O drevnei i novoi Rossii v ee politicheskom i grazhdanskom otnosheniiakh — sochinenie Karamzina;* cf. *Russkaia podpol'naia i zarubezhnaia pechat' — bibliograficheskii ukazatel'*, I (Moscow, 1935), 62.

[14] *Russkii Arkhiv*, IX (1871), 1138; M. Pogodin, *Nikolai Mikhailovich Karamzin*, II (Moscow, 1866), 70–77.

[15] *Russkii Arkhiv*, VIII (1870), 2225–2350.

[16] *Ibid.*, IX (1871), 1138 n.

which he had been able to examine inside Russia.[17] Apparently, however, some issues did escape the censor: the Harvard College Library copy of the *Russkii Arkhiv* for 1870 has it intact; that of the Library of Congress, on the other hand, lacks it.

The integral text of the *Memoir* became widely known in Russia only through the books of the historian and ethnographer, Alexander Pypin, who appended it to post-1900 editions of his intellectual and social history of Russia in the reign of Alexander I.[18] His was the first complete and unexpurgated version of the *Memoir* printed in Russia. Pypin also failed to indicate the source of his text, but his statement that the original was "presumably" available at the St. Petersburg Public Library[19] implies that he, too, had recourse to secondary copies. A close comparison of the Bartenev and Pypin versions points to many similarities, and suggests that both these versions came from the same source. Pypin took occasional liberties with the text, and felt free to make slight changes where the language struck him as unclear or too archaic.

The next — and, so far, the last — edition of the *Memoir* published in Russia, appeared in 1914 under the editorship of V. V. Sipovskii,[20] who had previously established himself as an authority on Karamzin with his study of the literary sources of the *Letters of a Russian Traveler*. Sipovskii resumed the search for the original manuscript, but he too was unsuccessful: it was to be found neither in the Public Library of St. Petersburg, nor in any other public collection. He finally had to settle on a copy made for the personal use of the imperial household, which he had located in the private imperial library. This copy may well have been transcribed directly from the original, and for this reason, as well as for its faithful rendering of Karamzin's lan-

[17] S. I. Ponomarev, "Materialy dlia bibliografii literatury o N. M. Karamzine," *Sbornik Otdeleniia Russkogo iazyka i slovesnosti Imperatorskoi Akademii Nauk*, XXXII, No. 8 (1883), p. 37.

[18] A. N. Pypin, *Obshchestvennoe dvizhenie v Rossii pri Aleksandre I* (St. Petersburg, 1908), pp. 479–534.

[19] *Ibid.*, p. 185.

[20] N. M. Karamzin, *Zapiska o drevnei i novoi Rossii*, ed. V. Sipovskii (St. Petersburg, 1914).

guage and spelling, it may be regarded as the best presently available. Sipovskii's editorial technique, unfortunately, left much to be desired: his proofreading was slipshod, and he felt free to make a number of corrections in the text without troubling to inform the reader precisely where he had done so. For this reason it has seemed necessary to the present editor to collate his version with the principal earlier editions. On the whole, the variants are neither numerous nor significant, and this provides some assurance that the text as we know it is for all practical purposes identical with the original.

N. M. KARAMZIN

A MEMOIR ON ANCIENT AND
MODERN RUSSIA

*"There is no flattery in
my tongue."*

(Psal. CXXXVIII)

[*1. The Kiev and Mongol Periods*]

The present is a consequence of the past. To judge the former one must recollect the latter; each, so to say, completes the other, and viewed together, the two present themselves to the mind more clearly.

From the Caspian Sea to the Baltic, from the Black Sea to the Arctic, amid deserts known to the Greeks and Romans more from fairy tales than from the correct descriptions of eyewitnesses, there lived a thousand years ago peoples given to nomadism, hunting, and agriculture. From these diverse tribes it pleased Providence to create the most spacious state in the world.

Rome, once strong with valor, had weakened from luxury, and collapsed, shattered by the might of the northern barbarians. New epochs followed; new peoples, new customs appeared, and Europe acquired a new appearance, the principal features in which are still to be seen in her political system. In a word, upon the ruins of Roman dominion there established itself in Europe the dominion of the Germanic peoples.

Russia also joined this new, general system. Scandinavia, the lair of restless knights — *officina gentium, vagina nationum* — furnished our fatherland with its first sovereigns, whom the Slavic and Finnic tribes dwelling on the shores of Lake Ilmen, the White Lake, and the River Velikaia accepted of their free will. "Come," the Finns and the Slavs told them, having wearied of internecine wars, "come to reign and rule over us. Our land is rich and great, but there

is no order in it." This took place in 862, and at the end of
the tenth century European Russia was already as large as it
is today; that is, she had matured from infancy into extraordinary greatness. The Russians, as hirelings of the Greeks,
fought in 964 against the Arabs in Sicily and later in the
environs of Babylon.

What caused such an unusual historical phenomenon?
The fervent, romantic passion of our early princes for conquests, and monocracy,[1] which they founded on the ruins of
this multitude of weak, quarreling democratic states of which
Russia had previously been made up. Rurik, Oleg, Sviato-
slav, Vladimir, gave the citizens no opportunity of recovering
from the rapid succession of victories, from the constant din
of military encampments, compensating them with glory
and with booty for the loss of their previous liberty, which
had brought them poverty and conflict.

In the eleventh century the Russian state, resembling a
sprightly, impassioned youth, could look forward to a long
life and to glorious deeds. Its monarchs held in their firm
hands the fate of millions. Illumined by the lustre of victories, surrounded by a martial, noble retinue, they seemed
demigods to the people. They judged and ruled the land.
With a wave of the hand they raised an army, and with a
motion of a finger they pointed the way to the Thracian
Bosphorus or to the Carpathian Mountains. In the happy
respite of peace, the monarch feasted with the lords and the
people like the father of a large family. Cities populated with
chosen inhabitants began to adorn the deserts; Christianity
was softening the fierceness of wild customs; Byzantine arts
made their appearance on the shores of the Dnieper and
Volkhov. Iaroslav gave the people a scroll of simple and
sagacious civil laws, which conformed to the laws of the
ancient Germans. In one word, Russia became not only the

[1] See above, page 62.

most spacious of all states, but also, compared to others, the
most civilized.

Unfortunately, during this age of sprightly youth, Russia
failed to protect herself against the common political plague
of that period, a plague communicated to Europe by the
Germanic peoples: I have in mind the appanage system. The
good fortune and character of Vladimir, the good fortune
and character of Iaroslav, could do no more than postpone
the destruction of the state which monocracy had founded
by conquest. Russia fell apart.

The disappearance of the source of Russia's power, of
that power which is indispensable to prosperity, was accompanied by the extinction of both the power and the prosperity of the people. There followed wretched internecine wars
of fainthearted princes, who, oblivious to the glory, good of
the fatherland, slaughtered each other and ravaged the people, in order to add some insignificant town to their appanage. Greece, Hungary, Poland received respites; our
internal troubles provided them with a guarantee of their
own security. They who had previously feared the Russians,
now treated them with contempt. In vain did some high-
minded princes — Monomakh, Vasilko — speak in the name
of the fatherland at solemn gatherings; in vain did others —
Bogoliubskii, Vsevolod III — make attempts to acquire authority over the entire country. Their efforts were weak,
uncoordinated, and Russia for two centuries rent her en-
trails, and drank her own blood and tears.

This evil was attended by another equally fatal one. The
people now lost respect for the princes. Could the ruler of a
Toropets or a Gomel loom in their eyes with the same importance as the monarchs of all Russia? Once the princes
began to sacrifice their blood for empty, selfish ends, the
people lost zeal for them, and they looked with indifference
on the downfall of princely thrones, ever ready to side with

him who was the more successful, or else to betray him when his good fortune betrayed him too. And the princes, who by now neither trusted nor loved the people, thought only how to enlarge their military retinues, which they allowed to oppress peaceful villagers and merchants. The princes themselves engaged in plunder in order to obtain more money for their treasury for every contingency, and, having by means of this policy divested themselves of the moral dignity of sovereigns, came to resemble extorting judges, or tyrants, rather than legitimate rulers. And thus, the weakening of the power of the state was accompanied by the weakening of the inner bonds that unite the citizens with authority.

In view of these circumstances, is it surprising that the barbarians subjugated our fatherland? It is more surprising that it should have been able for so long a time to appear and to function as a self-sufficient political body, while its organs and its heart were dying — a fact which can be explained only by the weakness of our neighbors. For the steppes of the Don and Volga were in the hands of Asiatic and nomadic hordes, capable only of brigandage. Poland herself was expiring from internecine conflicts. The kings of Hungary had tried but failed to establish their dominion across the Carpathian Mountains, while Galicia, having left Russia several times, was reunited to her. The Order of the Bearers of the Sword scarcely held ground in Livonia. But when, having seized China, a part of Siberia, and Tibet, the warlike nation formed by the victories of the khan of the Mongols turned against Russia, all that was left for her was the glory of a noble perdition. Our brave but foolhardy princes went into battle with a handful of men to die as heroes. Baty, leading half a million men, trampled their corpses, and in a few months shattered the state. In the art of war our ancestors were second to none, having for four centuries fought both without and within the country. But, weakened by the division of forces, unable to unite even in the face of common misfortune, they had to content themselves with crowns of martyrs earned in unequal battles and in defense of perishable cities.

Russia, soaked with blood, strewn with ashes, became the home of the slaves of the khans; its sovereigns trembled before the *baskaki*. Nor was this the end. In the regions of Dvina and Niemen, amidst thick forests, lived an impoverished, savage nation which for over two hundred years had paid the Russians a scanty tribute. Oppressed by the Russians as well as by the Prussian and Livonian Germans, it had learned the art of war, and commanded by certain brave knights emerged in orderly battle array from the forests onto the stage of world events. This nation not only regained its independence, but, having formed a civil society and founded a powerful state, seized the better half of Russia; that is to say, while the northern half of Russia remained a tributary of the Mongols, the southern half went entirely, up to the very Kaluga and River Ugra, to *Lithuania*. Vladimir, Suzdal, Tver were *Ulusy of the khan;* Kiev, Chernigov, Mtsensk, Smolensk, were Lithuanian cities. The former, at any rate, preserved their customs; the latter adopted even the usages of the aliens. It seemed that Russia had perished forever.

[2. *The Emergence of Moscow*]

A miracle! A small town, scarcely known before the fourteenth century, long called from contempt for its insignificance *"village Kuchkovo"* raised its head and saved the fatherland. Honor and glory to Moscow! The thought of re-establishing monocracy in tormented Russia originated and matured within its walls. The shrewd Ivan Kalita, who won for himself the title of *"The Gatherer of the Russian Lands,"* was the founding father of Russia's glorious resur-

rection, unparalleled in the annals of mankind. But his successors were still required in the course of the following
century to adhere with remarkable consistency and firmness
to a single course of action — a course best adapted to the
circumstances: to transform the khans themselves into instruments of our liberation. Having gained the special favor
of Uzbek, and with it the title of Grand Prince, Kalita first
succeeded in persuading the khans not to send his officials to
our cities for the collection of the tribute, but to receive it
instead at the Orda from the Prince's boyars; for indeed the
Tatar lords, surrounded by warriors, used to come to Russia
not so much to collect the khan's tribute, as to carry out impudent robberies. No one dared to get in their way; as soon
as they appeared the tillers fled from their plows, the merchants from their wares, the burghers from their homes.
Everything revived when these beasts of prey ceased to terrify
the people with their presence; the villages and cities became calm, and trade, domestic as well as foreign, was restored; relieved of the burden of the khan's tribute, the
people and the treasury grew rich. Kalita's second important
plan was to annex private appanages to the Grand Principal-
ity. Showered with favors by the rulers of Moscow, the khans
acting with a childish innocence made them presents of entire provinces, and granted them authority over other Russian princes, until the time came when power, nurtured by
cunning, completed by sword the task of our liberation.

The profound policy of the princes of Moscow was not
content with assembling the parts into one whole. It was still
necessary to bind the parts firmly together, and to fortify
monocracy with autocracy. The Russian Slavs, although they
had renounced democratic rule at the time when they had
recognized the Norman princes as their sovereigns, retained
many democratic habits. On important occasions all our
ancient cities convoked the so-called *veche,* or popular coun-

cil; in all the cities the *tysiatskie,* or captains, were elected
not by the prince but by the people. These republican institutions had not prevented Oleg, Vladimir, or Iaroslav from
ruling Russia as autocrats; the glory of their deeds, the nobility and size of their devoted military retinues, had served
as bridles on popular impetuosity. But when the state disintegrated into numerous independent provinces, the citizens, lacking in respect for weak princes wanted to regain
for themselves the ancient right of calling the *veche* and of
exercizing the supreme legislative power. In Novgorod and
certain other localities they took occasionally to judging and
solemnly exiling their princes. This libertarian spirit prevailed in Russia until Baty's invasion, and although it could
not disappear at once in a time of distress, it did weaken
perceptibly. Thus, the history of our country furnishes new
evidence of two truths: 1) firm autocracy requires a strong
state, and 2) political slavery is incompatible with civil
freedom.[2] The princes crawled on their knees at the Orda,
but returning thence with a gracious *iarlyk* of the khan they
commanded with greater boldness than they used to do in the
days of our political independence. The nation, humbled by
the barbarian yoke, thought only how to save its life and
property, and felt little concern for its civil rights. The Moscow princes took advantage of this attitude and situation,
and, uprooting little by little all the survivals of the ancient
republican order, established genuine autocracy. The *veche*
bell was silenced in all the cities of Russia. Dmitrii Donskoi
deprived the people of the right to elect the *tysiatskie,* and,
notwithstanding his unusual humanitarian inclinations, introduced the solemn death penalty for political offenders in
order to instill fear into audacious rebels. At last, what Ivan I
Kalita had begun, Ivan III completed: the capital of the

[2] N. Turgenev translates this passage: "La liberté du peuple ne peut exister
là où le pouvoir qui gouverne est esclave d'un pouvoir étranger." (A people
cannot be free when the ruling power is the slave of a foreign power.)

khans on the shores of the Akhtuba, where the descendants of Rurik had for so many years been in the habit of bending their knees, disappeared forever, destroyed by the vengeance of the Russians. Novgorod, Pskov, Riazan, and Tver were rejoined to Moscow, as were certain provinces which had been seized by Lithuania. The ancient southwestern principalities belonging to the descendants of Vladimir still remained in Polish hands; but, on the other hand, a new and regenerated Russia acquired in the reign of Ivan IV three kingdoms: Kazan, Astrakhan, and endless Siberia, previously unknown to Europe.

The Moscow princes accomplished this great deed not by their personal heroism, since, except for Donskoi, none of them could boast of it, but solely by utilizing the wise political system, that is, in accord with the needs of the period. Russia was founded by victories and by monocracy, she perished from the division of authority, and was saved by wise autocracy.

Situated in the depths of the north, rearing her head between Asiatic and European kingdoms, Russian society contained elements derived from both these parts of the world. It was a compound of ancient customs of the east, carried to Europe by the Slavs and reactivated, so to say, by our long connection with the Mongols; of Byzantine customs which we had adopted together with Christianity; and of certain German customs, imparted to us by the Normans. These German customs, distinguishing a brave and free people, could still be seen in the custom of trials by battle, in knightly amusements, and in the spirit of *mestnichestvo*, derived from the tribal love of glory. The confinement of women and severe *kholopstvo* were remnants of ancient Asiatic customs. The court of the tsar resembled the court of Byzantium. Ivan III, the son-in-law of a Paleologus, wanted, as it were, to bring Greece back to life in Russia by observing all her ecclesiastical and courtly ceremonials. He surrounded himself with Roman Eagles, and received foreign ambassadors in the *Golden Chamber* which recalled that of *Justinian*. The Russians considered such an amalgam of customs brought about by accidents and circumstances as indigenous, and they loved it as their own national heritage.

Although the two-century-long yoke of the khans was not propitious for the development of civic arts or of culture in our country, yet Moscow and Novgorod did take advantage of the important discoveries of their time; thus paper, gunpowder, and book printing were known to us shortly after they were invented. The libraries of the tsar and of the metropolitan, stocked with Greek manuscripts, deserved the envy of other Europeans. In Italy there was a revival of architecture — and Moscow attracted as early as the fifteenth century celebrated architects, invited from Rome; she had magnificent churches as well as the *Granovitaia Palata*. Ikonpainters, engravers, and goldsmiths grew rich in our capital city. In the days of our slavery, laws were silenced — but now Ivan III issued new civil statutes, and Ivan IV a complete code, whose principal departure from the laws of Iaroslav consisted in the introduction of the *punishment by the knout,* an institution which the ancient independent Russian had not known. The same Ivan IV founded a large and alert standing army, divided into provincial regiments, which we had not had before.

The eyes of Europe turned to Russia. Kings, popes, and republics entered with her into friendly relations — some for the benefit of their merchants, others in the hope of harnessing Russia's might in order to curb the dreadful Turkish empire, Poland, and Sweden. Ambassadors came to Moscow even from the depths of Hindustan, from the shores of the Ganges, and there was a widespread notion of routing Indian trade through Russia. The political system which the Mos-

cow princes had established deserved to be admired for its
wisdom: aspiring only to bring welfare to the people, they
made war only of necessity, and were always ready for peace;
they kept out of the affairs of Europe, meddling in which
pleases more the vanity of monarchs than it benefits the
state; and, once they succeeded in re-establishing the Russian state within sensible frontiers, they displayed no yearn-
ing for false or perilous conquests, preferring to preserve
rather than acquire.

Internally, autocracy struck root. No one beside the
monarch could either judge or invest; all authority derived
from that of the monarch. Life and property depended on
the arbitrary will of the tsars, and the title of *tsar's servitor*
replaced the titles of prince and boyar as the highest in the
land. The people, delivered by the princes of Moscow from
the disaster of internecine wars as well as from the foreign
yoke, felt no regrets for the ancient *veche* or for the dignitaries who used to restrain the sovereign's authority; satisfied
with the uses of authority, the people did not argue over
rights. Only the boyars, having been accustomed to lording
it in the appanage domains, grumbled at the severity of
autocracy; but the flight and executions of such boyars
demonstrated how firm that authority had become. In the
end, all the Russians began to look upon the tsar as a terrestrial god.

This was not affected by the policies of Ivan IV. This
monarch, who had ruled well until his thirty-fifth year, was
moved by some hellish inspiration, and began to take delight
in blood, slaughtering for no reason, and beheading men
known for their virtue. Neither the boyars nor the people
presumed to plot anything against him. They merely prayed
humbly, deep in their hearts, that the Lord would calm the
tsar's fury, this scourge for their sins! Except for the villains
known to history as the Oprichniks, all those who enjoyed

eminence by virtue of their wealth or their office prepared themselves for death, and took no steps to save their lives! What a memorable time and disposition! Nowhere did awe-inspiring tyranny ever expose national virtue, loyalty, or obedience to such cruel temptations; yet this virtue did not even hesitate in choosing between death and resistance.

[3. The Time of Troubles]

A crime, plotted secretly but uncovered by history, cut off the dynasty of Ivan. Godunov, a Tatar by origin, a Cromwell by disposition, assumed the throne with all the prerogatives of a legitimate monarch, and under the same regime of integral monarchy. This unfortunate man, overthrown by the shadow of the tsarevich he had slain, perished amid deeds of great wisdom and apparent virtue, the victim of an immoderate, illicit thirst for power, as an example for ages and peoples. Troubled by his conscience, Godunov sought to stifle its sacred reproaches by means of gentle deeds, and as a consequence began to loosen the reins of autocratic power. Blood ceased to flow at the place of execution — exile, incarceration, or compulsory monkhood were the only forms of punishment inflicted on boyars guilty or suspected of evil intentions. But Godunov lacked the advantages which are at the disposal of those who command either love or respect, such as the preceding, hereditary monarchs had enjoyed. The boyars, once his peers, envied him; the people still remembered him as a servant of the court. The moral strength of tsardom was weakened in the hands of this elected ruler.

Few monarchs were ever welcomed so joyously by the people as was the False Dmitrii on the day of his triumphal entry into Moscow. Tales of his alleged miraculous rescue, memories of the terrible natural disasters of Godunov's reign, and the hope that heaven, having restored the throne

to the descendants of Vladimir, would also restore prosperity
to Russia, inclined hearts favorably toward the young monarch, the favorite of fortune.

But the False Dmitrii was a secret Catholic, and his lack
of discretion betrayed this secret. He did have certain merits
and a kindly disposition, but his temperament was romantic,
and on the throne he resembled more a tramp than a king.
He was passionately fond of foreigners, and, though ignorant
of the history of his alleged ancestors, he mastered the most
minute details of the life of Henry IV, the French king,
whom he idolized. Russia's monarchic institutions of the
fifteenth and sixteenth centuries now underwent a change.
The small Boyar Duma, which previously had functioned
merely as a tsar's council, transformed itself into a tumultuous assembly of a hundred rulers, lay and ecclesiastical,
whom the unconcerned and lazy False Dmitrii entrusted
with the internal affairs of state, while he retained for himself the realm of foreign policy. Dmitrii occasionally appeared in person at sessions of the Boyar Duma, and, to the
amazement of all, engaged the boyars in arguments; for Russians were not accustomed to the sight of subjects solemnly
contradicting their monarchs. His jolly amiability altogether
overstepped the bounds of decorum and did violence to that
majestic modesty which autocrats require much more than
do Carthusian monks. Nor was this all. Dmitrii treated
Russian customs and religion with open contempt. When the
nation fasted, he revelled; in the Voznesenskii Monastery he
amused his spouse with the dances of clowns; he tried to
entertain boyars with viands which violated their supersti-
tions; he surrounded himself not only with a foreign guard,
but also with a band of Jesuits; he spoke of a merger of
churches, and praised that of the Latins. The peoples of
Russia first lost respect for him, then came to hate him, and,
at last convinced that a real son of Ivan would not have been

capable of profaning the temple of his ancestors, laid a hand on the impostor.

This deed had dreadful consequences for Russia, and they might well have been worse yet. Civil societies suffer greater harm from the arbitrary dispensations of justice by the people than from the personal iniquities or delusions of monarchs. The establishment of authority requires the wisdom of whole centuries; one hour of a mob's frenzy suffices to destroy the foundation of authority, which rests on the moral respect for the office of the ruler. The inhabitants of Moscow tore to pieces the man to whom a short time before they had sworn their loyalty. Woe to his successor and to the nation!

Vasilii Shuiskii, a collateral descendant of the ancient princes of Suzdal and of Monomakh, a sycophant of Tsar Boris, sentenced to death and then pardoned by the False Dmitrii, overthrew the careless Pretender. As a reward for this action he received from the Boyar Duma the blood-stained scepter of the latter. Shuiskii then solemnly betrayed autocracy, by swearing to execute no one, to deprive no one of his property, and not to declare war without the Duma's approval. With the frightful frenzies of Ivan still fresh in their memory, the sons of men who had been innocently slain by that fierce tsar were more concerned with their personal safety than with that of the state, and thus they thoughtlessly circumscribed the hitherto unlimited authority of the monarchs to which Russia had owed her salvation and her greatness. The complaisance of Shuiskii and the selfishness of the boyars appear in the eyes of posterity as crimes of equal weight. For Shuiskii too, was more concerned with himself than with the state, and, very eager to become tsar even with limited authority, he ventured upon a course of policy fraught with great danger to the realm.

The consequences were inevitable. The boyars, treating the semimonarch as their own handiwork, and desirous, so to

speak, of perpetuating their influence, restricted his authority more and more. By the time Shuiskii had realized what
was happening, it was too late, and his efforts to steady the
shaky throne with outbursts of magnanimity were futile. The
boyar disorders of old broke out once more, and the people,
incited in the square by the hirelings of certain insidious
lords, advanced in crowds on to the Kremlin palace to dictate
laws to the sovereign. Shuiskii stood firm. "Obey me or take
back the crown of Monomakh, which you have placed on my
head!," he told the Muscovites. The people were pacified for
a time, only to rise again in rebellion at the very moment
when Pretenders, encouraged by the successes of the original
Pretender, were rising one after another against Moscow.
Shuiskii fell, toppled not by these tramps, but by the unworthy lords; his fall was as noble as his rise had been
cowardly. Dressed as a monk, and handed over by villains to
foreigners, he felt greater regret for Russia than for the
crown he had lost; he replied with true tsarist pride to the
insidious demands of Sigismund, and died in exile, a national martyr, confined in a dungeon.

The many-headed hydra of aristocracy did not rule Russia
for long. None of the boyars enjoyed evident superiority;
they quarreled and interfered with each other in the per-
formance of political duties. At last they saw that they could
not manage without a tsar. Loath to elect a native for that
post for fear that his family might monopolize all the approaches to the throne, the boyars offered the crown to the
son of our enemy, Sigismund, who was taking advantage of
Russia's disorders to attempt a conquest of her western territories. But to this offer they attached conditions, for they
wanted to safeguard their religion as well as their power.
While the negotiations were still in progress, the Poles, assisted by traitors, entered Moscow and began prematurely to
tyrannize in Władysław's name. The Swedes captured Nov-

gorod. Pretenders and Cossacks ravaged other regions of
Russia. The government collapsed, the state was perish-
ing. . . .

History has named Minin and Pozharskii the "Saviors of
the Fatherland." Let us render justice to their zeal, but let
us also not forget the citizens who at this critical juncture
acted with remarkable unanimity. The faith, the love of
their native customs, and hatred of alien rule engendered a
general glorious uprising of the people under the leadership
of certain boyars who remained faithful to the fatherland.
Moscow was freed.

[4. The First Romanovs]

But Russia still had no tsar, and suffered from the oppression of rapacious foreigners. The fate of the fatherland was
settled by an assembly of prominent deputies from all the
towns, shepherds of the church, and boyars, which met at
the Church of the Assumption in Moscow. Never did the
nation act with greater solemnity and freedom, or from
holier motives. . . . All were inspired with the same desire,
the aim of which was the unity and the good of Russia.
There were no weapons to be seen; no threats to be heard;
briberies, disputes, and vacillations were absent. The assembly elected a youth, almost a boy, a recluse from the world.
Tearing him from the arms of his frightened mother, who
lived in a cloister, they raised him to the throne which was
stained with the blood of the False Dmitrii and the tears of
Shuiskii. This beautiful, innocent youth was like a lamb or a
sacrificial victim, and he trembled and cried. Without a
single powerful relative to stand by his side, estranged from
the proud, power-hungry great boyars, he considered the
latter not his subjects, but his future tyrants. Fortunately
for Russia, however, he proved mistaken. The sorrows caused
by the rebellious aristocracy had enlightened the citizens as

well as the aristocrats themselves. Both unanimously proclaimed Michael an autocrat, an unlimited monarch; both, fired with love for the fatherland, exclaimed merely *"God and the Sovereign!"* . . . They inscribed a charter which they laid at the throne. This document, inspired by the wisdom of experience and confirmed by the will of the boyars and the people, is the holiest of all the state charters. The princes of Moscow had instituted autocracy — the fatherland conferred it on the Romanovs.

The very election of Michael demonstrated the existence of a genuine desire to establish absolute monarchy. There can be no doubt that the ancient princely families had a far better claim to the crown than this son of a relative of Ivan's wife, whose unknown ancestors had come from Prussia. But a tsar elected from among these descendants of Monomakh or Oleg would have been surrounded by a host of eminent relatives, and might readily have granted them aristocratic power, thus weakening autocracy. The nation preferred a youth who had virtually no family. Yet this youth, who was related to the tsars, had a father — a man of wisdom, vigorous spirit, and inflexible counsel — whose task it was to serve him as a guardian during his occupancy of the throne, and to instill in him the principles of firm authority. Thus, the stern character of Philaret, which years of enforced monasticism had failed to mellow, contributed more to Michael's election than did Michael's kinship with Theodore Ivanovich.

These unforgettable men, whose pure hands held at this time the urn containing our destiny, curbed their own passions and the passions of others, and attained their goal. The rainbow of heavenly peace spread over the Russian throne. The fatherland, having ejected from its system the foreign despoilers, found peace under the canopy of autocracy. Russia expanded by acquisition, and assumed once more the shape of a civil society, which created, renovated and acted only of necessity, in accord with the popular spirit, and by means most closely related to the actual problems facing it. The Boyar Duma resumed its ancient role of a tsar's council which rendered advice on all matters of importance, political, civil, and fiscal. In old times the monarch used to administer the realm through viceroys, known as *voevody;* subjects who had cause to complain against them, went directly to the tsar, who judged their case together with the boyars. This *eastern simplicity* no longer corresponded to the level of Russia's political development, and the profusion of affairs called for a larger number of intermediaries between the tsar and his people. This need led to the establishment of the *prikazy* in Moscow whose duty it was to take charge of the affairs of all the cities, and to judge the viceroys. But the courts were still without a comprehensive legal code, since the code of Ivan had left much to the conscience and discretion of the judges. Realizing the importance of this matter, Tsar Alexis Mikhailovich appointed certain members of the Duma, and enjoined them, as well as the representatives of all the cities and estates, to correct the *Sudebnik*. He told them to supplement it with Greek laws long in use among us, with more recent royal decrees, and with the necessary addenda for cases which, although already encountered in courts, were as yet unsettled by a definite law. Russia received the *Ulozhenie,* countersigned by the patriarch, all the leading clergymen, secular officials, and representatives of cities. Next to Michael's electoral charter, the *Ulozhenie* constitutes today our country's most important political legacy.

In general, the reign of the Romanovs — Michael, Alexis, Theodore — helped to draw Russians closer to Europe as concerned civic institutions and manners. This was a consequence of frequent diplomatic contacts with European courts, and the arrival of many foreigners, some of whom came to enter into Russian service, and some to settle in Moscow. Our ancestors still adhered loyally to their customs; but the example began to have its effect, and obvious advantage, obvious superiority triumphed over ancient habit in the military and diplomatic establishments, in the method of education, and in the very manners of society; for there can be no doubt that between the thirteenth and seventeenth centuries Europe had left us far behind in civil enlightenment. This transformation occurred gradually, quietly, almost imperceptibly, by a means of a natural evolution, without paroxysms and without violence. We borrowed but as if unwillingly, adapting the foreign to the native, and blending the new with the old.

[5. Peter I]

At this point Peter appeared. In his childhood, the license of the lords, the impudence of the *Streltsy*, and the ambition of Sophia had reminded Russia of the unhappy times of boyar troubles. But deep inside of him the youth already had the makings of a great man, and he seized hold of the helm of state with a mighty hand. He strove toward his destination through storms and billows. He reached it — and everything changed!

His goal was not only to bring new greatness to Russia, but also to accomplish the *complete* assimilation of European customs. . . . Posterity has praised passionately this immortal sovereign for his personal merits as well as for his glorious achievements. He was magnanimous and perspicacious, he had an unshakable will, vigor, and a virtually inexhaustible supply of energy. He reorganized and increased the army, he achieved a brilliant victory over a skillful and courageous enemy, he conquered Livonia, he founded the fleet, built ports, promulgated many wise laws, improved commerce and mining, established factories, schools, the academy, and, finally, he won for Russia a position of eminence in the political system of Europe. And speaking of his magnificent gifts, shall we forget the gift which is perhaps the most important of all in an autocrat: that of knowing how to use people according to their ability? Generals, ministers, or legislators are not accidentally born into such and such a reign — they are chosen. . . . To choose good men one must have insight; only great men have insight into men. Peter's servants rendered him remarkable assistance on the field of battle, in the Senate, and in the Cabinet. But shall we Russians, keeping in mind our history, agree with ignorant foreigners who claim that Peter was the founder of our political greatness? . . . Shall we forget the princes of Moscow, Ivan I, Ivan III, who may be said to have built a powerful state out of nothing, and — what is of equal importance — to have established in it firm monarchical authority? Peter found the means to achieve greatness — the foundation for it had been laid by the Moscow princes. And, while extolling the glory of this monarch, shall we overlook the pernicious side of his brilliant reign?

Let us not go into his personal vices. But his passion for foreign customs surely exceeded the bounds of reason. Peter was unable to realize that the national spirit constitutes the moral strength of states, which is as indispensable to their stability as is physical might. This national spirit, together with the faith, had saved Russia in the days of the Pretenders. It is nothing else than respect for our national dignity. By uprooting ancient customs, by exposing them to ridicule, by causing them to appear stupid, by praising and introducing foreign elements, the sovereign of the Russians humbled Russian hearts. Does humiliation predispose a man and a citizen to great deeds? The love of the fatherland is bolstered by those national peculiarities which the cosmopolite considers harmless, and thoughtful statesmen beneficial. Enlightenment is commendable, but what does it consist of? The knowledge of things which bring prosperity; arts, crafts, and sciences have no other value. The Russian dress, food, and beards did not interfere with the founding of schools. Two states may stand on the same level of civil enlightenment although their customs differ. One state may borrow from another useful knowledge without borrowing its manners. These manners may change naturally, but to prescribe statutes for them is an act of violence, which is illegal also for an autocratic monarch. The people, in their original covenant with the king, had told them: "Guard our safety abroad and at home, punish criminals, sacrifice a part to save the whole." They had not said: "Fight the innocent inclinations and tastes of our domestic life." In this realm, the sovereign may equitably act only by example, not by decree.

Human life is short, and the rooting of new customs takes time. Peter confined his reform to the gentry. Until his reign all Russians, from the plough to the throne, had been alike insofar as they shared certain features of external appearance and of customs. After Peter, the higher classes separated themselves from the lower ones, and the Russian peasant, burgher, and merchant began to treat the Russian gentry as Germans, thus weakening the spirit of brotherly national unity binding the estates of the realm.

Over the centuries the people had become accustomed to treat the boyars with the respect due to eminent personages. They bowed with genuine humbleness when, accompanied by their noble retinues, with Asiatic splendor, to the sound of tambourines, the boyars appeared in the streets on their way to church or to the sovereign's council. Peter did away with the title of boyar. He had to have ministers, chancellors, presidents! The ancient, glorious Duma gave way to the Senate, the *prikazy* were replaced by colleges, the *diaki* by secretaries, and so it went. Reforms which made just as little

sense for Russians were introduced into the military hierarchy: generals, captains, lieutenants took the place of *voevody, sotniki, piatidesiatniki,* and so forth. Imitation became
for Russians a matter of honor and pride.

Family customs were not spared by the impact of the tsar's
activity. The lords opened up their homes; their wives and
daughters emerged from the impenetrable *teremy;* men and
women began to mingle in noise-filled rooms at balls and
suppers; Russian women ceased to blush at the indiscreet
glances of men, and European freedom supplanted Asiatic
constraint. . . . As we progressed in the acquisition of social
virtues and graces, our families moved into the background;
for when we have many acquaintances we feel less need of
friends, and sacrifice family ties to social obligations.

I neither say nor think that the ancient Russians who had
lived under the grand princes or the tsars were in all respects
superior to us. We excel them not only in knowledge, but
also in some ways morally; that is to say, we are sometimes
overcome with shame by things which left them indifferent, and which indeed are depraved. However, it must be
admitted that what we gained in social virtues we lost in civic
virtues. Does the name of a Russian carry for us today the
same inscrutable force which it had in the past? No wonder.
In the reigns of Michael and of his son, our ancestors, while
assimilating many advantages which were to be found in
foreign customs, never lost the conviction that an Orthodox
Russian was the most perfect citizen and *Holy Rus'* the foremost state in the world. Let this be called a delusion. Yet
how much it did to strengthen patriotism and the moral fibre
of the country! Would we have today the audacity, after
having spent over a century in the school of foreigners, to
boast of our civic pride? Once upon a time we used to call all
other Europeans *infidels;* now we call them brothers. For
whom was it easier to conquer Russia — for *infidels* or for

brothers? That is, whom was she likely to resist better? Was it conceivable in the reigns of Michael and Fedor for a Russian lord, who owed everything to his fatherland, gaily to abandon his tsar forever, in order to sit in Paris, London, or Vienna, and calmly read in newspapers of the perils confronting our country? We became citizens of the world but ceased in certain respects to be the citizens of Russia. The fault is Peter's.

He was undeniably great. But he could have exalted himself still higher, had he found the means to enlighten Russians without corrupting their civic virtues. Unfortunately, Peter, who was badly brought up and surrounded by young people, met and befriended the Genevan Lefort. This man, whom poverty had driven to Moscow, quite naturally found Russian customs strange, and criticized them in Peter's presence, while lauding to high heaven everything European. The free communities of the German settlement, which delighted the untrammeled youth, completed the work of Lefort, and the ardent monarch with his inflamed imagination, having seen Europe, decided to transform Russia into Holland.

National inclinations, habits, and ideas were still sufficiently strong to compel Peter, in spite of his theoretical liking for intellectual liberty, to resort to all the horrors of tyranny in order to restrain his subjects, whose loyalty, in fact, was unquestionable. The Secret Chancery of the Preobrazhenskoe operated day and night. Tortures and executions were the means used to accomplish our country's celebrated reform. Many perished for no other crime than the defense of the honor of Russian caftans and beards, which they refused to give up, and for the sake of which they dared to reproach the monarch. These unfortunates felt that by depriving them of their ancient habits Peter was depriving them of the fatherland itself.

The extraordinary efforts of Peter reflect all the strength of his character and of autocratic authority. Nothing frightened him. The Russian church had had since time immemorial its head, first in the person of the Metropolitan, and lastly in that of the Patriarch. Peter proclaimed himself the head of the church, abolishing the Patriarchate as dangerous to unlimited autocracy. But, let us here note, our clergy had never contended against secular authority, either princely or tsarist. Its function had been to serve the latter as a useful tool in affairs of state, and as a conscience at times when it occasionally left the path of virtue. Our primate had one right: not to act, not to rebel, but to preach the truth to the sovereigns — a right which carries blessings not only for the people, but also for the monarch whose happiness consists in justice. From Peter's time on the Russian clergy had deteriorated. Our primates turned into mere sycophants of the tsars, whom they eulogized in biblical language from the pulpits. For eulogies we have poets and courtiers. The clergy's main duty is to instruct the people in virtue, and the effectiveness of this instruction depends on the respect which the clergy commands. If the sovereign presides over the assembly of the chief dignitaries of the church, if he judges them and rewards them with secular distinctions and benefits, then the church becomes subordinated to secular authority, and loses its sacred character. Its power of appeal weakens, and so does faith, and with the weakening of the faith the sovereign deprives himself of the means with which to govern the hearts of the people on extraordinary occasions, when it is necessary to forget everything, to abandon everything for the sake of the fatherland, and when the only reward which the spiritual shepherds can promise is the crown of martyrdom. Spiritual authority ought to have a separate sphere of action, apart from secular authority, but it should function in close union with it. I have in mind the realms of justice and law. Where the welfare of the state is involved, a wise monarch shall always find a way of reconciling his will with that of the metropolitan or the patriarch. But it is better for this conciliation to appear as an act of free choice and of inner persuasion than of obvious humility. An overt, complete dependence of spiritual authority on secular authority derives from the assumption that the former is useless, or, at any rate, not essential to political stability — an assumption throughly disproven by the experience of ancient Russia and of contemporary Spain.

Shall we close our eyes to yet another glaring mistake of Peter the Great? I mean his founding a new capital on the northern frontier of the state, amidst muddy billows, in places condemned by nature to barrenness and want. Since at that time he controlled neither Riga nor Reval, he might have founded on the shores of the Neva a commercial city for the import and export of merchandise; but the idea of establishing there the residence of our sovereigns was, is, and will remain a *pernicious* one. How many people perished, how much money and labor was expended to carry out this intent? Truly, Petersburg is founded *on tears and corpses*. A foreign traveler, upon entering a country, usually looks for its capital in localities which are most fertile and most propitious for life and health. In Russia, he sees beautiful plains, enriched with all the beauties of nature, shaded by groves of linden trees and oaks, traversed by navigable rivers whose banks please the eye and where, in a moderate climate, the salutary air favors long life. He sees all this, and regretfully turning his back on these beautiful regions, enters sands, marshes, sandy pine forests, where poverty, gloom, and disease hold sway. This is the residence of the Russian sovereigns, who must strive to the utmost to keep the courtiers and guards from starving to death, as well as to make good the annual loss of inhabitants with newcomers, future victims of premature death! Man shall not overcome nature!

But a great man demonstrates his greatness with his very errors. They are difficult if not impossible to undo, for he creates the good and the bad alike forever. Russia was launched on her new course with a mighty hand; we shall never return to bygone times! It would have taken another Peter the Great at least twenty or thirty years to establish the new order much more firmly than all the successors of Peter I up to the time of Catherine II had done. Notwithstanding his marvelous diligence, Peter left much to be finished by his successors. Menshikov, however, was concerned only with his personal ambition, and so were the Dolgorukis. Menshikov intrigued to pave the road to the throne for his son, while the Dolgorukis and Golitsyns wanted to see the pale shadow of a monarch on the throne, and to rule themselves in the name of the Supreme Council. Impudent and dastardly plots! Pygmies contending for the legacy of a giant. The aristocracy, the oligarchy was ruining the fatherland. . . . And could Russia at this time have dispensed with monarchy, after she had changed her time-sanctioned customs, and undergone internal disorders as a result of new, important reforms which, by dissociating the customs of the gentry from those of the people, had weakened spiritual authority? Autocracy became more essential than ever for the preservation of order.

[6. Anne]

For this reason the daughter of Ivan, after a few days of dependence on eight aristocrats, accepted from the people, gentry, and clergy unlimited authority. This sovereign wanted to rule in accord with the ideas of Peter the Great, and she hastened to correct the many deficiencies which had weakened the Petrine system since his death. The reformed Russia seemed at this time, as it were, a great unfinished edifice on which appeared already some signs of impending collapse. The departments of the judiciary and the military, as well as our foreign policy, were in a state of decay. But Ostermann and Münnich, driven by an ambition to win for themselves in their adopted fatherland the epithets of great men, worked tirelessly and with brilliant success. The former regained Russia her place of eminence in the European state system, to which Peter's efforts had aspired; the latter improved and revitalized the military establishment, and brought us victories. For the perfection of its glory Anne's reign required yet a third wise statesman, one capable of bringing to the Russians laws and civil enlightenment. But Anne's ill-fated attachment to a soulless, base favorite, cast a shadow over her life as well as her place in history. The Secret Chancery at the Preobrazhenskoe with its tortures was reactivated; in its caves and on city squares flowed rivers of blood. And who was it that they tormented? Enemies of the queen? None of them wished her ill even in his thoughts; the Dolgorukis themselves had sinned only against the fatherland, which reconciled itself with them in their misfortune. Biron, unworthy of authority, wanted to secure through terror a good grip on power. The slightest suspicion, an ambivalent word, even silence itself seemed to him at times a crime calling for execution or exile. He undoubtedly had enemies. Could good Russians look indifferently while a Courland noble virtually seized the throne? But these enemies of Biron were genuine friends of the throne and of Anne. They perished; the enemies of Biron's informer perished; and anyone who presented him the gift of a stately horse had the right to expect royal favor.

[7. *Elizabeth*]

In consequence of two conspiracies, the wicked Biron as well as the kindly regent lost their power and freedom. A

French doctor and a few drunken Grenadiers raised Peter's daughter to the throne of the world's greatest empire with shouts of *"death to foreigners! honor to Russians!"* The beginning of this reign was distinguished by the impudence of the famous Own Company of Her Majesty, the bestowal of the Blue Ribbon on a Little Russian choir boy, and the tragedy of the benefactors of our country, Ostermann and Münnich, who never were greater than at that moment when standing on the scaffold they wished happiness to Russia and to Elizabeth. Their crime was their devotion to the Empress Anne, and their conviction that Elizabeth, idle and lascivious, could not make a good ruler. Notwithstanding all this, the Russians praised her reign. She showed more confidence in them than in Germans; she re-established the authority of the Senate, she abolished the death penalty, had good-natured lovers, a passion for merrymaking and tender poems. Though she was of a humane disposition, Elizabeth intervened in a war which was as bloody as it was useless for Russia. The foremost statesman of her time was Chancellor Bestuzhev, a man endowed with wisdom and energy, but avaricious and partial. Soothed by indolence, the Queen gave him freedom to traffic in the politics and forces of the realm. At last she had him removed, and then she committed a new blunder by solemnly announcing to the people that this minister, who had personified her whole reign, was the most infamous of all mortals! Fortune, dealing kindly with the reign of the gentle-hearted Elizabeth, protected Russia from those extraordinary evils which no human wisdom can avert, but it was unable to protect her from the covetous greed of P. I. Shuvalov. The dreadful monopolies of this period survived long in the memory of the people, who were oppressed for the benefit of private persons, and to the detriment of the treasury itself. Many of the institutions of Peter the Great fell into disuse from neglect, and the reign of Elizabeth altogether earned no distinctions for the brilliant accomplishments of the art of statesmanship. A few victories, won more by the steadfastness of the warriors than by the skill of the military commanders, the University of Moscow, and the Odes of Lomonosov are the loveliest monuments of this period. Under Anne as well as under Elizabeth, Russia stayed on the course which had been charted for her by the hand of Peter, departing ever further from her ancient customs, and coming closer to those of Europe. Secular tastes made rapid strides. The Russian court dazzled with its splendor, and, having spoken German for several years, now turned to French. In matters of dress, carriage equipment, service, our lords vied with Paris, London, and Vienna. But the terrors of autocracy still frightened the minds of the people; they looked about whenever the name of the most gentle Elizabeth or a powerful minister came up; tortures and the Secret Chancery continued to exist.

[8. Catherine II]

Another conspiracy, and the unfortunate Peter III lay in the grave, together with his pitiful vices. . . . Catherine II was the true inheritor of Petrine greatness, and the second architect of the new Russia. The main achievement of this unforgettable queen was to soften autocracy without emasculating it. She flattered the so-called *philosophes* of the eighteenth century, and admired the character of the ancient republicans, but she wished to command like a terrestrial goddess — and she did. Peter, having violated national customs, had to have recourse to cruel methods. Catherine could do without them, to the satisfaction of her gentle heart: for she required of Russians nothing contrary to their conscience or civil tradition, and endeavored only to exalt either the fatherland, given her by heaven, or her own fame — and this she tried to achieve by victories, laws, and enlightenment. Her proud, noble soul refused to be debased by timid suspicion, and so vanished the dread of the Secret Chancery. With it left us also the spirit of slavery, at any rate among the upper classes. We accustomed ourselves to pass judgment, to praise in the actions of the sovereign what was praiseworthy, and to criticize what was not. Catherine listened to our opinions, and there were times when she struggled within herself, but she always overcame the desire for revenge — a virtue of great excellence in a monarch! Catherine was confident of her greatness, and firm, unshakable in her declared purposes. Constituting the sole spirit of all the political movements in Russia, and holding firmly in her hands the reins of power, she eschewed executions and tortures, and imbued the hearts of ministers, generals, and all state officials with a most lively fear of arousing her displeasure, and with a burning zeal to win her favor. For all these reasons Catherine could scorn idle gossip; and when sincerity spoke words of truth, the queen thought — "I have authority to demand silence of this generation of Russians, but what will posterity say? And shall thoughts, confined by fear to the heart, be less offensive to me than the spoken word?" This manner of thought, demonstrated by the actions of a reign which lasted for thirty-four years, distinguished her reign from all those which had preceded it in modern Russian history. That is to say, Catherine cleansed autocracy of the stains of tyranny. This calmed men's hearts, and led to the development of secular pleasures, knowledge, and reason.

Having raised throughout her realm the moral value of man, Catherine re-examined all the inner parts of our body politic, and left none unimproved. She emended the statutes of the Senate, the gubernii, the courts, as well as those of the economy, army, and commerce. Special praise is due to the foreign policy of her reign. Under Catherine Russia occupied with honor and glory one of the foremost places in the state system of Europe. In war we vanquished our foes. Peter had astounded Europe with his victories — Catherine made Europe accustomed to them. Russians began to think that nothing in the world could overcome them — a delusion which brought glory to this great queen! Although a woman, she knew how to choose commanders as well as ministers and administrators. Rumiantsev and Suvorov were equals of the most illustrious generals in the world. Prince Viazemskii earned for himself the reputation of a worthy minister with his prudent political economy and the preservation of order and integrity. Shall we reproach Catherine for her excessive love of military glory? Her triumphs assured the external security of the realm. Let foreigners condemn the partition of Poland — we took what was ours. The queen followed the policy of noninterference in wars which were of no concern to Russia and of no use to herself, yet she succeeded in maintaining in the empire the martial spirit which victories had bred.

In his endeavor to please the gentry, the weak Peter III had granted them the freedom to choose whether or not to enter state service. The sagacious Catherine did not abrogate this law, but she was able to neutralize its politically harmful consequences. The queen wanted to supplant the love of Holy Rus', weakened by the reforms of Peter the Great, with civic ambition. To achieve this end she combined new attractions and benefits with service ranks, and devised symbols of distinction, the value of which she endeavored to maintain by bestowing them only on people of merit. The Cross of St. George could not produce valor, but it did bolster it. Many served in order to keep their seat and the right to speak at Assemblies of the Nobility; many, notwithstanding the spread of luxury, greatly preferred titles and ribbons to material gains. All these factors strengthened the necessary dependence of the gentry on the throne.

But we must admit that the most brilliant reign of Catherine was not without its dark side. Morals continued to deteriorate ever more in the palaces as well as in the cottages — in the former from the example set by the dissolute court, in the latter from the spread of taverns, which brought income to the treasury. Do the examples set by Anne and Elizabeth absolve Catherine? Do the riches of the state belong to a man whose only distinction is a handsome face? A hidden weakness is only a weakness; an overt one is a vice, because it seduces others. The violation of canons of morality diminishes the very dignity of the sovereign's office, for no matter how depraved they may be themselves, people cannot inwardly respect those who are depraved. And is it necessary to demonstrate that the people's sincerest respect for the monarch's virtue helps strengthen his authority? We must regretfully concede that while zealously praising Catherine for the excellencies of her soul, we unwillingly recall her foibles, and blush for mankind. We must also note that justice did not flourish at that time. When a lord knew that he was in the wrong in a law suit against a squire, he used to have the case transferred to the Cabinet, where it went to sleep, never to reawaken. The very political institutions devised by Catherine reveal more sparkle than substance; the choice fell not upon the best in content, but the prettiest in form. This holds true of the institution of the gubernii, which, though elegant in theory, were badly suited to the conditions of Russia. Solon was in the habit of saying: "My laws may not be perfect, but they are the best for the Athenians." Catherine sought in laws theoretical perfection, but she failed to consider how to make them function most smoothly and most usefully. She gave us courts without having trained judges; she gave us principles but without the means with which to put them into practice. Many of the harmful consequences of the Petrine system also emerged more clearly in the reign

of this queen. Foreigners secured control over our education;
the court forgot how to speak Russian; the gentry sunk into
debt from the excessive emulation of European luxury; dis-
honest deals, inspired by a craving for fancy were more common; the sons of Russian boyars dispersed abroad to squan-
der their money and time on the acquisition of a French or
English appearance. We possessed academies, institutions of
higher learning, popular schools, wise ministers, a delightful
society, heroes, a superb army, an illustrious fleet, and a great
queen — but we lacked decent upbringing, firm principles,
and social morality. The favorite of a great lord, even though
of low birth, was not ashamed to live in splendor; the lord
himself was not ashamed of corruption. People traded in
truth and ranks. Catherine — a great statesman at principal
state assemblies — proved a woman in the minutiae of royal
activity. She slumbered on a bed of roses, she was deceived
or else deceived herself. She either did not see, or did not
wish to see many abuses, perhaps considering them unavoidable, and she felt satisfied with the over-all successful, glorious progress of her reign. Yet when all is said and done,
should we compare all the known epochs of Russian history,
virtually all would agree that Catherine's epoch was the
happiest for Russian citizens; virtually all would prefer to
have lived then than at any other time.

The events which occurred after her death silenced those
who had severely judged this great queen. For it is true that
in her last years, years which were indeed the weakest in
principle as well as in execution, we were particularly prone
to censure her. Having grown accustomed to the good, we
failed to appreciate its full value, and perceived all the
stronger its contrary; the good seemed to us to follow naturally, as if inevitably from the order of things rather than
from the personal wisdom of Catherine, whereas the bad we
blamed on her.

[9. Paul I]

Paul came to the throne at that period, propitious for autocracy, when the terrors of the French Revolution had cured Europe of the dreams of civil freedom and equality. But what the Jacobins had done to the republican system, Paul did to the autocratic one: he made people to hate its abuses. As a result of a wretched mental delusion and of the many personal unpleasantries which he had experienced, he wished to turn into an Ivan IV. But Russia had had a Catherine II, and knew that the sovereign, no less than the people, must fulfill his sacred obligation, the violation of which breaks the ancient covenant between authority and obedience, and tumbles the nation from the level of civilized existence into the chaos of private natural law. The son of Catherine could have ruled sternly, and still have earned the fatherland's gratitude. But Paul, for no apparent reason and to the consternation of Russians, took to ruling by means of general terror, obeying no law save his own whim. He treated us not as his subjects but as his slaves. He executed the innocent and rewarded the worthless. His actions robbed capital punishment of the stigma of disgrace, and reward of its allure. Titles and ribbons, which he distributed with a lavish hand, declined in value. He thoughtlessly destroyed a ripe harvest of political wisdom, which he despised as the work of his mother. In the regiments he stamped out the noble spirit of war, nurtured by Catherine, substituting for it the spirit of martinetism. Heroes, accustomed to victories, he taught to parade. He infected the gentry with an aversion for military service. Scorning the soul, he respected hats and collars. Although inwardly disposed toward goodness, he secreted gall. He devised each day ways to frighten others, yet he himself was the most frightened of all. He wanted to build himself an inaccessible palace — and built himself a tomb instead! . . . Let us call attention to one striking fact.

It was thought abroad that during this reign of terror Russians were afraid even to think. But this was not so! They spoke up and boldly! Driven to silence only by the boredom of constant repetition, they trusted each other, and were not deceived. Something like a spirit of sincere brotherhood prevailed at that time in the capital cities. Common calamity drew hearts together, and a selfless wrath against the abuses of authority silenced the inner voice of prudence. Such were the consequences of the humanitarian reign of Catherine, consequences which four years of Paul's reign could not undo; they showed that we deserved a wise, lawful, and just government.

The people of Russia looked upon this monarch as if he were a dreadful meteor, counting each minute and impatiently awaiting the last. . . . It came, and throughout the kingdom the news of its advent was news of redemption. In houses and on the streets people cried with joy and embraced one another as on Easter Sunday. Who was less fortunate than Paul? Tears of sorrow were shed only within the circle of His Most August family, and by a few individuals whom he had showered with favors, but what men were they! Their regrets, no less than the prevalent joy, should have offended the soul of Paul, if, after its separation from the body, illumined at last by the light of truth, it could have gazed on the earth and on Russia! To acknowledge duly the honorableness of the most prudent men in Russia we must not omit to mention their judgment. Having learned of the deed, they regretted that the evil of a harmful reign was cut short by harmful means. Conspiracies are disasters which undermine the foundations of states, and furnish dangerous precedents for the future. If certain lords, generals or bodyguards should assume the authority secretly to kill or depose monarchs, what would become of autocracy? It would turn into a plaything of an oligarchy, and as such rapidly resolve itself into anarchy, which is more horrible than the worst

master, because it endangers all the citizens, whereas the
tyrant executes only some. The wisdom of the ages and the
interests of the nation have established for monarchies the
principle that the law ought to dispose of the throne, and
God, God alone, of the life of tsars! May he who believes
in destiny see in an evil autocrat the scourge of heavenly
wrath! We shall bear it as we bear a storm, an earthquake,
a plague or some other dreadful but uncommon occurrence;
for in the course of nine centuries we have had only two
tyrants, tyranny presupposing an extraordinary blinding of
the mind on the part of the sovereign, whose true happiness
is inseparable from that of the people's, from justice, and the
love of good. Let the people be frightened of conspiracies for
the sake of the tranquility of the sovereigns! Let the sovereigns
also fear them for the sake of the people's tranquility! Two
causes account for conspiracies: widespread hatred or widespread contempt for the ruler. Biron and Paul were victims
of hatred, the Regent Anne and Peter III of contempt.
Münnich, Lestocq, and the others would not have ventured
on a course contrary to the conscience, to honor, and all the
laws of the state, had the rulers whom they overthrew enjoyed the respect and love of Russians.

The people did not question Alexander's virtue. They
judged only the conspirators, who had been motivated by
the spirit of vengeance, and by concern for their personal
safety. They were particularly hard on those who had themselves participated in his cruelties and had received his favors. Most of these conspirators are already hidden from
human eyes by the darkness of the grave or the darkness of
oblivion. Few if any of them enjoyed the consolation of a
Brutus or a Cassius in solitude or on the deathbed. Russians
approved of the young monarch who rejected the company
of these men, and the nation turned its eyes most hopefully
on the grandson of Catherine, who had vowed to rule following the *dictates of her heart*.

[PART TWO: THE REIGN OF ALEXANDER I
FROM 1801 TO 1810]

[1. Introduction]

So far I have spoken of bygone reigns, now I shall turn to
the present reign, addressing myself to my conscience and to
my sovereign, to the best of my understanding. What entitles
me to do so? My love for the fatherland and for the monarch,
and some knowledge culled from the chronicles of the world
and from conversations with great men, that is, from their
works. What do I want? To test in good faith Alexander's
magnanimity, and to say what I consider just, and what history some day shall confirm.

Two schools of thought predominated at the time of Alexander's accession. Some urged that Alexander, to his eternal
glory, take steps to bridle the unlimited autocracy which
had had such disastrous consequences in the reign of his
father. Others, dubious of the practical value of such an
undertaking, wanted him only to restore the ruined system
of Catherine, which appeared so happy and sound in comparison with Paul's. In point of fact, can one limit autocracy
in Russia without, at the same time, emasculating the tsar's
authority, salutary for the country, and if so, how? Superficial
minds lose no time and answer: "Yes, one can. All one has
to do is to establish the supremacy of law over all, including
the monarch." But whom shall we entrust with the authority
over the inviolability of this law? The Senate? The Council?
Who will sit in these institutions? Will they be officials selected by the sovereign or by the country? In the former
event they will be an assembly of the tsar's sycophants; in

the latter they will want to argue with the tsar over authority — I see an aristocracy, not a monarchy. Furthermore, what will the senators do should the monarch violate the law? Will they expostulate with His Majesty? And should he have a good laugh at them, will they declare him a criminal? Will they incite the people? . . . Every good Russian heart shudders at this frightful prospect. Two political authorities in one state are like two dreadful lions in one cage, ready to tear each other apart; and yet law without authority is nothing. Autocracy has founded and resuscitated Russia. Any change in her political constitution has led in the past and must lead in the future to her perdition, for she consists of very many and very different parts, each of which has its own special civic needs; what save unlimited monarchy can produce in such a machine the required unity of action? If Alexander, inspired by generous hatred for the abuses of autocracy, should lift a pen and prescribe himself laws other than those of God and of his conscience, then the true, virtuous citizen of Russia would presume to stop his hand, and to say: "Sire! you exceed the limits of your authority. Russia, taught by long disasters, vested before the holy altar the power of autocracy in your ancestor, asking him that he rule her supremely, indivisibly. This covenant is the foundation of your authority, you have no other. You may do everything, but you may not limit your authority by law!" But let us assume that Alexander actually prescribes royal authority some kind of statute based on the principles of public good, and sanctions it by a sacred oath. Would such an oath be capable of restraining Alexander's successors unless it were strengthened with other means, means which in Russia are either unfeasible or dangerous? No, let us be done with schoolboy sophistries, and affirm that there is only one true method for a sovereign to make certain that his successors do not abuse their authority: let him rule virtuously, let him accustom his subjects to goodness! In this manner he will engender salutary customs, principles, and public opinions which will keep future sovereigns within the bounds of legitimate authority far more efficiently than all the ephemeral forms. How? By inspiring them with a fear of arousing universal hatred with a contrary system of government. It may be safe occasionally for one tyrant to follow another, but it is never safe for him to follow a wise king! "The sweet repels us from the bitter," said Vladimir's legates after becoming acquainted with European religions.

Russia was then unanimous in its high esteem of the young monarch's qualities. He has now ruled for ten years, and there is no reason to change this opinion. I will go further: there is general agreement that no monarch perhaps ever exceeded Alexander in his love for and dedication to the public good, that none was as impervious to the lustre of his office, or as capable of retaining simple human virtues on the throne. But here I need spiritual fortitude to speak the truth. Russia is seething with dissatisfaction. Complaints are heard in the palaces and in the cottages; the people lack confidence as well as enthusiasm for the government, and condemn strongly its aims and policies. An amazing political occurrence! Usually, the successor of a cruel monarch easily wins for himself general acceptance when he softens the political regime. How then shall we explain this woeful condition of public opinion among a people who have been calmed by Alexander's gentleness, whom he had freed from the threat of unjust persecution by the Secret Chancery and Siberian exile, and to whom he has given the freedom to enjoy all the pleasures permissible in civil societies? By the unfortunate situation in Europe, and by what I consider to be important mistakes of the government. For, alas, it is possible with good intentions to err in the choice of means. Let us see. . . .

[2. *Foreign Policy*]

Let us begin our discussion with foreign policy which had such an important impact on the internal life of the country. The dreadful French Revolution was already buried, but she had left behind a son who resembled her in his principal features. The so-called republic became a monarchy, the impelling force of which was the genius of ambition and victory. The shrewd British, having been hurt by the peace, resumed their efforts to rouse all Europe against the French, and pursued this task. Vienna longed for the Netherlands and Lombardy; for her, war entailed great risks as well as opportunities. Berlin played a cagey game and confined itself to pleasantries; prudence demanded that it pursue a peaceful policy. Russia had lost nothing and had nothing to fear; that is to say, she was in a most fortunate position. Austria, still strong like a mighty fortress, separated Russia from France; while Prussia was for her as it were a bridle to keep Austria in line. Russian policy should have aimed at general peace, insofar as war could have induced a change in the European situation: the success of France and Austria could have had equally undesirable consequences for Russia by strengthening either of them. Napoleon's love of power imposed a heavy burden on Italy and Germany. The former, as farther removed, had less of a bearing on Russian interests. As for Germany, our interests required that she remain independent, in order to shield us from French influence. No one better deserved Napoleon's respect than Alexander. The glory of the Italian hero still blazed throughout Europe, undimmed by the disgrace of Herman and Korsakov. In the Consul's eyes, England and Austria appeared to be the natural enemies of France; Russia, on the other hand, performed the role of a magnanimous arbiter of Europe, who, by continually interceding on behalf of Germany, was in a position to remind Napoleon of Trebbia and Novi whenever he failed to show the proper respect for our demands. Russia was represented in Paris by a minister who was well known for his diplomatic skill; the choice of such a man indicated the importance which Alexander attached to this post, and perhaps even flattered the Consul's vanity. But how amazed we were to learn that Count Markov placed his signature on a treaty calling for a repartition of the southern German provinces, helping in this manner to promote the interests and the honor of France, and to increase her influence in Germany! Our amazement was greater still when we heard that this same minister, who on an important issue had shown excessive servility to Napoleonic airs, submitted to Talleyrand threatening notes concerning some Genevan tramp arrested by the French. He annoyed the Consul with all kinds of trifles, and then, ousted from Paris, received the Blue Ribbon. The consequences were not difficult to divine. . . . But what had caused this shift in policy? Had we become aware of Napoleon's dangerous ambition? And did we not know this before? Here I am reminded of a conversation which took place at that time between a youthful favorite of the sovereign's and an old minister. The former, as yet more vain than clever, and quite unversed in the science of politics, declared unequivocally in my presence that Russia should make war in order to occupy the idle minds and maintain the military spirit in our armies; the latter let it be understood with a subtle smile that he had helped Count Markov to obtain the Blue Ribbon which so annoyed the Consul. The young favorite delighted in the thought of earning the Blue Ribbon in battle against the celebrated Bonaparte, while the old minister exulted, picturing to himself the impotent fury of Napoleon. Unfortunates! In fine, the whole Markov embassy, so inconsistent in its principles, was our first political mistake.

I shall never forget the dire forebodings which I felt when, suffering from a serious illness, I learned that our army had taken to the field. . . . Russia had set in motion all her forces to help England and Vienna, that is, to serve them as a tool in the quarrel with France, without any particular advantage to herself. Under the conditions then prevailing, Napoleon did not as yet directly menace our security, protected as we were by Austria, as well as by the size and glory of our military forces. What did we intend to do if we had won the war? To restore to Austria the great losses she had previously suffered? To liberate Holland and Switzerland? I concede that this would have been feasible, but only after we should have inflicted ten decisive defeats on the French, and completely exhausted their forces. What would have emerged in the new order? The greatness, the primacy of Austria, which from gratitude would have relegated Russia to a secondary position, and even that only until the time when she succeeded in pacifying Prussia, at which time she would have proclaimed us an Asiatic country, as Bonaparte had done. Such were the prospects in the event of a favorable outcome; what followed the unfavorable outcome is known already! The policy of our cabinet astonished by boldness; having raised one hand against France, with the other we threatened Prussia, demanding her cooperation! Too impatient to engage in preliminary negotiations with Prussia we wanted to settle everything in one move. What, I ask, would we have done had the Ministry in Berlin told Prince Dolgorukov: "Young man! You aspire to overthrow the despot Bonaparte, yet you yourself, even before you have disposed of him, dictate to independent powers how to conduct their politics! Go on your way — we are prepared to assert our independence by the sword." Would such a reply have caused Benningsen and Count Tolstoy to attack Prussia? A beautiful beginning which deserved a like ending!

But Prince Dolgorukov returned with a more pleasant reply; true, we were deceived, or deceived ourselves.

Everything turned out to our true advantage. Mack lost an army within a few days; Kutuzov, instead of Austrian colors, saw before him those of Napoleon, but he retreated with honor, glory, and victory to Olmütz. Two strong hosts stood poised for battle. The cautious, prudent Napoleon told his men: "Europe will now see who deserves the title to the greatest bravery, you or the Russians," and he gave us an opportunity to make peace. The Russian position was never more favorable, and never was there less reason to hesitate in the choice. Napoleon was in Vienna, but Charles was drawing near, and there were 80,000 Russians awaiting the command to bare their swords. Prussia was getting ready to join us. One word would have ended the war in a most glorious manner for us. The exiled Francis would have returned to Vienna by the grace of Alexander, without having to cede to Napoleon anything save perhaps only Venice; an independent Germany would have enjoyed the protection of the Rhine; and our monarch would have won for himself the titles of benefactor, the virtual restorer of Austria, as well as the savior of the German Empire. Victory was, to say the least, problematic; and what would it have given us anyway? Hardly anything except glory, which could have been ours in peace as well. And the cost of failure? Shame, flight, hunger, the total destruction of our army, the collapse of Austria, the enslavement of Germany, and so on. . . . The ways of the Lord are unfathomable; we wanted battle! Here was our second political mistake (I say nothing of the military ones).

The third mistake was the Peace of Tilsit. It was also the one most pregnant with consequences, because it reacted at once on the internal condition of the country. I do not want to go into the miserable story of the quasi minister Oubril, and I condemn neither the treaty which he had concluded (itself a consequence of Austerlitz), nor the ministers who had advised the sovereign to reject this brief agreement. Nor do I condemn the latest war with the French — in this case we had no choice but to defend the security of our possessions, which Napoleon menaced by inciting Poland. All I know is that in the course of the winter we should have dispatched Benningsen 100,000 fresh troops, or else we should have opened peace negotiations, which had every chance of success. Pultusk and Preussisch-Eylau heartened the Russians and amazed the French. . . . Instead, we ended up with Friedland. But at this point it was necessary to show courage, which on certain occasions is also the deepest form of wisdom: we should have forgotten Europe, which we had lost at Austerlitz and Friedland, and turned all thoughts to Russia, in order to safeguard her internal welfare. That is to say, we should have accepted no peace save on honorable terms, which would not have required us to break our profitable commercial relations with England or to fight Sweden, in violation of the holiest laws of mankind and of nations. We could have rejected Europe without suffering disgrace, but we could not maintain our honor by transforming ourselves into an instrument of Napoleon in Europe after we had pledged ourselves to rescue it from his tyranny. There was also a second peace condition indispensable to our security, one which we should have conceded only in the event of another disaster on the right bank of the Niemen: that there be no Poland under any shape or name. In politics, self-preservation is the supreme law. It would have been better to consent to Napoleon's seizure of Silesia than to have recognized the Duchy of Warsaw.

Thus, our mighty efforts, having led to Austerlitz and the Peace of Tilsit, consolidated French hegemony over Europe, and made us, through Warsaw, the neighbors of Napoleon. Nor was this all. The unprofitable Swedish war and the break with England resulted in an excessive increase in the quantity of assignats, in rising prices, and in widespread discontent in the country. We did conquer Finland; let the *Moniteur* praise this acquisition! We know what it had cost us apart from men and money. A state requires for its security not only physical but also moral might. Whenever we sacrifice honor and justice, we impair the latter. For our seizure of Finland we are hated by the Swedes and reproached by all the other nations; and I am not certain which did greater harm to Alexander's honor, to have been defeated by the French, or to have been compelled to follow their predatory system.

Having sacrificed to the alliance with Napoleon the moral dignity of a great empire, can we depend on the sincerity of his friendship? Shall we deceive Napoleon? Facts are facts. He knows that inwardly we detest him, because we fear him; he had occasion to observe our more than questionable enthusiasm in the last Austrian war. This ambivalence of ours was not a new mistake, but an inescapable consequence of the position in which we had been put by the Tilsit Peace. Is it easy to keep a promise to assist one's natural enemy and to increase his power? It seems to me that having seized Finland we would have had no scruples in conquering Galicia, had we been able to foresee Napoleon's real successes. But Charles might yet have won; and anyway we would have failed to gain Napoleon's good will even with the most sincere fulfillment of our obligations as allies; he would have given us a bit more, but he would not have given us the means to consolidate our independence. Shall we then argue that Alexander should have supported the Austrians? The Austrians did not support us when the exhausted Napoleon was departing from Preussisch-Eylau, and their army of 100,000 men could have dealt him the fatal blow. Of course, in politics there is no place for rancor, but could not thirty or forty thousand Russians also have arrived too late for a decisive battle, as the Archduke Jean had done at Wagram? Ulm, Austerlitz were fresh in memory. What would have been the consequence? Worse yet. Bonaparte, seeing our courage, would have taken the most direct and effective measures to curb it. In these circumstances it is better that he consider us merely timid, hidden enemies, that he merely forbid us to make peace with the Turks, that he merely frighten us indirectly with Sweden and Poland. What will happen next? God knows, but the people know the political mistakes we have committed, and ask: why did Count Markov annoy Bonaparte in Paris? Why did we allow an ill-advised war to bring distant clouds over Russia? Why did we fail to conclude peace before Austerlitz? The voice of the people is the voice of God. No one will be able to persuade Russians that in matters of foreign policy the counselors of the emperor have followed the principles of sincere, wise patriotism, and striven to advance the interests of the sovereign. These unfortunates, expecting disaster, were concerned only with their vainglory; each justified himself so as to shift the blame on the monarch.

[3. Political Institutions]

Let us now turn to internal policies, past and present. Instead of reverting at once to the order established by Catherine, an order affirmed by thirty-four years of experience, and vindicated, so to speak, by the disorders of Paul's reign; instead of abolishing only that which was superfluous and introducing that which was indispensable; in short, instead of first examining and then merely correcting, the counselors of Alexander developed a fancy to introduce novelties into the principal organs of royal authority. In so doing they ignored the wise precept which teaches that all novelty in the political order is an evil to which recourse is to be had only of necessity; for time alone gives statutes the requisite firmness, since we respect more that which we have respected for a long time, and do everything better from habit. Peter the Great had replaced the Boyar Duma with the Senate, and the *prikazy* with colleges; he spent much energy on making these institutions function properly. Time having revealed certain superior administrative methods, Catherine II issued the decree for the *Establishment of the Gubernii,* which she put into effect piecemeal and with great circumspection. The Colleges of the Judiciary and the Fisc were replaced by Boards; other colleges remained intact. And even if the justice and the economy of the country under Catherine were not all that a good citizen might have desired, still no one thought to blame the shortcomings on the form or organization of institutions. All complaints were directed at the individuals who ran them. Field Marshal Münnich observed in our political system a certain gap between the throne and the Senate, but he was by and large wrong. Like the ancient Boyar Duma, the Senate was entrusted with all the authority which a supreme governing body can possess in an autocratic system. The Senate took care of all those matters which came within the purview of royal authority, and linked itself with the person of the Sovereign through the office of the Procurator-General. The monarch, being humanly incapable of encompassing all his enormous responsibilities, supplied the Senate with his supreme deputy and overseer in the Procurator-General, having previously determined when this important institution was to act in accord with pre-established laws, and when to call for his Serene permission. The Senate issued laws, examined the work of the colleges, resolved their doubts, or inquired of the sovereign. Whenever a private citizen complained to the tsar against the Senate, the monarch threatened with dire punishment either the Senate, for its misuse of authority, or, if the complaint proved unjustified, the citizen who had the audacity to make the false charge. I can see no void here, and recent history from the time of Peter to that of Catherine II demonstrates that the establishment of Supreme Councils, Cabinets, and Conferences is incompatible with the original purpose of the Senate, limiting or circumscribing its field of action, one institution interfering with the other.

This system was second to none in Europe in orderliness, and it had in it not only features common to all the other systems, but also some which were particularly suited to the local needs of the empire. Paul, disliking his mother's work, re-established the colleges which she had abolished, and reformed the institution of the gubernii. But his reforms were prudent. He abolished the superfluous Upper Land Courts and their *Raspravy,* he deprived the Judiciary Boards of the authority to execute their judgments, and so on. . . .

Alexander, inspired with love for the common good, and with the best intentions, took counsel, and, in accord with the ideas of Field Marshal Münnich and the political system of foreign countries, established ministries. To begin with, let us call attention to the excessive haste with which this move was made. The ministries were created and set in motion before the ministers had been provided with an Instruction, that is, with a dependable, clear guide to help them carry out their important duties! Let us next inquire into their utility. Ministerial bureaus have replaced colleges. Where work had been carried out by eminent officials such as a president and several assessors, men with long training and with a strong sense of responsibility for their whole office, we came to see insignificant officials, such as directors, filing clerks, desk heads, who, shielded by the minister, operated with utter impunity. It may be countered that the minister did everything and answered for everything; but in fact only ambition has no bounds. Human capacity and ability are quite narrowly circumscribed. For example, was the Minister of the Interior, who appropriated for himself nearly all of Russia, capable of gaining a good insight into the endless stream of papers flowing through his office? Could he understand at all subjects of such diversity? [As a consequence of his inability to do so] committees began to mushroom; they were like a parody of the ministries, and demonstrated the latter's inability to provide an effective government. At last the government realized the excessive complexity of the Ministry of the Interior . . . and what did it do? It added a new ministry, one whose structure was as complex and incomprehensible to Russians. What? Wardship comes under the Ministry of the Police? And medicines too? Etc. etc. . . . This ministry is either a mere department of the Ministry of the Interior, or it has been misnamed. And can this second reorganization be said to have enhanced the government's reputation for wisdom? First it acts, and then it says: "Sorry, we have made a mistake; this matter belongs not to this but to that ministry." Such subjects must be first thought over, for otherwise people lose confidence in the firmness of laws.

In the second place, the ministers, having emerged upon the ruins of the colleges (since the isolated colleges of War and of Admiralty are of no significance in this order), wedged themselves between the sovereign and the people, eclipsing the Senate, and divesting it of its power and greatness. And although the ministers are subordinate to the Senate insofar as they must submit reports to it, yet by being able to say: "I had the pleasure to report to His Majesty!" they can silence the Senators, with the result that so far this alleged responsibility has proven but a meaningless ritual. Edicts and laws submitted by the ministers and approved by the sovereign are communicated to the Senate only for promulgation.

From this it follows that Russia is governed by ministers, that is, that within his own department every minister may act at will. We ask: who deserves more confidence: a single minister, or an assembly of most eminent statesmen, which we have come to regard as the supreme government, the principal instrument of royal power? True, the ministers constitute a Committee which is to approve every new establishment before its confirmation by the monarch. But does not this Committee resemble a council of six or seven different nationals, each of whom speaks his own language, and cannot understand the others? Must the Minister of the Navy grasp the subtleties of juridical science, or the principles of political economy and trade, and so forth? What is even more important is that every minister needs complaisant colleagues to satisfy his own needs, and therefore tends to acquire the habit of complaisance himself.

"Patience," reply the royal counselors, "we shall yet devise a method of curbing ministerial authority" — and they issue the act establishing the Council.

Catherine II, too, had a council following the precept that two heads are better than one. What mortal can do without advice where important matters are involved? Sovereigns need it most of all. In questions of war and peace, which call for an unequivocal *yes* or *no*, Catherine took the advice of certain select lords. This was her council, one essentially *secret*, that is, special, the empress' own. She did not transform it into a formal state council because she did not want to destroy Peter's Senate, which, as we have shown, cannot exist alongside another supreme governing institution. What is to be gained from debasing the Senate in order to elevate another organ of government? If the Senators are unworthy of royal trust, they need only to be replaced. The Senate cannot govern as long as the Council, acting in lieu of it, reviews affairs formally and also in its own name, and, to boot, issues laws jointly with the sovereign. Nowadays, royal decrees read: "having considered the Council's opinion. . . ." Thus, the Senate is left out? What is it then? Will it stay as a mere court of law? . . . We shall see, because we have been instructed to stand by for more supplementary state statutes, reforms of the Senate, gubernii, etc. "A monarchy," writes Montesquieu, "must have a repository of laws." "Le conseil du Prince n'est pas un dépôt convenable. Il est, par sa nature, le dépôt de la volonté momentanée du Prince qui exécute, et non pas le dépôt des lois fondamentales. De plus, le conseil du Monarque change sans cesse; il n'est point permanent; il ne sauroit être nombreux; il n'a point à un assez haut degré la confiance du peuple: il n'est donc pas en état de l'éclairer dans les tems difficiles, ni de le ramener à l'obéissance." The points we have raised here cannot be materially affected by the impending changes: the Council will either perform the functions of the Senate, or it will serve as its moiety, its department. All this is playing with names and forms, it is to ascribe to them a significance which objects alone possess. I congratulate the person who invented this new formula or preamble to laws: "Having considered the Council's opinion" — but the Russian sovereign will take wisdom under consideration wherever he happens to find it: in his own mind, in books, in the judgment of his best subjects. In an autocracy laws need no confirmation save the signature of the sovereign; the totality of power is his. The Council, the Senate, the committees and ministers are nothing more than the agencies by means of which this authority operates, they are the sovereign's proxies — where he himself acts, they are not consulted. The expression: "Le conseil d'état entendu" is meaningless to a Russian; let the French rightly or not, use it! . . . True, in Russia it also used to be written: "The sovereign commanded, and the Boyars concurred," but this legal formula had been for some time a sort of requiem for the defunct boyar aristocracy. Shall we revive the form when both the thing and the form itself have long ago been destroyed?

The Council, it is said, will curb the ministers. The emperor is going to submit to the Council for its consideration the most important ministerial proposals. In the meanwhile, however, the ministers will continue to govern the country in the sovereign's name. The Council does not intercede in the normal course of events, because it is consulted only on extraordinary occasions, and yet it is this everyday course of political activity which determines whether our time is blessed or cursed.

Only those laws are salutary which had for long been desired by the best minds of the country, and of which, so to say, the people have had a premonition, insofar as they represent the readiest remedy for an acknowledged evil. The establishment of the ministries and the Council were not anticipated by anyone. The least the authors of this reform might have done was to have explained the advantages of these new institutions. I read and see nothing but dry forms. They draw lines for my eyes, leaving my mind undisturbed. Russians are told: "So far it has been thus — now it will be different." Why? This they fail to say. Whenever Peter the Great carried out important political reforms, he used to give the nation an account; take a look at his Church Statutes, in which he opens to you his whole heart, in which he reveals to you all the motives, all the causes as well as aims of this statute. On the whole, Russia's new legislators are distinguished more for the art of clerkship than for that of statesmanship. They issue a project of Ministerial Instruction. What could be more important or interesting? Here, no doubt, one can find defined the competence, purpose, method, and obligations of every minister? . . . But nothing of the kind! A few words are tossed out on the principal matter, and everything else consists of secretarial trivia: they tell how ministerial departments are to correspond with each other, how papers are to come and go, how the sovereign is to open and close his rescripts! Montesquieu suggests the symptoms which indicate the rise and decline of empires — the author of this project provides with similar airs the criteria with which to gauge the success or failure of a chancery. I sincerely acclaim his knowledge of this matter, but I condemn the following resolution: "If the sovereign issues an edict which is contrary to the judgment of the minister, then the minister is free not to countersign it." It follows that in an autocratic state the minister has the legal right to advise the public that in his opinion an edict is harmful? The minister is the monarch's arm, and nothing else! the arms does not judge the head. The minister affixes his signature to Personal Imperial Edicts not for the benefit of the public but for the emperor, as assurance that they are written, word for word, as he has commanded. Such mistakes in fundamental political conceptions are scarcely excusable. In defining an important ministerial responsibility, the author writes: "The minister is tried in two instances; when he oversteps the bounds of his authority, or when he fails to make use of the means at his disposal to forestall harm." But where are these bounds of authority and these means defined? One should first make the law, and then speak of punishing the offender. And can this notorious ministerial responsibility really be a subject of trial in a Russian solemn court? Who selects the ministers? The sovereign. Let him then reward with his favor those who deserve it, and dismiss those who do not, without ado, quietly and discreetly. A bad minister is the sovereign's mistake; such mistakes ought to be corrected, but in secret, so that the nation retains trust in the personal choices of the tsars.

This is the light in which our good Russians view the new

political institutions; realizing how unripe these institutions are they long for the old order. In the brilliant reign of Catherine II, when we had a Senate, colleges, and a Procurator-General, our affairs made satisfactory progress. Prudent legislators of the past, when compelled to introduce changes into the political systems, tried to depart as little as possible from the old. "If you have no choice but to alter the number of officials and their authority," says the sage Machiavelli, "then, for the sake of the people, do at least keep their titles unchanged." We do quite the opposite: leaving the thing itself unchanged, we invent titles, and contrive different methods to produce the same effect! An evil to which we have grown accustomed bothers us much less than a new evil, while new benefits do not wholly inspire confidence. The reforms accomplished so far give us no reason to believe that future reforms will prove useful; we anticipate them more with dread than with hope, for it is dangerous to tamper with ancient political structures. Russia, after all, has been in existence for a thousand years, and not as a savage horde, but as a great state. Yet we are being constantly told of new institutions and of new laws, as if we had just emerged from the dark American forests! We require more preservative than creative wisdom. Peter's excesses in imitating foreign powers are justly condemned by history, but are they not worse yet in our own time? Where, in what European country, do the people prosper, where does justice flourish, where does good order prevail, where are hearts content and minds at rest? In France? It is true, they have a Conseil d'État, Secrétaire d'État, Sénat conservateur, Ministres de l'Intérieur, de la Justice, des Finances, de l'Instruction publique, de la Police, des Cultes; it is equally true that Russia of Catherine II had neither these institutions nor these officials. Yet where do we find a civil society fulfilling its true mission — in the Russia of Catherine II, or in the France of Na-

poleon? Where do we find more arbitrary power and absolutist whim? Where are the affairs of state handled with
greater legality and order? We perceive in Alexander's beautiful soul a fervent desire to institute in Russia the rule of
law. He could have attained this aim more readily, and
made it more difficult for his successors to deviate from the
lawful order, had he left the old institutions intact but
imbued them, so to say, with a constant zeal to serve the
public interest. It is far easier to change new things than
old ones. Alexander's successors are much more likely to be
impressed with the power which is heightened in the Senate
than that which is attributed to the present Council. Novelties breed novelties, and encourage despotic licentiousness.

Let us say once and let us say again that one of the main
reasons for the dissatisfaction of Russians with the present
government is its excessive fondness for political changes,
changes which shake the foundations of the empire, and the
advantages of which are still an open question.

[4. Some Internal Measures and Laws]

Let us now turn to some provisional and individual decrees enacted in Alexander's reign. Let us take a look at
measures taken to deal with important problems, and at
their consequences.

After Napoleon had shattered with one blow the previously celebrated Prussian state, he began to advance toward our frontiers. All good Russians felt anxiety; all felt
the need for extraordinary efforts, and waited to see what
the government would do. It came out with — the Manifesto
on the Militia. . . . I believe that the sovereign's counselors
were inspired by good intentions, but they knew little of
Russia's condition. To arm 600,000 men while disposing of
no spare weapons! To feed them without the means of sup-
plying them with bread, or of storing it in the places to

which they were to go! Where were the gentry to command these men? Many provinces could not raise even half the required officers. The gentry were astounded; the tillers were frightened; deliveries and work ceased; sorrow drove peasants to drink; further violence was also expected. But the Lord protected us. The noble sons of the fatherland were at that time unquestionably prepared for magnanimous sacrifices, but the general enthusiasm soon subsided, for they saw that the government desired the impossible. People began to lose confidence in it, and those who had at first read the Manifesto with tears in their eyes, a few days later ridiculed the miserable militia! Finally, the government reduced the number of reservists. . . . It had seven long months at its disposal, and yet it failed to furnish strong reinforcements to the army! Instead, it furnished us the Tilsit Peace. . . . If the government, instead of appealing for the militia, which is unfamiliar to us, had appealed for 150,000 recruits, with bread, carts, and money, it would not have caused the slightest stir in Russia, and yet it might have been able to strengthen our army before the battle of Friedland. All that the situation required was prompt action. When the state faces extraordinary dangers and sacrifices, the main thing is to act rashly, to give the people no time to come to their senses, not to retract policies, not to waver. I have read the correspondence of the Russian *voevody* from the time of the False Dmitrii, when we had had no tsar, no Boyar Duma, and no capital. These men had little knowledge of writing, but much knowledge of Russia, and they saved her with the simplest means, demanding that each do what he could do best considering the special circumstances of his command. I shall conclude this section with a special observation. At the time when the militia edict was issued, everybody complained of the shortage of weapons, and blamed it on the carelessness of the command. I do not know, but have we profited from this experience for our future security? Are the arsenals being stocked with cannon and guns for every contingency? I hear only that the renowned Tula works are deteriorating, that the new steam engines do not work too well, and that the new models of weapons bring ruin to artisans. . . . Is this not so?

The intentions of Alexander demonstrate consistently his desire to promote the public good. Abhorring the senseless principle which holds that the tranquility of the sovereign entails the ignorance of his subjects, he has spent millions to found universities, gymnasia, and schools. . . . Alas, these measures turn out to cause greater loss to the treasury than they bring benefit to the fatherland. The professors have been invited before there were students to hear them, and though many of these scholars are prominent, few are really useful; for the students, being but poorly acquainted with Latin, are unable to understand these foreign instructors, and are so few in number that the latter lose all desire to appear in class. The trouble is that we have built our universities on the German model, forgetting that conditions in Russia are different. At Leipzig or Göttingen a professor need only to appear on the platform for the lecture hall to fill with an audience. In Russia there are no lovers of higher learning. The gentry perform service, while the merchants care only to obtain a thorough knowledge of mathematics or of foreign languages for purposes of trade. How many young men in Germany study to become lawyers, judges, pastors, professors! Russian scribes and judges, on the other hand, have no need to know Roman laws. Our priests are given an education of sorts at the seminaries, and proceed no further. As for the academic profession, its rewards are yet so unfamiliar in Russia, that it will be a long time before parents will decide to prepare their sons for it. Instead of the sixty professors whom we had called from Germany to Moscow and the other cities, I would have invited twenty at most, but I would have spared no expense to increase the number of government scholarships at the gymnasia; needy families, enrolling their sons there, would bless the sovereign's generosity, and thus, poverty aided by charity, would produce in Russia in a decade or two a profession of scholars. I dare say no other method can be as effective in bringing this undertaking to a successful conclusion. The constructing and purchasing of buildings for universities, the founding of libraries, cabinets, and scholarly societies, and the calling of famous astronomers and philologists from abroad — all this is throwing dust in the eyes. What subjects are not being taught today even at such places as Kharkov and Kazan! And this at a time when it takes the utmost effort to find in Moscow a teacher of Russian, when it is virtually impossible to find in the whole country a hundred men who know thoroughly the rules of orthography, when we lack a decent grammar, when imperial decrees make improper use of words; the important Bank Act, for instance, says: "to give money without time limit," instead of *"à perpetuité,"* *"without repayment,"* and the Manifesto on Commercial Tariffs speaks of *"shortening* the importation of merchandise," etc., etc. Let us also call attention to certain strange features of this new educational system. The best professors, who should devote their time to science, are busy furnishing candles and firewood to the university! Their economic responsibilities comprise also the upkeep of the one hundred or more schools which are subordinated to the University Council. In addition, the professors are required annually to travel around the provinces to inspect schools. How much wasted money and effort! Previously, the economy of the university was entrusted to the care of a special university chancery, and properly so. Let the superintendent of schools inspect the district schools in his province once every three years, but it is absurd as well as pathetic to see these poor professors being shaken up and down in kibitkis on their annual peregrinations! They can learn the condition of every gymnasium or school from the latter's reports, without ever stepping outside the Council: well-attended schools are good, poorly attended schools are bad, and bad schools are almost always the result of one and the same cause, namely poor teachers. Why not appoint good ones? Are there none? Or are they in short supply? . . . What is responsible for this? The inactivity of the local Pedagogical Institute (I speak only of the one in Moscow, with which I am acquainted). Professorial jaunts will not remedy this shortcoming. Altogether, so far the Ministry of so-called Education in Russia has done nothing but slumber, as if it were unaware of its importance and wanting a course of action, waking up from time to time only to demand of the sovereign money, distinctions, and medals.

Having done much to promote in Russia the cause of learning, and noting with displeasure the gentry's lack of interest in university studies, the government resolved to make academic pursuits mandatory, and issued the ill-advised Examination Act. Henceforth, no one is to be promoted to the rank of Counselor of State or Collegiate Assessor without a certificate of studies. In the past, functionaries of the most enlightened states had been required to know only what was essential to their work: the engineer, engineering, the judge, law, and so on. But in Russia, the official presiding in the Civil Court must know Homer and Theocritus, the Senate Secretary — the properties of oxygen and all the gasses, the Deputy Governor — Pythagorean geometry, the superintendent of a lunatic asylum — Roman law, or else they will end their days as Collegiate or Titular Counselors. Neither forty years of state service, nor important accomplishments exempt one from the obligation of having to learn things which are entirely alien and useless for Russians. Never before had love of knowledge led to an act so contrary to the spirit of knowledge! It is amusing that the author of the Instruction which commands everyone to master rhetoric, should himself be guilty of grammatical errors! . . . But let us leave alone the ridiculous, and turn to the harmful prospects of this act. Heretofore, the gentry and the other classes of Russia sought in the service either distinctions or emoluments. The former motive is harmless; the latter dangerous, since inadequate salaries expose covetous men to all the temptations of graft. Under conditions now in force, what can provide a Titular or Collegiate Counselor with an inducement for service in case he happens to be ignorant of physics, statistics, or the other sciences? The better, i.e., ambitious officials, will retire; the inferior, i.e., greedy ones will remain in the service to fleece the living and the dead. Instances of this are occurring already. Instead of enacting this new decree, one need only have enforced the provisions of the University Act, which requires young men, prior to entry into the service, to show proof of studies. From beginners one may ask anything, but it is unfair to confront an old official with new conditions of service: he has turned gray on his job, relying on the rules of honor, and hoping some day to obtain the rank of Counselor of State, promised him by law — and now you violate this state contract. Moreover, instead of general knowledge, every man should be required to know only that which is necessary for the service to which he wants to devote himself. Examine the lower officials of the College of Foreign Affairs in statistics, history, geography, diplomacy, and languages; others only in their native tongue and in Russian law, and not in Roman law, which is of no use to us; others yet in geometry in case they aspire to becoming surveyors, etc. To seek the superfluous is as bad as to reject the necessary.

[5. Serfdom and the Problem of Emancipation]

The Examination Act was everywhere greeted with sarcastic ridicule. The act to which I want to turn next has
offended many and gladdened no one, although the sovereign, when he issued it, was inspired by the most sacred hu-
manitarianism. We have heard of monstrous landowners who
engaged in an inhuman traffic with people. Having purchased a village, these men picked the peasants fit for military service, and then sold them without land. Let us assume
that there still are such beasts today. Trade of this kind
should then be outlawed by a strict decree, containing a
proviso that the estates of the unworthy landowners engaging in it are to be placed under guardianship. The enforcement of such a law could be entrusted to the governors. Instead of doing this, the government outlaws the sale and
purchase of recruits. In the past, the better farmer toiled
gladly for ten, twenty years in order to accumulate 700 or
800 rubles with which to purchase a recruit, so as to keep his
family intact. Now he has lost his most powerful incentive to
engage in beneficent hard work and stay sober. Of what use
is wealth to a parent if it cannot save his beloved son? Yes,
inn-keepers rejoice, but the heads of families weep. The
state must have its recruits — it is better to draw them from
miserable than from happy people, for the latter are in-
comparably worse off in the army than they were before. I
would like to ask whether the peasants of a tyrannical landlord — one whose greed is such that he would be capable of
selling them as recruits — prosper from the prohibition of
such sales? If anything, their lot may be less miserable in
the regiments! But as for the landowners of modest means,
they have now lost an opportunity of ridding themselves of
unsatisfactory peasants or household serfs, to their own and
to society's benefit; under the old system the lazy, intem-

perate peasant would mend his ways in the strict military school, while the diligent, sober one would remain behind the plow. Moreover, the example itself exercised a salutary effect, and other peasants swore off the bottle knowing the master's rights to sell them as recruits. What means has a petty landowner nowadays with which to frighten his dissolute peasants when it is not his turn to furnish recruits? The cane? Backbreaking labor? Is it not more useful to have them frightened of the cane in the ranks of the military company? One may argue that our soldiers have improved as a result of this decree, but have they indeed? I inquired of generals — they have not noticed it. At any rate, it is true that the village peasants have deteriorated. The father of three or even two sons readies in good time one of them for the draft, and keeps him unmarried; the son, knowing what awaits him, drinks, because good behavior will not save him from military service. The legislator should view things from a variety of angles and not merely from one; or else, extirpating one evil, he may occasion yet greater evil.

Thus we are told that the present government had the intention of emancipating proprietary serfs. One must know the origins of this bondage. In Russia in the ninth, tenth, and eleventh centuries the only bondmen were the *kholopy*, i.e., either foreigners captured in war or purchased, or criminals deprived by law of citizenship, together with their descendants. But rich men, disposing of a multitude of *kholopy*, populated their lands with them, and in this manner arose the first serf villages in the modern sense of the word. Furthermore, proprietors also admitted into servitude free peasants on terms which more or less constrained the latter's natural and civil liberties; some of these peasants, upon receipt of land from the proprietor, committed themselves and the children to serve him forever. This was the second source of slavery in the countryside. Other peasants

— and they constituted the majority — rented land from the owners in return for a payment consisting only of money or a set quantity of cereals, while retaining the right to move on elsewhere after the expiration of a fixed period of time. These free movements, however, had their drawbacks, for great lords and wealthy men lured free peasants away from weak landlords, and the latter, left with deserted fields, were unable to meet their state obligations. Tsar Boris was the first to deprive all peasants of this freedom to move from place to place, that is, he bound them to their masters. Such was the beginning of general bondage. This law was changed, limited, and made subject to exceptions; it was tried in courts for many years; at last it attained to full force, and the ancient distinction between serfs and *kholopy* disappeared entirely. It follows: 1) that the present day proprietary serfs were never landowners; that is, they never had land of their own, which is the lawful, inalienable property of the gentry; 2) that the serfs who are descended of the *kholopy* are also the lawful property of the gentry and cannot be personally emancipated without the landlords receiving some special compensation; 3) that only the free peasants who were bound to their masters by Godunov may, in justice, demand their previous freedom; but since 4), we do not know which of them are descended of the *kholopy,* and which of free men, the legislator faces no mean task when he tries to untie this Gordian knot, unless he is bold enough to cut through it by proclaiming all to be equally free: the descendants of war captives, purchased, lawful slaves, as well as the descendants of enserfed peasants, the former being freed by virtue of the law of nature, and the latter by virtue of the power of the autocratic monarch to abrogate the statutes of his predecessors. I do not want to pursue this controversy further, but I should like to point out that as far as the state is concerned, natural law yields to civil law, and that the prudent autocrat abrogates only those laws which have become harmful or inadequate, and which can be replaced by superior ones.

What does the emancipation of serfs in Russia entail? That they be allowed to live where they wish, that their masters be deprived of all authority over them, and that they come exclusively under the authority of the state. Very well. But these emancipated peasants will have no land, which — this is incontrovertible — belongs to the gentry. They will, therefore, either stay on with their present landlords, paying them quitrent, cultivating their fields, delivering bread where necessary — in a word, continuing to serve them as before; or else, dissatisfied with the terms, they will move to another, less exacting, landlord. In the first case, is it not likely that the masters, relying on man's natural love for his native soil, will impose on the peasants the most onerous terms? Previously they had spared them, seeing in the serfs their own property, but now the greedy among them will try to exact from the peasants all that is physically possible. The landlords will draw up a contract, the tiller will renege — and there will be lawsuits, eternal lawsuits! In the second case, with the peasant now here, now there, won't the treasury suffer losses in the collection of the soul-tax and other revenues? Will not agriculture suffer as well? Will not many fields lie fallow, and many granaries stay empty? After all, the bread on our markets comes, for the most part, not from the free farmers but from the gentry. And here is one more evil consequence of emancipation: the peasants, no longer subjected to seignorial justice from which there is no appeal and which is free of charge, will take to fighting each other and litigating in the city — what ruin! . . . Freed from the surveillance of the masters who dispose of their own *zemskaia isprava,* or police, which is much more active than all the Land Courts, the peasants will take to drinking and villainy

— what a gold mine for taverns and corrupt police officials, but what a blow to morals and to the security of the state! In short, at the present time, the gentry, dispersed throughout the realm, assist the monarch in the preservation of peace and order; by divesting them of this supervisory authority, he would, like Atlas, take all of Russia upon his shoulders. Could he bear it? A collapse would be frightful. The primary obligation of the monarch is to safeguard the internal and external unity of the state; benefiting estates and individuals comes second. Alexander wishes to improve the lot of the peasants by granting them freedom; but what if this freedom should harm the state? And will the peasants be happier, freed from their masters' authority, but handed over to their own vices, to tax farmers, and to unscrupulous judges? There can be no question that the serfs of a sensible landlord, one who contends himself with a moderate quitrent, or with labor on a *desiatina* of plowland for each household, are happier than state peasants, for they have in him a vigilant protector and defender. Is it not better quietly to take measures to bridle cruel landlords? These men are known to the governors. If the latter faithfully fulfill their obligations, such landlords will promptly become a thing of the past; and unless Russia has wise and honest governors, the free peasants will not prosper either. I do not know whether Godunov did well in depriving the peasants of their freedom since the conditions of that time are not fully known. But I do know that this is not the time to return it to them. Then they had the habits of free men — today they have the habits of slaves. It seems to me that from the point of view of political stability it is safer to enslave men than to give them freedom prematurely. Freedom demands preparation through moral improvement — and who would call our system of wine-farming and the dreadful prevalence of drunkenness a sound preparation for freedom? In conclusion, we have this to say

to the good monarch: "Sire! history will not reproach you
for the evil which you have inherited (assuming that serfdom actually is an unequivocal evil), but you will answer
before God, conscience, and posterity for every harmful consequence of your own statutes."

I do not condemn Alexander's law permitting villages to
gain their freedom with their masters' permission. But are
many of them sufficiently rich to avail themselves of it? Will
there be many prepared to surrender all they have in return
for freedom? The serfs of humane landlords are content with
their lot; those who serve bad landlords are impoverished —
the situation of both categories renders this law ineffectual.

[6. Financial Policies]

Among the more important activities of the present government one must mention measures designed to balance
income and expenditure, and to improve trade and the national economy in general. Two ill-fated wars with the
French, the war with Turkey, and especially the war with
Sweden, had compelled the treasury to multiply assignats.
The inevitable result followed: the price of things went up,
while the value of the currency went down. This calamity
was made complete by the rupture of relations with England.
Russian merchandise can be shipped abroad only by sea; but
while fewer foreign vessels entered Russian ports, the products of European factories, light in weight and expensive,
kept on entering Russia by sea and land. This destroyed all
equilibrium between exports and imports. Such was the
situation when the Tax Manifesto came out. Instead of
saying simply: "the unavoidable growth of fiscal expenditures forces us to raise more revenue, yet we do not want to
issue any more new assignats," the government informed us
solemnly that assignats represented not money but an indeterminate quantity of state debts, payable in specie which the

exchequer happens to lack! The result was a further increase in the price of all things and a fall in the rate of exchange. The former was caused by new taxes, the latter by the loss of confidence which our assignats suffered in the eyes of foreigners as a result of their being solemnly proclaimed questionable promissory notes. Let us say a few words about both these issues.

New taxes are a very unreliable and purely provisional method of increasing state revenue. The agriculturalist, the factory owner, the manufacturer, assessed with new taxes invariably raises the price of his products — products indispensable to the exchequer — and a few months later, the exchequer suffers from new shortages. As a result of supplementary taxes, for instance, the contractors now demand 15,000 rubles for goods for which they had charged the commissary 10,000 rubles earlier in the year! Again taxes must be raised, and so *ad infinitum!* The economy of the state is different from that of the private citizen. I can become richer by raising the rent of my peasants, but the government cannot, because its taxes are general, and always result in high prices. The exchequer can enrich itself in two ways only: by increasing the quantity of things, or by reducing expenditures, by industry or by thrift. If we produce each year greater quantities of bread, cloth, leather, and linen, then the upkeep of the army will be cheaper. A carefully run economy yields more riches than do gold mines. A million saved in the exchequer from expenditures turns into two million; a million acquired through taxes at first decreases to half a million, and then turns into nothing. And while sincerely praising the government for its desire to promote agriculture and animal husbandry in Russia, shall we also praise it for its frugality? Where do you see it? In the reduction of court expenditures? But the thrift of the sovereign and the thrift of the government are two different things! If anything, Alexander has a reputation of a miser. Yet how many new posts have been invented, how many unnecessary officials created! Here three generals guard the slippers of Peter the Great; there a man draws salary from five places; everyone draws food allowances, they loan money which is never repaid, and to whom? — to the richest men! They deceive the sovereign with projects and paper establishments, in order to loot the exchequer. . . . Inspectors, Senators, and other officials travel continuously at government expense, without accomplishing the slightest good with their rounds. All demand that the Emperor grant them residences, and then purchase them at twice their worth with government money, supposedly for the public good, but in fact, for their own private benefit, and so on, and so forth. . . . In short, Russia has never, not since her beginning, known either a sovereign as modest in his private expenditures as Alexander, or a reign as extravagant as his. Let us note a further incongruity: at the very time when in decrees we enjoin the gentry to be thrifty, hussar officers in the army wear uniforms covered with silver and gold! What wages are paid to these people? And how much does a uniform cost? Deeds, not clothes, adorn regiments. It is not enough to suspend certain constructions and works undertaken by the government, it is not enough to save this way twenty million. It is also necessary to deal firmly with the shameless greed of many eminent personalities, to refrain from founding new establishments, to cut down the number of parasites carried on the payroll, to learn to send away empty-handed all the ignoramuses who demand money for the alleged advancement of science, and, wherever possible, to restrain the luxury of private citizens —. that luxury which, in the present condition of Europe and Russia, is more injurious to the state than it ever was before.

Let us turn to assignats. Many naive, yet by no means stupid, people still think that the counselors of the government have acted in this matter for their own secret ends, and have sought deliberately to undermine the state's credit. As for me, I explain this riddle, like so many others, entirely by the well-known fondness of superficial minds for boasting and smart talk. Until now, the term "state debt" was applied in Russia only to the sums which our government borrowed in Holland and in other foreign countries. No one included among them assignats which everybody treated as money because they served as such in making purchases. The inhabitants of the Maldive Islands know no money but worthless shells, yet they engage in internal and external trade. What gives value to money? The government, by declaring itself ready to accept it as a tribute of the nation in lieu of such and such objects. If the sovereign offered us marked chips, and ordered that they circulate instead of rubles, having previously devised a method of protecting us from counterfeit wooden coins, we would accept the chips as well. Coins have been introduced not to be made into vessels, buttons, or snuffboxes, but to help us appraise things and compare them with each other. Let us concede that metallic coins, as Büsch and others argue, are the best, having been known already in Job's time. But must a strong government, rich in things, deem itself a beggar, must it deprive itself of an army and fleet simply because it does not happen to dispose of a surplus of silver and gold? The value of gold itself is far more imaginary than intrinsic. Who would exchange in the winter a warm shirt for gold beads, if the latter were to be valued entirely for their usefulness? But I give up the shirt and accept the beads when I can get along without the shirt, and use the beads to purchase a coat. If I can obtain a coat for a piece of paper as well, then the paper and the beads are to me of equal value. Assignats lose in value because they are too many; so does gold and silver. The discovery of America had an effect on the price of European

merchandise similar to that which assignats have now produced in Russia. This interdependence of prices and the
quantity of money in circulation is unchangeable. Our ancestors got along from the ninth to the fourteenth centuries
without metallic coins of their own, using only leather scraps
which were sealed by the government and called *kuny,* that
is, assignats; and they traded with the East and the West,
with Greece, Persia, and the German Hansa. From the ninth
century until 1228 these scraps suffered no decline in relation to silver, because the government kept on issuing them
in sensible quantities. But when they were inordinately
multiplied later on, they fell drastically. It is well worth
noting that these leather assignats were replaced in Russia
by silver and copper coinage during the most turbulent and
barbaric periods of our servitude to the khans, at a time
when the *baskaki* enjoyed greater respect than the princes.
The Tatars refused to accept the *kuny,* demanding silver instead. A Russian could purchase his exemption from torture,
from death, and from slavery with a piece of this metal; he
gave for it all that he had, and suspiciously rejected the
kuny, with the result that they disappeared of themselves.
Silver had originally reached Kiev from Greece, and later
Novgorod from Siberia, by way of Iugra, as well as from
Germany by way of the Hanseatic towns; at last it reached
Moscow from the Horde itself, with which it had opened
commercial relations. But the quantity of metals which the
merchants were able to obtain was so insignificant that the
Russians, having done away with the *kuny,* were compelled
inside the country to resort largely to barter — a procedure
most unfortunate for trade, and a consequence of barbarism!
Tsar Ivan Vasilevich, having ruined the exchequer with his
many and unprecedented expenditures, and being faced with
a shortage of silver, thought of introducing leather money
once more. Peter the Great was also short of bullion, al-

though we had accumulated much of it from commerce with England, as well as from the acquisition of Siberia with its rich mines; in his time silver in Russia was dearer than anywhere else in Europe — the reason why foreign merchants liked to send their ducats and thalers here. Nevertheless, the scarcity of money favored internal trade. Bread and other cheap merchandise came by land to the capital from the remotest provinces because it could not be disposed of locally. Gold and silver abounded in Petersburg, Archangel, Moscow — in Simbirsk, Penza, or Voronezh they were rarely to be seen. Documents from the reigns of Empress Anne and the Regent voiced the complaints of the wisest of Russian ministers concerning the severe shortage of small change: Ostermann suggested repeatedly that we purchase in Holland large quantities of silver, but he gave no thought to assignats, being perhaps unaware that in modern Europe we had used them first and for so long a time. Finally, Catherine II, by issuing assignats, astonished the nation at first, but it was not long before her move was seen to facilitate the transaction of payments and other commercial dealings. The people came to realize the convenience and utility of the assignats. In the past, loan and commercial operations in Russia had been conducted with promissory notes — now assignats replaced the promissory notes and resulted in the expansion of internal trade. The government was committed to redeem them in specie, but it knew that as soon as the public became firmly persuaded of the soundness of paper money it would demand from the bank only the small quantities needed for petty expenses. And so it was in the reign of Catherine, to the benefit of the state and the nation. The exchequer acquired a considerable capital, and could, in exceptional circumstances, get by without raising taxes, while the people had enough currency. As for silver, it was less in demand now than previously, and remained for a long time

on parity with assignats, then it rose a trifle, then more, and
finally one and one-half times, keeping pace with the gradual
rise of all other prices, which followed inevitably from the
increase by 200 million of the quantity of money circulating
in Russia. Where money is scarce, things are cheap — where
it is plentiful, they are dear. Silver coins, having been super-
ceded by assignats, became more expensive in relation to
them not as coins, preferred to paper, but as a commodity.
One noticed a general high level of prices which, however,
neither got out of hand nor constituted an unmitigated evil.
In the last years of Catherine's reign, when the government
was unable to meet the popular demand for coinage of small
denominations, the people justly complained against it. The
reign of Paul brought no significant change whatever to the
national economy, because the treasury did not increase the
quantity of assignats. But in the present reign they have
poured forth like a flood, with the result that the price of
goods has doubled and tripled. We do not blame the government for having issued perhaps as many as 500 million paper
rubles. Was there another, better method of meeting state
requirements? I do not know, and even doubt it! But once
the unavoidable evil was done, one should have acted with
thought and discretion, without sighing and beating of the
alarm, for those actions intensify the evil. Let the ministers
speak frankly only to the monarch, never to the people! God
help us if they should follow a different principle: to deceive
the sovereign and tell every truth to the nation! Announce
that as of now the factory printing assignats will be idle. Very
well, but why interpret the words: "The State Bank will
pay the bearer" etc.? I would consent to your saying that
assignats are not money if you were able to throw open banks
and coffers filled with silver for the redemption of the paper.
I would consent to your saying that assignats are not money
if we had other money. But what have we? Silver? Copper?

How much of such money is there in Russia right now? And do you think that this paltry sum could meet the requirements of the country's trade turnover? In ancient Russia *kuny* circulated together with silver and gold, in the new Russia assignats circulate together with metals, which then as now are in short supply. A scrap of leather is no better than a scrap of paper, but the ancient princes of Kiev, Smolensk, or Novgorod, did not try to persuade the people that *kuny* were promissory notes, and Russia made good use of them for five centuries, blessing this happy invention. Custom is stronger than sophistry. Despite the fact that assignats came in the form of promissory notes, we did not consider the sovereign our debtor, we did not expect him to pay for the papers, we did not study the treasury's condition, being satisfied that assignats obtained for us everything we wanted. Let us even concede that assignats are promissory notes — but then they are state notes, different in their properties from commercial or private ones. The government puts them into circulation in the form of promissory notes, but once in general use they turn into coinage where coinage is in short supply. Necessity binds the government no less than the people. If a merchant were to say of his note what the manifesto says of assignats, that is, if he were solemnly to declare that he had issued them in excessive quantities, and feared greatly the consequences — then the next day hardly a soul would consent to sell him an estate for a promissory note. For our assignats, on the other hand, everything is being sold even now. The value of assignats declined in relation to goods not because their trustworthiness or credit has fallen, but because of the operation of the general law regulating the relationship between prices and goods. In short, the manifesto notwithstanding, assignats continue to serve in Russia as money at this very moment, for they are the only money we have. But as a consequence of the manifesto, foreign traders, who are much better acquainted than Russians with the language and symptoms of national bankruptcy, began to have misgivings over their trade with Russia, with the result that the rate of exchange continued to fall, lowering the prices of Russian produce for foreigners, and raising them for us.

What is to be said of the so-called *Spirit of the Manifesto* sent everywhere together with it? The *Spirit* ought to be contained within the manifesto itself, and not in a separate work of some apprentice secretary who, with absurd airs, expounds words to us by repeating or transposing them, and declares haughtily that only imbeciles deem it necessary to mint coins in accord with their current value, and that a pood of copper, worth forty rubles in everything else, should circulate in money at sixteen rubles, because if we should make two copper rubles from one all prices would double. No, Mr. Interpreter, our copper coins are nothing but small change which right now we need badly, and which is short because copper coins are secretly melted into objects or exported abroad. A ruble's worth of copper should not be made into ten rubles except for some compelling reason, so as to prevent counterfeiting; but neither should forty rubles' worth of copper be made into sixteen rubles, so as to prevent coins from being melted into stills, etc. Nowhere do metals circulate in the form of money below their intrinsic value. Disregarding this *Spirit,* the government ordered a reform of the copper currency and decreed that sixteen rubles of copper be minted into twenty-four rubles; why not forty or fifty? Counterfeiting will be no easy matter, even if the price of copper should before long decline appreciably; this is proven by Russia's own experience, copper money having circulated in our country since the time of Peter the Great much above its intrinsic value. Everybody criticizes the government for allowing money changers to rob the people, although it has

the means to provide us with all the copper coinage necessary for change. Assignats of low denomination are also
traded — do bank counselors, perhaps, find it difficult to
sign them, or are they conserving paper?

I have looked into books of political economy, I have
heard learned men give estimates of the contemporary economic condition of Russia, and I found more verbiage than
ideas, more sophistries than clear conceptions. The evil is not
as great as they imagine. Everything is expensive, that is
true, but have not incomes kept pace with expenses? A landowner with villages under the plow, or with factories, does
not suffer from high prices, nor do merchants; the master of
peasants paying quitrent does suffer somewhat; and capital-
ists and salaried personnel lose most of all. Weighing the
advantages and disadvantages, I conclude that, on the whole,
the present high prices are an evil, and, insofar as they are
caused by the increase of assignats, there arises the question
whether the quantity of assignats should be reduced.

The government feels that it should, and it takes steps to
found a Loan Bank, as well as to dispose of treasury estates.
One can only hope that this undertaking will not be fully
realized, or else it will in turn engender a new evil, one which
could scarcely have been foreseen last summer.

The rise of prices has occurred not only in proportion to
the emission of new assignats, but also in proportion to the
likelihood of future emissions, new taxes, and the low rate
of exchange. Prices have mounted daily. On Friday merchandise cost more than on Thursday; on Saturday more
than on Friday, sometimes going up from habit, and sometimes from unscrupulous greed. The force which had set the
ball in motion was gone, but the ball kept on rolling. . . .
The people could not make up their minds whether or not
to trust the treasury's promise that it would suspend further
emission of assignats. Finally, a surprise occurred: a major

shortage of money, that is, of assignats! Moscow merchants asked one another with astonishment what had become of them, and offered money lenders 3 per cent a month. In fact, there were just as many assignats as before, but that was not enough owing to high prices; that is, the unwarranted rise of prices in recent times was out of proportion to the quantity of available assignats. For instance, a merchant who had previously owned a capital of 10,000 rubles, now owned 15,000, but since the price of the merchandise which he was purchasing has doubled, he found that in order to keep his business from declining he had to borrow 5,000 rubles.

If the treasury at this point, through the bank and the sale of estates, withdraws from circulation 200 million rubles, we shall experience a frightful shortage of currency; the wine-farmers will be ruined, the peasants will cease paying quitrent to their masters, merchants will refuse to buy and to sell goods, and the treasury revenues will fall in arrears. Do not expect cheapness to follow at once — no! it will be some time before vendors consent to sell you something for half its previous price. Rather, there will occur a suspension of trade and payments. There will be no end to dissatisfaction and complaints, and many will declare themselves bankrupt before we attain at last a new system of appraising things, commensurate with the quantity of money circulating in the country. Great breaks are dangerous. It is just as harmful suddenly to decrease the quantity of paper money as it is suddenly to increase it. What then is to be done? Suspend all further emission of assignats! . . . This is enough. Prices will undoubtedly fall, for, as we had previously said, they had risen out of proportion to the quantity of assignats; but they will fall gradually, without a crisis, as long as Russia is not subjected to further calamities.

The second idea of the government is to reduce the price of silver by promising to redeem in a few years through the so-called *Bank for the Liquidation of Debts* every two paper rubles with one silver ruble. Should this bank succeed in acquiring deposits to the value of 200 million paper rubles, the government will find itself upon the expiration of the stated period in extreme difficulty. It is no easy matter to prepare 100 million rubles in silver for redemption! Fortunately, the deposits in this bank have been small, for there is no idle capital in Russia; but what is the merit of a policy which benefits the country only by failing? The author of this edict apparently assumed that in the course of the next six years the silver ruble would fall to the equivalent of, say, 150 kopecks in assignats, and that the holders of state bonds would therefore gladly accept the entire sum in paper. Very well, but what if this should not be the case? Let us note that in Russia silver has risen out of proportion to other prices. Four years ago a bag of flour cost in Moscow four and one-half silver rubles, whereas now it costs less than two and one-half. Look also at other Russian produce, and you will find that it all costs in silver almost half of what it had cost previously. This is due to the upkeep of foreign armies, and the clandestine import of foreign goods both of which have increased the outlay of silver. Do you want to reduce the price of silver? Then refrain from using it in making purchases for the army, suppress the illegal trade which is carried on exclusively in hard currency, and give us small change — or else you demand the impossible. The present high price of precious metals hurts not the population at large but the treasury and the wealthy men who need foreign merchandise, the price of which rises in accordance with the price of silver. In Russia silver circulates only in the capitals, in the border towns, and in the seaports — inside the country it is neither seen nor demanded, in sharp contrast to the claim made by the manifesto that in Russia the only legal tender is the silver ruble. No, in Russia, silver is a commodity, not money!

Legal foreign trade also does not demand precious metals. An Englishman does not care what currency circulates in Russia, whether copper, gold, or paper. If a scrap of paper will procure for him in Russia an object for which he will find it profitable to give us an object priced at a guinea, then the English guinea will have a course at par with the Russian paper, because the commerce of states is really based on the exchange of things. The exchange rate of currencies is determined not by their intrinsic but by their commercial value. For instance, should the metallic content of our ruble diminish but the ruble's purchasing power inside Russia remain constant, then the diminution of the intrinsic worth of the ruble would have no influence on its rate of exchange, as long as other factors did not cause its decline. On the other hand, should we require more foreign currencies than foreigners required rubles, should we let in more merchandise than we sent out, then our exchange rate would drop. These reasons explain how the ruble could have turned into eighteen sous or eight stivers! Another factor in the decline of the exchange rate of the ruble, in addition to the fall of the purchasing power of the paper ruble inside Russia and the lack of balance in our foreign trade, was the activity of foreign merchants, who, fearing that our paper currency would depreciate further, transferred their capital from Russia to England and other countries.

Our government is extremely anxious to raise the exchange rate, but it wants the impossible. Until free maritime trade is restored there will be no balance between imports and exports, and foreigners will not need Russian currency to purchase sizable quantities of our produce. With the newly issued Manifesto on Tariffs we do permit the free exportation of all goods, imposing at the same time serious restrictions on imports. But shall we find many ships to carry our goods abroad? And here is another shortcoming of this manifesto: we permit, for example, the exportation of wool, and thus place foreign traders in competition with our own. This is a most unequal contest. A foreigner finds it profitable to offer two ducats for a pood of wool, as he did in the past, for a ducat then equaled three and one-half rubles, whereas now it equals twelve. In consequence, we too, requiring wool for the manufacture of textiles, have to pay twenty-five rubles a pood, which is much more than three times its previous price, and almost twice its present one! Now we ask: does the government intend to raise the price of military cloth in Russia, as must needs follow from the exportation of wool? Had the exchange rate of Russian currency declined only in proportion to the decline of paper money in the country, we would have been able to trade with Europe on equal terms, and to transact business in the price of our own produce. But as things stand, the French, Dutch, and Germans enjoy too many advantages over us, and in joint trade are in a position to ruin Russian buyers. Let us learn from the shrewd British: when public interest demands that the prices of certain goods be lowered, then they forbid their exportation. Will the exportation of wool improve appreciably the exchange rate? [No.] It will, though, appreciably raise the price of wool inside Russia. How long is it since the government has had recourse to the most unfair means of procuring cheap cloth for the army? Private factories were assessed with rents, and their proprietors compelled by force to sell at the very lowest prices. And now, of a sudden, the treasury must pay double for cloth!

In view of the insignificance of Russian exports, the idea of limiting the importation of merchandise is quite sensible. I would not criticize the government if, together with cloth, silk, and cotton textiles, it forbade also the importation of such items as diamonds, tobacco, Dutch herrings, and pickled lemons. My only regret is that the Manifesto set no time limit on the sale of the forbidden goods. As it is, shops will sell, in the guise of old wares, freshly imported articles as well — of course, in secret. True, these articles will lack the seal — and what of forged ones? Anyway, what customer looks for the seal? Altogether, it is imperative that the strictest measures be taken against the clandestine trade; it carries off millions. Everyone talks about it, but the ears of high customs officials are sealed with gold! Another evil is the fact that shopkeepers, being exempt from a deadline before which the sales have to be completed, increase each day the price of forbidden cloth and fabrics, and we all keep on buying as long as the supply lasts. One should not encourage such avid and unconscionable greed!

Anyway, the severity of the authorities and the loyalty of the customs can do something to improve our exchange rate, but not much. This rate is useful only in a country which sells more than it buys, and which, in addition, enjoys political stability, freedom from internal and external threats, and an administration imbued with the spirit of firm orderliness; a country which is not exposed to dangerous changes, which does not expect every minute edicts enunciating new policies concerning the national economy, new interpretations of assignats, new proofs that they are not money. It is not only necessary that our harbors be thrown open to all the ships of the world, but also that foreigners want to bring capital to Russia, to exchange their guineas and ducats for Russian assignats, and that they stop treating assignats as suspect promissory notes.

Leaving the subjects of state income, assignats, and commerce, I want to mention the manifesto which, I think, was issued in 1806, and defined the rights of the commercial classes. Known as the *Korennoi Ustav*, it should have been inscribed in golden letters on a charter, and placed in the repository of laws for the memory of centuries. I speak not of the style or the arrangement of ideas; but what is most perplexing is that the legislator, having described both the rights and the privileges of each category, postponed the task of defining the obligations, or conditions on which merchants could secure these rights, only threatening them indirectly with an increase in merchants' taxes. Why was this manifesto promulgated if it was too early to state the obligations of those who might wish to avail themselves of its benefits? Who can tell? Persons of melancholy inclinations, however, were saying: "It's very simple — they want to confuse all the estates! They have not as yet figured out the tax, but they rush to announce it, and as consolation promise the right to carry the saber!" But now we have a Council to review projects of general state laws. We expect in the future more mature legislative ideas.

[7. *Codification of Russian Law*]

We shall soon see how well founded is this hope, for Russia is about to receive a code of civil laws.

The inadequacy of the Ulozhenie, became apparent as early as the reign of Tsar Theodore Alekseevich, for which reason this code was supplemented in his time with additional articles. The all-embracing Peter the Great wanted a comprehensive book of laws, and informed the Senate of this wish in a personal edict in which he stated that the principles of these laws should be determined by a thorough examination of all native and foreign statutes. Catherine I repeatedly urged the Senate to occupy itself with this important task. Peter II ordered that every province send to Moscow for that purpose several well-informed and public-minded representatives of the gentry. Empress Anne broadened this body by adding to it representatives of merchants. Nevertheless, Count Ostermann exhorted the Regent [Anna Leopoldovna] in these words: "Although the Senate has been laboring over the preparation of a book of laws for twenty years, it is doubtful that it will ever succeed unless it forms for this purpose a special commission composed of two clergymen, five or six nobles, burghers, and several experienced jurists. . . ." The reign of Elizabeth went by, as did the brilliant reign of Catherine II, and we still had no code, notwithstanding the good will of the government, notwithstanding the establishment in 1754 of a special legislative commission, notwithstanding the project of a code presented by Catherine II to the Senate, the tumultuous assembly of deputies in Moscow, and Catherine's eloquent Instruction, studded with quotations from Montesquieu and Beccaria. What was wanting? — able men! Were there none in Russia? — anyway, they were not found; perhaps no one looked for them hard enough.

Alexander, eager to realize the ambition of every previous Russian monarch, formed a new commission. Many secretaries, editors, and assistants were engaged, but the one most indispensable thing was lacking: a man capable of serving as its soul, of conceiving the best plan or method, and of best carrying it out. More than a year went by and nothing was heard of this commission's work. At last the sovereign sent an enquiry to the chairman, and in reply was advised that it was necessary to move slowly, that Russia had hitherto known only decrees, not laws, and that instructions had been given to translate the Code of Frederick the Great. This reply did not sound too encouraging. The success of every endeavor depends on its object being clearly and soundly understood. What? we have no laws, only decrees? and are *ukazy* (*edicta*) not laws? . . . And Russia is not Prussia: of what use to us is a translation of Frederick's Code? Knowing it can do no harm, but by the same token one should study the Codes of Justinian or of the Kingdom of Denmark, that is, to find general conceptions and not guidance in formulating our own laws. We waited for two years. The director was changed, and a whole volume of preparatory work came out. We looked and rubbed our eyes, blinded by classroom dust. We saw a lot of learned verbiage and phraseology culled from books, but not a single idea derived from observation of the peculiar social complexion of Russia. Good Russians could not make any sense of it. All they knew was that the authors' heads were up in the clouds and not down to Russian earth, and all they wished was that these theoreticians should either come down to us or else give up writing our laws. Again a change of scenery, and the making of laws is entrusted to different hands! We are promised a speedy end to the voyage and a secure haven. The Manifesto announced that the first part of the Code was ready, and that the remainder would follow soon. Indeed, two booklets under the title, *Project of a Code,* are issued. What do we find? . . . A translation of the Code Napoléon!

What a surprise for Russia! What grist for the mills of evil gossip! Thanks to the Almighty we have not yet buckled under Napoleon's iron sceptre — we have not, as yet, turned into a Westphalia, or a Kingdom of Italy, or a Duchy of Warsaw, where the Napoleonic Code, translated amid tears, serves as the civil statute. Is it for this that Russia has been in existence as a powerful state for some one thousand years? Is this why we have toiled for one hundred years or so to produce our own comprehensive code, in order now to confess solemnly to all Europe that we are fools, and bow our gray heads to a book pasted together in Paris by six or seven ex-lawyers and ex-Jacobins? Peter the Great also liked foreign things, but he did not prescribe that we simply take, say, Swedish laws, and call them our own, because he knew that

the laws of a nation must be an outgrowth of its own ideas,
customs, habits, and special circumstances. If translations
were all that was needed, we would have had by now nine
codes. Although it is true that the sage authors of this project
every now and then realized the impossibility of transcribing
directly from the French original, and, having arrived with
their translation at the chapters dealing with *marriage and
divorce,* turned from Napoleon to the *Kormchaia Kniga,* it
is still evident everywhere that they cut our coat to a foreign
pattern. Is it advisable, for instance, to open the Russian
code with a chapter on *civil rights,* which, properly speaking,
Russia neither had nor has? We have only political rights,
that is the specific rights of the various estates of the realm;
we have gentry, merchants, townfolk, peasants, and so forth
— they all enjoy their specific rights, but they have no right
in common, save for that of calling themselves Russians. In
the Code Napoléon I read: *Participation aux droits civils
ci-après.* Further down the legislator discusses the rights of
property, inheritance, and testation. Such are civil rights in
France. But are proprietary or even state peasants in Russia
in possession of such rights, even if they do call themselves
Russians? These passages are mere translations, which, moreover, in places are unclear. For instance, in the original it
is said of a man deprived of civil rights: *"Il ne peut procéder
en Justice, ni en défendant, ni en demandant,"* whereas in
the translation it says that he cannot appear in court either
as plaintiff or as defendant; it follows that he may assault
and rob you with impunity? . . . The translators condense
much. They might also have omitted the following clause,
retained by them in the description of movable and immovable property: "Les glaces d'un appartement sont censées
mises à perpétuelle demeure, lorsque le parquet sur lequel
elles sont attachées fait corps avec la boiserie. . . . Quant aux
statues, elles sont immeubles lorsqu'elles sont placées dans

une niche pratiquée exprès pour les recevoir, encore qu'elles puissent être enlevées sans fracture ou detérioration." They could also have left out reference to *Alluvion*. Russia since its founding has known no contests over matters such as these, and no Russian, reading this project, would guess that he was reading our own Civil Code, did not the title say so: everything is un-Russian, everything is non-Russian, content as well as presentation. Who can tell why our guardianship institutions require a Family Council? But in the appropriate section of the French Code there is reference to a *conseil de Famille*. . . . Who can understand this terseness in essentials, where clarity demands that no words be spared, and this turgidity in the description of cases which are entirely inapplicable to us? I have heard by no means stupid men express the opinion that these two printed booklets merely hint at the contents of the future code by sketching certain ideas. I did not want to point out their mistake and prove that this was the code itself, because they would not have readily believed me, to such an extent is this Napoleonic legislation alien to the Russian mind. The project even contains absurdities, as, for example, when it says, "A stillborn child does not inherit." If the legislator will pronounce such truisms he will need a hundred, a thousand volumes. I looked for this axiom in the Code Napoléon, and found, instead: "Celui là n'est pas encore constitué enfant, qui n'est pas né viable." In this instance translators have turned into authors. I do not want to carp on neologisms, but I must say that in a book of laws it does seem strange to speak of a *lozhe reki* (*le lit de la rivière*), instead of *zhelobovina, ruslo*. Even the extract from our church statutes on lawful marriages and divorces is hastily done, so that, for instance, the principal cause of divorce, namely sexual impotence, is omitted. The authors seems to be very afraid to suggest any changes in the realm of spiritual affairs. But the code should at least have said that bishops are to have the discretionary authority to permit within their dioceses marriages between couples whose blood relationship is open to question, or else the extension of kinship ties in small villages will soon be such that no one will be able to get married. I approve of the law dealing with the division of landed property among brothers and sisters, children and parents, which public opinion has been urging for a long time. I doubt whether, apart from this one clause, anything else in this project deserves praise.

Putting aside all other considerations, let us enquire: is this the time to present Russians with French laws, even if they should be capable of being conveniently adapted to Russia's social conditions? We all, all who love Russia, her sovereign, her glory and well-being, so strongly detest this nation, bespattered with the blood of Europe and covered with the dust of so many demolished kingdoms — how can we then, at the very time when Napoleon's name makes hearts shudder, place his code at the holy altar of the fatherland?

An old nation has no need of new laws. Common sense tells us to ask of the Commission a systematic presentation of our own laws. The Russian *Pravda* and the *Sudebnik* have outlived their age, and survive as mere curiosities. Although the *Ulozhenie* of Tsar Alexis Mikhailovich still retains the force of law, is not much of it also antiquated, senseless, and ill-suited for us? There remain the edicts and decrees issued from the time of Tsar Alexis to our own — here is the content of the Code! The materials must be classified, with criminal matters referred to criminal matters, civil to civil, and then the two principal parts must be divided into articles. Once every edict has been subsumed under its proper article, then one should proceed to the next phase, which is to gather the related parts into a whole, into a concordance of edicts. This phase will demand that some items be explained, and others changed or amended, in the event that court experience should indicate the existing laws are either contradictory or inadequate. The third phase calls for a general critique of the laws: are they the best we can have, given the present social condition of Russia? At this stage we shall see that certain laws will need to be corrected, especially criminal laws of a cruel and barbaric character; since they have long ago fallen into disuse, why let them remain on the books and discredit our legislation?

The laws, thus assembled, classified, supplemented, and emended, should be presented systematically in book form, together with expositions of the reasoning behind them. It is not enough to describe cases: one should also settle all potential cases, and this is done by means of *general rules,* which alone make laws complete and endow them with the highest degree of perfection. Such rules are not to be found in the *Ulozhenie* of Tsar Alexis, and in many of the edicts. It is said: "Should this case arise, decide thus." And what does one do when a case arises for which the legislator had made no provision? . . . One must report! In formulating such rules do not philosophize grandiloquently, but think, so as to enlighten the judge. It is more advantageous as well as expedient to instill in his mind simple rules than their diverse applications. Russian law has its principles as much as does Roman law — define them, and you will give us a system of laws. This final phase of lawmaking I shall call *systematic presentation.* I will not insist much on the order of arrangement of the subject matter; begin with civil laws or criminal laws, with men or with things, with the reasoning or with the ordinance itself. . . . But I do think that it is better to begin with what is the most important, and to follow not the Codes of Napoleon or of Frederick, but those of Justinian and of Tsar Alexis Mikhailovich. Protect with the sacredness of the law the inviolability of the church, the sovereign, the officials, and the personal safety of all Russians; strengthen our civic bonds; attend to the inalienability of property, to inheritance, purchase, testaments, mortgages, and so forth; and finally, provide us with a manual of legal procedure.

This is an enormous undertaking, yet it is of such a nature that it cannot be entrusted to a large number of people. A single man must create the Russian Code; others may only serve him, be it as his advisers, assistants, or employees. In this case perfection of the parts and of the whole presupposes oneness of ideas, and ultimate success presupposes oneness of will. We shall either find such an individual, or else wait for the code a long time to come!

There is yet another method of preparing a code. So far we have been discussing systematic legislation. But if you lack men capable of carrying out such a task, then lower your requirements and you will still do a great deal for the country. Instead of a pragmatic code, issue a comprehensive summary collection of Russian laws or edicts of all the judiciary departments, reconciling contradictions, and replacing superfluous laws with necessary ones, so that judges will not refer in one and the same case to the *Ulozhenie* of Tsar Alexis Mikhailovich, to the Maritime Statute, and to twenty other edicts, some of which cannot be found without difficulty in the Senate itself. Such a compilation will not require mighty intellectual effort, genius, or exceptional learning, nor will it earn us the plaudits of Europe — but it will facilitate the execution of justice in Russia, without obstructing the work of the judges with Gallicisms, and without exposing us to foreign compassion, which we must evoke with our translation of the Code Napoléon.

Let us add to our discussion of Russian legislation one more point. Our state consists of diverse nations, such as Livonia, Finland, Poland, and even Little Russia, which have their own distinct civil statutes. Is it absolutely necessary to impose on them uniform laws? Yes, it is, but only as long as by so doing we do not produce in these provinces great and lasting disaster — otherwise, no. To achieve such legal uniformity it is best of all to prepare it in advance by means of preliminary policies, avoiding compulsion, and working on the impressionable minds of youth. Require the young men who reside in these provinces and wish to devote themselves to jurisprudence to take additional examinations in Russian laws, and particularly in the Russian language — this is the very best preparation for the desired uniformity of the civil laws! Furthermore, one should make exhaustive inquiries to determine why, for instance, Livonia or Finland happen to have a certain special law. Is the cause which produced it still operative, and is it compatible with the well-being of the state? If the answer be in the affirmative, one should inquire next whether the same result could not be obtained with different means. Would not morals suffer from innovation, or the bonds binding the various social estates in this land, weaken? . . . "What does it matter," asks Montesquieu, "whether the citizens follow identical laws, as long as they follow them faithfully?" In issuing a general code, Frederick the Great had no desire to destroy the separate statutes which were of particular benefit to certain provinces. Beware of superficial minds, who think that one has only to command and everything will become alike!

[PART THREE: RECOMMENDATIONS]

We have indicated the principal actions of the present government, and shown wherein they had failed. If we add to this picture the personal mistakes of ministers in matters affecting the welfare of the realm, such as the resolutions concerning salt, textile manufactures, and the driving of cattle to pasture, mistakes which have had so many evil consequences; further, the general fearlessness caused by a belief in the gentleness of the sovereign; the indifference of local officials to all kinds of misdeeds, the thievery in the courts, the impudent graft of district police captains, board directors, deputy governors, and, most of all, of the governors themselves; finally, if we complete the picture by pointing out the disturbing prospects for the future and the external dangers — should one then be surprised at the intensity of public anger at the government? We must not conceal the evil, we must not deceive ourselves or the sovereign, we must not try to explain away the discontent by saying that people like to complain and are always dissatisfied with their own time. These complaints are striking in their consistency and in their effect on the state of mind of the whole country.

I am by no means a melancholic, and I differ with those who, perceiving the weakness of the government, expect imminent destruction. No! States are sturdy, especially Russia, which is impelled by autocratic power! As long as we suffer no external calamities, we may keep on boldly blundering in our internal politics for a long time. I still see much room for all kinds of innovation on the part of egotistic and inexperienced minds. But is this not a dismal prospect? Must one exhaust one's strength simply because one has enough of it in reserve? Even the worst physicians have a hard time disposing of a strongly constituted patient. But every inappropriate medicine causes much injury and shortens life.

Having discussed the injuries, let us now turn to the remedies. And which can we suggest? The simplest!

The past cannot be retrieved. There was a time (we spoke of it in the beginning) when Alexander could easily have resuscitated Catherine's system, which at that time still lived

in the minds and hearts of those who had been molded by
it. Had this been done, the stormy reign of Paul would have
vanished from memory like a nightmare. Now it is too late.
Most of the people and things have changed, and so many
innovations have been introduced that now even the old
would strike us as dangerous novelty, for we are no longer
accustomed to it. Furthermore, the sovereign's glory would
suffer were he to admit solemnly to a decade of blunders
brought about by the selfishness of his most superficial advisers, who with their creative wisdom wished to eclipse
Catherine, the woman, and Peter, the man. What is done, is
done; one must try to find the means best suited to the
present situation.

[1. The Importance of Finding Proper Men for Government Service]

The main trouble with the legislators of the present reign
is their excessive reverence for political forms. This weakness accounts for the invention of various ministries, the
founding of the Council, and so forth. The work itself is
performed no better — it is merely performed in offices and
by officials of a different designation. Let us follow a different principle, and say that what matters are not forms, but
men. Retain the ministries and the Council: they will prove
useful as long as they are staffed throughout with wise and
honest men. Thus, our first good wish is: may God favor
Alexander in the successful choice of men! The greatness of
the internal policies of Peter was due to his ability to make
such choices, and not to the establishment of the Senate or
the colleges. This monarch was passionately fond of able
men. He looked for them in monastic cells and in dark ship
cabins: there he found Feofan and Ostermann, men celebrated in our political history. Alexander is faced with different circumstances and endowed with different spiritual

qualities of modesty and serenity from Peter, who went everywhere alone, spoke to everyone, listened to everyone, and ventured to assess the quality of a person from a single word, a single glance. But let the rule remain the same: *seek men!* Let him who enjoys the sovereign's confidence spot such men even from afar, and appoint them to the very highest positions. Appointments must be made strictly according to ability not only in republics, but also in monarchies. Some men are gradually led, others are lifted to great heights by the omnipotent arm of the monarch; the law of gradual progress holds for most, but not for all men. A person endowed with a ministerial mind must not end up as a head clerk or secretary. Rank depreciates not from the rapidity of promotion, but from the stupidity or disrepute of the dignitaries who hold it; and as for the envy which a meritorious person provokes, it dissipates quickly. You do not form a useful ministry by composing an instruction, but by preparing good ministers. Although it is true that their proposals are examined by the Council, yet what assurance have you of the wisdom of its members? Over-all wisdom comes only of individual wisdom. In short, what we need now above all, is men!

But these men are needed not only for the ministries and Council, but also and particularly for the office of governor. Russia consists not of Petersburg and not of Moscow, but of fifty or more subdivisions known as gubernii. If all goes well there, then the ministers and the Council can rest on their laurels; and it will go well there if you find in Russia fifty wise and conscientious individuals to devote themselves zealously to the well-being of the half million Russians entrusted to each of them, to curb the rapacious greed of minor officials and cruel landlords, to re-establish justice, pacify the landtillers, encourage merchants and industry, and to protect the interests of the exchequer and the nation. If the governors cannot or will not accomplish these things, they are badly chosen; if they lack the means to do so, then the structure of gubernatorial authority is unsound. 1) What manner of men are most contemporary governors? Men without talent, who allow their secretaries to profit from all kinds of wickedness, or men without conscience, who derive profit from wickedness themselves. One need not leave Moscow to be aware that the head of a certain province is a fool, and has been one for a long time! While in another he is a thief, and has been one for a long time! . . . The land buzzes with rumor, but the ministers either do not know it, or do not want to know it! What is the use of your new ministerial institutions? Why do you write laws — for posterity? Men, not documents, govern. 2) In the past, the governor was subordinated only to the Senate; now, he must, in addition, deal with various ministers. How much bother and writing! And, worst of all, many branches of the provincial administration are outside his competence, such as schools, imperial domains, state forests, highways, waterways, and the mail. What a great diversity and profusion! In consequence of this arrangement, the gubernia has not one chief, but many, some of whom reside in Petersburg and some in Moscow. Such a system of government is in violent conflict with our ancient, truly monarchic system, in which unity and forcefulness of power was attained by having it concentrated in the hands of the viceroy. Each gubernia represents Russia in microcosm. We want the whole country to be governed by a single authority, and its constituent parts by many. We fear abuses in the central government, but do they not exist in the local government? As a large house cannot be run in an orderly fashion unless it has a steward who accounts for everything to the master, so the gubernii will be put in order only when we terminate the regime which permits so many officials to function independently of the governors who answer to the sovereign for the tranquility of the country, and do so to a far greater extent than all the ministers, counselors, and Senators living in St. Petersburg. Is this one consideration not proof enough that we must raise the dignity of the governor's office by endowing it with universal respect? Model your governors on the viceroys of Catherine; give them the dignity of senators, and reconcile their authority with that of the ministers, whose true function should be merely to serve as secretaries of the sovereign in the various branches of government — and then all you will need to know is how to choose men!

[2. *The Importance of Knowing How to Deal with Men*]

This is the principal rule. A second and equally essential one is *know how to deal with men.* There are few angels and few villains in this world; what prevails is largely a mixture of the good and bad. A wise government finds the means to encourage the good tendencies in public officials, and to restrain the inclination toward evil. The first of these aims is attained by rewards and distinctions, the latter by instilling a fear of punishment. Anyone who knows the human heart as well as the composition and evolution of civil societies must acknowledge the soundness of Machiavelli's dictum that fear is the most efficacious and common of all human motives. If in your travels you happen to be in a land where all is tranquil and in order, where the people are content, the weak protected from oppression, and the innocent secure, then you can boldly say that in this country crime does not go unpunished. How many lambs would turn into tigers were it not for fear! To love goodness for its own sake is something of which only highly ethical men are capable; it is a rare occurrence in the world, or else why would people devote altars to virtue? Common men observe the canons of honesty not so much because they hope to gain thereby some special advantage, but because they fear the penalty which follows an open violation of these canons. One of the worst political evils of our time is the absence of fear. The country is filled with robbers, yet who is punished? The government waits for denunciations, for evidence; it dispatches senators to conduct investigations — and nothing gets done! Swindlers do the denouncing; honest people suffer in silence, for they want to be left in peace. It is no easy matter to convict through evidence a clever thieving judge, particularly under our law which prescribes equal penalties for the bribe-taker and the bribe-giver. The thieves are pointed out, and then the government lavishes on them titles and ribbons in the expectation that someone will lodge a complaint against them. And these worthless officials, relying on other like-minded protectors in Petersburg, keep on violating the law, openly contemptuous of decency and the good name of which they had been fictitiously deprived. In a few years they succeed in amassing a fortune worth several hundred thousand rubles, and, once penniless, they now proceed to buy up villages! Occasionally, the sovereign, notwithstanding his gentleness, also displays traits of severity: he has ordered the dismissal of two or three senators, and of a few other officials charged with extortion. But what are these instances compared to the infinite amount of extortion practiced in our time? A scoundrel reasons as follows: "My colleague X has been punished with dismissal; but such and such of my colleagues live in the lap of luxury. The exception proves the rule. If I, too, should suffer expulsion from the service, a rich hoard for a rainy day should be able to provide me with many a consolation in life." A sensitive heart, no doubt, is averse to severity, but where severity alone can establish order, there gentleness is not appropriate. How do painters depict a king? As a warrior brandishing a sword — not as a shepherd with flowers! . . . Russia will have no justice if the sovereign, having entrusted it to the courts, fails to keep an eye on the judges. Russia is not England. We have grown accustomed for many centuries to regard the monarch as the judge and to acknowledge his good intention as the supreme law. Let the sirens chant around the monarch: "Alexander, enthrone in Russia the rule of law . . . etc." I will interpret the meaning of this chorus: "Alexander! Let us rule in the name of the law over Russia, while you relax on the throne; only be sure to lavish favors and to give us ranks, ribbons, and money!" In Russia the sovereign is the living law. He favors the good, and punishes the bad, and he wins the love of the former by the fear of the latter. Not to fear the sovereign means not to fear the law! In the Russian monarch concentrate all the powers: our government is fatherly, patriarchal. The father of the family judges and punishes without protocol. The monarch, too, must in conditions of a different nature, follow only his conscience and nothing else. What is beyond Alexander's ken when he wishes to know? Let him also use his power to punish the culprits! Let him also punish those who promote culprits to positions of eminence! Let the minister answer at least for the choice of leading officials! Salutary fear must be spread out: where ten are liable for one, there ten mind one. Begin always at the top: when the district police captains are bad, then the blame rests on the governors and ministers! This was not the principle followed by those men who advised the sovereign to disgrace all the officials of the Commissariat and the Office of Provisions, except for their director, by depriving them of uniforms. Equals cannot be responsible for each other. If all the officials were responsible for the disasters suffered by the army then it was not enough to deprive them of uniforms; if, on the other hand, the guilty ones have not been found, then one should have waited with punishment. The indiscriminate punishment of the guilty together with the innocent deprives punishment of the stigma of disgrace. The lightest punishment used to no purpose is more despotic than the severest punishment founded on justice and intended for the common good. The tyrant is despised, but a soft heart in a monarch is counted as a virtue only when it is tempered with the sense of duty to use sensible severity. Forgiveness is praiseworthy in a sovereign only when extended to offences of a personal or private nature, and not to offences which impinge upon the interests of society. But if frequent use of the right to pardon is harmful, tolerance is even more so — the former is ascribed to weakness, the latter to indifference or imperviousness. We have alluded to offences against the person of the monarch. It is rare that they do not cause some injury to the state as well. No one in Russia, for instance, should be permitted openly to display dissatisfaction, or to show disrespect for the monarch, whose sacred person symbolizes the fatherland. Give people freedom and they cover you with mud — whisper a word in their ear and they lie at your feet!

Having shown how indispensable fear is in warding off evil, let us say something of rewards. Rewards are beneficial when awarded with moderation; otherwise they are either useless or harmful. I see every general bedecked with stars, and wonder: How many victories have we won? How many kingdoms have we conquered? . . . Today they award the Blue Ribbon — tomorrow they deprive of command! . . . Does the Cross of St. George, once a proud distinction, adorn an outstanding warrior? Not at all — a coward, who is despised by the entire army! Who in the future will feel himself adorned by the Cross of St. George? If the value of ranks and ribbons has gone down in the reign of Paul, then in the reign of Alexander it has, to say the least, not gone up, with the result that the sovereign was and continues to be subjected to pressures for other rewards, pecuniary in character, to the detriment of the exchequer, the nation, and political virtue. Of continence we had spoken elsewhere. Here let us recall two axioms: 1) Nothing great is done for money; and 2) overabundance inclines man to idle comfort, which runs contrary to all greatness. Russia was never famous for her wealth. In Russia service used to be performed from a sense of duty and of honor, for a piece of bread, and nothing more! In our day, not only the military but also the civil servants want to live on a grand scale at government expense. And what great diversities in pay: identical ranks provide such different emoluments, that one official goes hungry, while another gives exquisite dinners, the reason being that the former is entered on the old and the latter on the new list, that the former works in the Senate, or in the gubernia, while the latter is employed in the chancery of a minister or in some other new post. No one pays any attention to destitute officers, while greedy generals are offered rents and pensions. For a model they take the French — and why not the Russians of the time of Peter or Catherine? Anyway, the French generals are also most discontented with Napoleon because, having enriched them, he deprives them of the leisure and the means wherewith to enjoy their wealth. Honor, honor should be the main reward! The Romans conquered the world with oaken garlands. The main features of human nature have not changed: attach to any symbol the idea of superior virtue, that is, bestow it only on individuals of superior quality, and you will see it turn into an object of general desire, notwithstanding its low pecuniary value. Thank God, we still have ambition, our eyes still shed tears at the thought of Russian sorrows; in the very chorus of discontent, in the very impudence of the complaints levied at the government, you can often discern the voice of grateful love for the fatherland. The men are available, know only how to bridle their inclinations to wickedness and to

encourage their inclinations to goodness by means of a prudent system of punishments and rewards! But, let us repeat,
of the two the former is the more important.

This skill in choosing and handling men is the foremost
among the skills which a Russian sovereign must possess. If
you lack it, you will vainly seek to find national well-being
in new organic statutes! [i.e. constitutions]. Ask not, how
are the laws of a state written? How many ministers are
there? Is there a supreme council? But ask: what sort of
judges, what sort of landlords are there? . . . Phrases are for
newspapers — for governments, there are only principles.

Let us supplement these thoughts with a few special observations.

[3. The Role of the Gentry in the Russian System]

Autocracy is the Palladium of Russia; on its integrity depends Russia's happiness. But from this it does not follow
that the sovereign, in whose hands rests the plenitude of
power, should degrade the gentry, who are as ancient as
Russia herself. The gentry were never anything except a
brotherhood of outstanding men serving the grand princes
or tsars. It is bad when a servant obtains mastery over a weak
lord, but a prudent lord respects his choice servants, and
considers their honor his own. The rights of the well-born
are not something apart from monarchical authority — they
are its principal and indispensable instrumentality by means
of which the body politic is kept in motion. Montesquieu
said: "point de Monarque — point de noblesse; point de
noblesse — point de Monarque!" The gentry are an hereditary estate. Some people must be trained to fulfill certain
obligations so as to maintain order and provide the monarch
with a source whence to draw the servants of the state. The
people labor, the merchants trade, and the gentry serve, for
which they are rewarded with distinctions and benefits,

respect and comfort. Personal changeable ranks cannot replace the hereditary, permanent nobility, and, necessary as they are to mark grades in the state service, in a sound monarchy they must not be allowed to encroach upon the fundamental rights of the nobility, or to acquire its privileges. Noble status should not depend on rank, but rank on noble status; that is, the attainment of certain ranks should be made unconditionally dependent on the candidate being a gentleman, a practice we have failed to observe from the time of Peter the Great, an officer being *ipso facto* a nobleman. Superior talent, which is not related to class origin, must not be barred from higher office — but let the sovereign knight a person before bestowing upon him high rank, and let him do so with some solemn ceremony, on the whole seldom, and with utmost selectivity. The advantages of such a practice are evident: 1) Frequent promotion of commoners to the rank of minister, lord, or general, must be accompanied by a grant of wealth, which the aureole of eminent office requires. This drains the treasury. . . . The gentry, on the other hand, having inherited wealth, can manage even in the higher posts without financial assistance from the treasury. 2) The gentry feel offended when they find the steps of the throne occupied by men of low birth, where, since the days of old, they had been accustomed to see dignified boyars. This is unobjectionable when these men are distinguished by uncommon and sublime talents; but if they are men of ordinary ability, then it is better that their positions be given to gentlemen. 3) The mind and heart are furnished by nature, but they are formed by upbringing. A gentleman, favored by fortune, is accustomed from birth to feel self-respect, to love the fatherland and the sovereign for the advantages of his birth-right, and to be powerfully attracted to distinctions which his ancestors have earned and he himself will earn by his own accomplishments. These attitudes and feelings imbue him with that nobility of spirit which, among other things, was the reason for the institution of the hereditary nobility. It is an important excellence which the natural gifts of a commoner can but seldom supplant, because a commoner, dreading scorn even when he enjoys an eminent status, usually dislikes the gentry, and hopes with personal arrogance to make others forget his base origin. Virtue is rare. You must seek in the world common rather than superior souls. It is not my opinion, but that of all deep-thinking statesmen, that a monarchy is buttressed by firmly established rights of the wellborn. Thus, I wish that Alexander would make it a rule to enhance the dignity of the gentry, whose splendor may be called a reflection of the Tsar's aureole. This aim is to be attained not only by means of state charters, but also by those, so to say, innocent, effortless signs of consideration, which are so effective in an autocracy. For instance, why should the emperor not appear occasionally at solemn assemblies of the nobility as their chairman, and not in the uniform of a guards officer, but in that of a nobleman? This would be far more effective than eloquent letters and wordy assurances of royal esteem for the society of the wellborn. But the most effective method of elevating the gentry would be a law admitting every nobleman into military service in the rank of an officer, conditional only on his knowing well the essentials of mathematics and of Russian. Limit the payment of wages to recruits — and all the wellborn, in accord with the interests of the monarchy founded on conquests, shall take to swords instead of the penholders with which the rich and poor alike among them equip their sons to serve in chanceries, archives, and courts, much to the detriment of the state; for at present the gentry feel a revulsion to the barracks where their youths, sharing with common soldiers menial work as well as menial amusement, may suffer corruption of health and morals. Indeed, what is there among things necessary for the service that one cannot learn in an officer's rank? And it is much pleasanter for a noble to acquire learning at this rank than as a noncommissioned officer. Were this done, our armies would profit from the influx of young, well-educated nobles, who now waste away as court clerks. The guards would remain an exception — in the guards only would nobles begin service as noncommissioned officers. But in the guards, too, a sergeant of gentle birth should be distinguished from the son of a soldier. Military discipline which does not help us win victories can and ought to be relaxed. Severity in trifles destroys the zeal for work. Keep the warriors busy with games or guard parades, but not to the point of exhaustion. Work on the soul even more than on the body. The heroes of the guard parade turn into cowards on the battlefield; how many examples have we known! In Catherine's time, officers sometimes went about in evening clothes, but they went bravely into battle as well. The French are no pedants, and win. We saw the Prussian heroes!

[4. The Role of the Clergy]

As with the gentry, so with the clergy: its usefulness to the state is proportionate to the general respect which it enjoys among the people. I do not propose to re-establish the Patriarchate, but I should like to see the Synod have a more important body of members and sphere of action. I wish it consisted entirely of archbishops, and that it met in joint sessions with the Senate on important occasions when the state issues new fundamental laws in order to hear them read, to accept them into their repositories of law, and to promulgate them — of course, without any contradiction. Efforts are being made right now to increase the number of clerical schools, but it would be better yet to pass a law which would prohibit the investiture of eighteen-year-old

pupils, and introduce a strict examination as a prerequisite of
every investiture whatsoever; also one which would insist
that bishops show greater concern for the morals of the
parishioners, employing for this purpose the sensible and the
efficacious means furnished them by the Synod, and conceived as well by Peter the Great. The character of these
important spiritual dignitaries is always a good indicator of
a people's moral condition. Good governors are not enough.
Russia also needs good priests. Having both we shall require
nothing more, and envy no one in Europe.

[5. Concluding Remarks]

The gentry and the clergy, the Senate and the Synod as
repositories of laws, over all — the sovereign, the only legislator, the autocratic source of authority — this is the foundation of the Russian monarchy, which the principles followed
by the rulers can either strengthen or weaken.

States, like human beings, have their definite life spans:
thus believes philosophy, and thus teaches history. As a sensible mode of life prolongs a man's age, so a sensible political
system prolongs the age of states. Who will estimate the
years which lie ahead of Russia? I hear the prophets of imminent disaster, but my heart, thank God, refuses to believe
them. I see danger, but not as yet destruction!

Russia is still forty million strong, and the autocrat is a
sovereign inspired with zeal for the public good. If, being
human, he commits errors, he undoubtedly does so with
good intentions — this itself is an indication that they will
probably be corrected in the future.

If, in general, Alexander should in the future be more
cautious in introducing new political institutions, striving
above all to strengthen those already in existence, and paying
more attention to men than to forms; if, applying severity
judiciously, he should induce the lords and officials zealously

to fulfill their obligations; if he should conclude peace with Turkey and save Russia from a third, most dangerous war with Napoleon, even at the cost of so-called honor — a luxury only strong states can afford, and one which is by no means identical either with their basic interests or with their self-preservation; if, without further multiplying paper notes, through the application of prudent economy, he should reduce the expenditures of the treasury, and devise some means of raising the pay of impoverished military and civil officials; if, through the strict enforcement of custom regulations, he should create a balance between the import and export of merchandise, and if, as must needs follow from these premises, high prices should gradually fall — then Russia would bless Alexander, uncertainty would come to an end, disaffection would evaporate, habits useful to the state would emerge, the progress of things would become more even and regular, the new and the old would blend into one, the past would be recalled ever less frequently, and evil gossip, though present, would lose a sympathetic ear! . . . The fate of Europe does not at present depend on us. Whether France will change her dreadful system, or whether God will change France, no one can tell, but storms do not last forever! The day when we perceive clear skies over Europe, and Alexander enthroned over an *integral* Russia, we shall extol that good fortune of Alexander which he well deserves by virtue of his uncommon kindness!

Loving the fatherland, loving the monarch, I have spoken frankly. I now revert to the silence of a loyal subject with a pure heart, praying to God: may He protect the Tsar and the Russian Empire!

NOTES AND COMMENTS

AND

SELECTED BIBLIOGRAPHY

NOTES AND COMMENTS

All the words in SMALL CAPITALS refer to the text of Karamzin's *Memoir on Ancient and Modern Russia* in the present edition. For the sake of clarity, the commentary is divided into sections corresponding to those listed in the Table of Contents.

Motto

THERE IS NO FLATTERY. . . . This passage is not in the Psalms. Similar words, but expressing a different sentiment, can be found in Psalm CXXXIX.4 (Russian Psalter CXXXVIII.4): "For there is not a word in my tongue/ But, lo, O LORD, Thou knowest it altogether."

[PART ONE: HISTORICAL INTRODUCTION]

1. The Kiev and Mongol Periods

COME TO REIGN. . . . A paraphrase of the well-known passage in the Russian Primary Chronicle, in which the Slavs and Finns are quoted as having said to the Normans in 862: "Our land is great and rich but there is no order in it. Come to reign and rule over us." Cf. *The Russian Primary Chronicle — Laurentian Text*, translated and edited by S. H. Cross and O. P. Sherbowitz-Wetzor (Cambridge, Mass. [1953]), p. 59.

THE RUSSIANS . . . FOUGHT IN 964. . . . The source of Karamzin's reference to alleged Russian participation in the Sicilian wars of the tenth century is the fourteenth-century Arabic historian, Ahmad Ibn 'Abd al-Wahhab al-Nuwairi, quoted in B. de Riedesel's *Voyages en Sicile, dans la Grande Grèce et au Levant* (Paris, 1802), pp. 424–25: "Ce fut dans le milieu de shoual 353 (25 Octobre 964 è.v.), que Manuel s'avança à la tête d'une armée composée principalement de Mages, d'Arméniens et de Russes, et plus nombreuse que toutes celles qu'on avoit vues jusque-là en Sicile." This statement, however, refers to Normans, not to Slavs, for the term "Rus" was often applied in the Middle Ages to peoples of Scandinavian origin. Another Arabic historian, al-Ja'qūbī, writing in the ninth century, also ascribed to "Rus" the pillage of Seville, actually perpetrated by Normans; *cf.* T. Lewicki, *Zródła arabskie do dziejów Słowiańszczyzny,* I (Wrocław-Kraków, 1956), 128.

It is more difficult to trace the source of Karamzin's equally erroneous statement concerning alleged Russian participation in Babylonian wars. In the seventeenth and eighteenth centuries there were current in Russia numerous legends telling of Russian exploits in Babylon, often derived from Byzantine chronicles. *Cf.* I. Zhdanov, "Povesti o Vavilone i 'Skazanie o kniaziakh Vladimirskikh'," *Zhurnal Ministerstva Narodnogo Prosveshcheniia,* Nos. 8–10 (1891).

IAROSLAV GAVE THE PEOPLE A SCROLL OF . . . CIVIL LAWS. . . . Karamzin refers to the *Russkaia Pravda,* whose authorship is traditionally ascribed to Grand Prince Iaroslav I of Kiev (978–1054). This code, however, was modeled not so much on Germanic law, as on the systematic condensed legal compendia used in contemporary Byzantium.

VASILKO — Prince Vasilko Rostislavovich lived in the late eleventh and early twelfth centuries.

VSEVOLOD III — Georgievich, Grand Prince (ruled 1177–1212). On these two princes, see Karamzin's *History,* volume II, chapter 6, and volume III, chapter 3, respectively.

BASKAKI (fr. Tatar *basquaq*) — representatives of the khans and tribute collectors.

ULUS — Mongolian term denoting the nomadic encampment as well as a tribe with its territory.

2. *The Emergence of Moscow*

VILLAGE KUCHKOVO — a tract of land in Moscow first mentioned in the chronicles in the fourteenth century. Its name was probably derived from that of Boyar Kuchka who ruled the shores of the Moscow River in the twelfth century.

UZBEK — Khan of the Golden Horde (1313–1340).

ORDA (Turk. *urdu*) — the khan's tent and residence in general.

IARLYK — a written decree or any other document issued in the name of the Tatar-Mongol khans.

AKHTURA — Sarai, the CAPITAL of the KHANS of the Golden Horde was located on the left bank of the River Akhtuba, near Astrakhan. It was destroyed numerous times.

MESTNICHESTVO — in Moscow, the system of making state appointments with strict regard to the relative social standing of a person's family; it also entailed the right to refuse positions considered incompatible with such standing. Mestnichestvo was abolished at the end of the seventeenth century.

KHOLOPSTVO — the most severe form of bondage in pre-Petrine Russia; slavery.

GOLDEN CHAMBER (*Zolotaia Palata; Zolotaia Podpis'naia Palata*) — a reception hall in the imperial palace in Constantinople; also, a large chamber for official functions in the Moscow Kremlin.

GRANOVITAIA PALATA (lit. "Faceted Chamber") — a reception hall in the Moscow Kremlin, built by Italian architects at the end of the Fifteenth century. With a floor space of 4,500 square feet, it was in its time the largest covered hall in all Russia. The name refers to the facets cut in the masonry of its principal façade.

IVAN III ISSUED NEW CIVIL STATUTES — the so-called *Sudebnik* (Code) of 1497.

AND IVAN IV A COMPLETE CODE — the so-called Second, or *Tsarskii Sudebnik* issued in 1550.

STANDING ARMY — refers to the army reforms carried out by Ivan IV in 1556 which, among other things, established a regular infantry, later known as the *streltsy*.

FROM THE DEPTHS OF HINDUSTAN — In his *History* (volume VII, chapter 3) Karamzin describes a mission which Khan Babur, the founder of the Moghul dynasty in India, sent to Moscow to inquire about the possibilities of opening commercial relations with Russia. The mission failed, partly because the Indian legates could not establish to their hosts' satisfaction whether Babur was a *samoderzhets,* that is, a full-fledged sovereign, or merely a vassal, and hence, whether he should be addressed by Ivan IV as "brother." In the *Russkaia letopis' po Nikonovu spisku*, VI (St. Petersburg, Imperatorskaia Akademiia Nauk, 1790), 250, from which Karamzin probably drew this information, Babur's embassy is dated September 1534; Karamzin, in his *History*, incorrectly transcribes it as "September 1532."

THIRTY-FIFTH YEAR — Ivan IV was born in 1530, and instituted the *Oprichnina* in 1565, when he was thirty-five.

3. The Time of Troubles

THE SHADOW OF THE TSAREVICH HE HAD SLAIN — refers to the death of Dmitrii, the probable heir to the Russian throne, at Uglich in 1591. Karamzin's account of this event (cf. *History*, volume X, chapter 2) served as the basis of Pushkin's *Boris Godunov*.

MIRACULOUS RESCUE — the Pretender claimed to be Dmitrii, miraculously saved from death.

TERRIBLE NATURAL DISASTERS — refers probably to the great famine of 1601–03.

SHUISKII . . . SOLEMNLY BETRAYED AUTOCRACY — In his coronation oath, taken in 1606, Shuiskii swore to uphold the Orthodox faith, to execute no one without the approval of the Boyar Duma, to respect property rights, not to punish the innocent friends and relatives of convicted criminals, and to pay no heed to informers. None of the sources which cite this oath make any mention of a pledge not TO DECLARE WAR without the Duma's approval, and it is likely that Karamzin confused Shuiskii's oath of 1606 either with the alleged "charter" of 1613 or with the so-called "conditions" of 1730, both of which did include such a clause (see below, note on p. 213). In the *History* (volume XII, chapter 1), Karamzin reported Shuiskii's oath correctly, that is without the alleged war clause.

THEY ATTACHED CONDITIONS — refers to the agreement of February 1610, between the boyars and Władysław, the son of the Polish king, SIGISMUND, and the successor to the Polish crown, invited to the throne of Russia.

4. The First Romanovs

HIS FRIGHTENED MOTHER — Michael's mother, Martha, had been forced to take the veil, and in 1613, at the time of Michael's election to the throne, lived with him at a Kaluga cloister.

THEY INSCRIBED A CHARTER — This statement alludes to one of the two charters which Michael, according to an opinion prevalent in the eighteenth century, was supposed to have signed at the time of his coronation in 1613. Neither of these charters survived; neither, according to modern authorities, ever existed; in fact, each precludes the existence of the other.

1. Some seventeenth- and eighteenth-century books on Russia maintain that Michael was compelled by the nobility to grant them formal concessions, similar to those conceded by Shuiskii seven years earlier. One of these sources, Ph. J. von Strahlenberg's *Das Nord-und Ostliche Theil von Europa und Asia* (Stockholm, 1730), p. 209, lists a five-point charter requiring the tsar to maintain the established religion, to pardon past offences, not to tamper with laws, but to obey them, not to make war, and to transfer the title to his private properties either to his relatives or to the state.

2. Other eighteenth-century sources mention an entirely different coronation charter, one which is supposed to have granted the Romanov dynasty absolute power. This "charter" was frequently used in evidence by advocates of Russian absolutism as a legal justification of this system. Thus, for instance, A. L. Schlözer wrote in his *Historische Untersuchung über Russlands Reichsgrundgesetze* (Gotha, 1777), p. 11: "Gibt es wirklich Russische Reichsgrundgesetze, so müssen sie aus der Wahlurkunde vom Jahre 1613 geholt werden" ("If Russia really possesses a state constitution, it can only be derived from the document on the election of 1613"). Another German historian, B. von Wichmann, following Schlözer, was of the same opinion: "Einziges russisches Grundgesetz ist gegenwärtig also nur derjenige Theil der, im Vorhergehenden beleuchteten Wahlacte [von 1613], welcher den Russischen Monarchen die Autocratie zuspricht" ("Thus the Russian constitu-

tion is to be found only in that part of the aforesaid electoral act of 1613, which bestows on the Russian monarch the power of autocracy"); (*Urkunde über die Wahl Michael Romanow's,* Leipzig, 1819, p. XVI).

Karamzin obviously refers to the latter of these two alleged charters. The opinion prevailing among modern historians is that both these versions were invented in the eighteenth century, the first in connection with contemporary attempts to impose formal limitations on the Russian monarchy (especially 1730), the second in an effort to discover a satisfactory juridical basis of Russian statehood, whose nonlegal character puzzled many historians and constitutional scholars, particularly those of German origin.

PRIKAZY — administrative establishments of the Moscow state, put in charge of departments or regions, and abolished in 1717 to give way to colleges.

ULOZHENIE — the Russian Code of 1649.

5. Peter I

PETER CONFINED HIS REFORM TO THE GENTRY — refers only to Peter's cultural reforms.

DIAKI — secretaries of *prikazy*.

TEREMY (fr. Greek *teremnon*) — living quarters located in the upper floors of the house, or in a separate building, usually shaped as a tower, occupied by female members of the family.

LEFORT — François (1656–1699), Swiss officer in Russian service, and an intimate friend of Peter I.

GERMAN SETTLEMENT (*Nemetskaia sloboda*) — a Moscow suburb inhabited, since the sixteenth century, by foreigners.

PREOBRAZHENSKOE (*Preobrazhenskii Prikaz*) — an extraordinary chancery, established by Peter I in 1697, which with time came to be used for summary trials of political offenders, real and imaginary, who could not be punished under existing statutes. In its principal features it resembled the English Star Chamber. In 1803 Karamzin visited the village of Preobrazhenskoe, where it had been originally located, and tried to convey to his readers the terror with which its name was associated; but at

that time he still felt that Peter was compelled by circumstances to use cruel methods, and tended to exonerate this
tsar; see *Sochineniia Karamzina* (Smirdin, ed.; St. Petersburg,
1848), I, 425.

MENSHIKOV — Alexander Danilovich (1663?–1729), Peter's favorite. After Peter's death, he was instrumental in elevating
Catherine, Peter's widow, to the throne. During her short reign
(1725–1727), he virtually ruled Russia.

THE DOLGORUKIS AND GOLITSYNS — two ancient Russian families,
who played a prominent role in Russian politics from the
death of Peter I (1725) to the accession of Anne (1730). In
1726, in the reign of Catherine I, they helped establish
the SUPREME Privy COUNCIL (*Verkhovnyi Tainyi Sovet*), a
committee of several aristocrats (including three Dolgorukis
and one Golitsyn) and high officials, which for a time governed
Russia. In 1730, upon the death of Peter II, the Supreme
Council invited to the Russian throne Anne of Courland, but
only if she agreed to sign a set of "conditions," which imposed
severe limitations on her authority in favor of the Council. To
secure the crown Anne complied, but shortly after her arrival
in Moscow she reneged on her promise, and assumed autocratic
power, acting with the support of the gentry, officialdom, and
high clergy which suspected and distrusted the aristocrats in the
Council. The events of 1730 are traditionally regarded as the
final effort of the ancient Russian aristocracy to secure an
active voice in the central government.

6. Anne

DAUGHTER OF IVAN — Anne of Courland, daughter of Ivan V.

OSTERMANN — Count Andrei Ivanovich (1686–1747), a Russian
statesman of Westphalian origin. He entered Russian service
under Peter I, and in the reign of Anne exerted great influence
on Russian administration and diplomacy. Overthrown in
1741 in consequence of French court intrigues, he was condemned to death, then pardoned and exiled to Siberia, where
he remained until his death.

MÜNNICH — (Minikh) Count Burkhard Christoph (1683–1767), a

German officer in Russian service. He settled in Russia in the late 1720's, and in the reign of Anne fought many successful campaigns, especially against the Ottoman Empire. Condemned to death in 1741, together with Ostermann, he shared the latter's fate, but he outlived Ostermann, and spent the last years of his life in the service of Catherine II.

SOULLESS, BASE FAVORITE — Ernst Johann BIRON (real name: Biren or Bühren) (1690–1772), the third influential German at the court of Anne. A petty Courland noble, he came to Russia with Anne as both her chief adviser and her lover. Although he held no official position in government, he wielded all through her reign enormous power, which he used far less beneficially than either Ostermann or Münnich. Greatly hated for his cruelty and greed, he was disgraced in 1740 through Münnich's intrigues, and exiled to Siberia.

THE DOLGORUKIS THEMSELVES — In 1739 several prominent members of the Dolgoruki family were executed in Novgorod, allegedly for plotting to overthrow Anne in favor of Elizabeth, but in reality as punishment for their actions in 1730.

A STATELY HORSE — Biron was passionately fond of horses.

THE GOOD-NATURED REGENT — Anna Leopoldovna, the Princess of Brunswick-Bevern-Lüneburg, appointed Regent during the brief reign of Ivan VI (1740). She was deposed and exiled in the palace coup of November 25, 1741 which brought

7. Elizabeth

PETER'S DAUGHTER — to the throne. This coup was engineered by Elizabeth's

FRENCH DOCTOR — Johann Herman Lestocq (Lestok) (1692–1767). Lestocq figured prominently in Russian politics until 1745, when he lost favor as a result of the discovery of his intrigues with the French Ambassador. He was arrested and exiled in 1748, and recalled from exile by Peter III in 1762.

OWN COMPANY OF HER MAJESTY (*Leib-kompaniia*) — the Grenadier Company of the Body-Guards of the Preobrazhenskii Regiment. This company played a decisive role in the coup which brought Elizabeth to the throne, and in return received extensive privileges: all of its members were granted estates and patents of hereditary nobility. It was dissolved by Peter III.

LITTLE RUSSIAN CHOIR BOY — Alexis Grigorevich Razumovskii (1709–1771), a Cossack from the Chernigov province. Brought to St. Petersburg as a young man to sing in the palace chapel, he became Elizabeth's lover, and exerted considerable political influence until her death.

BESTUZHEV — Count Alexis Petrovich Bestuzhev-Riumin (1693–1766), statesman and diplomat. He served as Chancellor during most of Elizabeth's reign, and between 1742 and 1758 directed Russia's administration. A sworn enemy of Prussia and France, he was instrumental in bringing Russia into the Seven Years' War, the BLOODY AND . . . USELESS WAR, to which Karamzin refers, and which, indeed, cost Russia over 300,000 casualties and thirty million rubles. He fell from favor in 1758, was sentenced to death, then pardoned and exiled. Catherine II restored to him his lost titles and recalled him from exile.

SHUVALOV — Peter Ivanovich (1711–62), Russian statesman and soldier active in the reign of Elizabeth, especially in the fields of military and economic policy. To raise revenue, he established state MONOPOLIES over salt and over alcoholic beverages, which led to a sharp rise in the price of these articles. He left behind personal debts exceeding one million rubles.

THE UNIVERSITY OF MOSCOW — founded in 1755.

LOMONOSOV — Mikhail Vasilevich (1711–65), Russia's universal talent. Among his numerous accomplishments were ODES on official themes.

8. Catherine II

RUMIANTSEV — Count Peter Alexandrovich Rumiantsev-Zadunaiskii (1725–96), general, active in Turkish wars of Catherine II.

SUVOROV — Alexander Vasilevich (1730–1800), general, active in the wars against Poland (1772), the Ottoman Empire (1768–74, and 1787–91), in the suppression of the Polish insurrection

(1794), and the campaign against the French (1799–1800).

VIAZEMSKII — Prince Alexander Alekseevich (1727–96). In 1764 he was appointed Procurator-General with extremely broad powers, resembling those of a Prime Minister. Viazemskii centralized the administration of Russian finances, and introduced the custom of annual statements of state income and expenditure; he also participated in the Commission for the preparation of a new code of laws.

Karamzin was related to the Viazemskii family through his marriage to Prince Andrei Ivanovich Viazemskii's illegitimate daughter, K. A. Kolyvanova. He did much of his research on Russian history at the Viazemskii estate at Ostafevo, and was appointed legal guardian of the Prince's son, P. A. Viazemskii, the future writer.

WE TOOK WHAT WAS OURS — i.e., the eastern provinces of the Polish-Lithuanian Commonwealth, which Karamzin regards as the rightful property of the Russian Empire, because they had once belonged to Kievan Rus'. His views on the Polish question are more fully expounded in an essay submitted to Alexander in 1819 "Mnenie Russkogo grazhdanina" ("A Russian citizen's opinion"); *Neizdannye sochineniia i perepiska Nikolaia Mikhailovicha Karamzina* (St. Petersburg, 1862), pp. 3–8.

THE FREEDOM TO CHOOSE WHETHER . . . TO ENTER . . . SERVICE — In 1762 Peter III freed the Russian gentry from the compulsory state service which Peter I had imposed on them.

SOLON WAS IN THE HABIT OF SAYING — Karamzin's quotation (one of his favorite), is probably derived from Plutarch ("The Life of Solon") by way of Montesquieu: "On demanda à Solon si les lois qu'il avoit données aux Athéniens étoiant les meilleures. 'Je leur ai donné, répondit-il, les meilleures de celles qu'ils pouvoient souffrir.'" *Cf.* Montesquieu, *The Spirit of Laws,* Book XIX, Chapter 21.

9. Paul I

ONLY TWO TYRANTS — i.e. Ivan IV and Paul I.

2. *Foreign Policy*

Broadly speaking, the European peace settlement completed by the Treaty of Amiens (1802) was shattered by the incompatibility of the commercial and strategic interests of France and Great Britain; this, in turn, was exacerbated by certain specific disagreements, such as the dispute over Malta. The precarious peace was formally broken by the British declaration of war in May 1803; yet this event of itself might perhaps not have led to the long and sanguinary military conflicts which followed, since neither side felt strong enough to assert its claims by force, had it not been for the inopportune intervention of Russia.

Russian interests were not directly involved in the Anglo-French dispute of 1803. As Karamzin correctly observes, Russia had "lost nothing and had nothing to fear." Indeed, the conflicts of these two powers worked to Russia's advantage by strengthening her international position: this was clearly brought out by the readiness of England and France to resolve their dispute over Malta by offering to hand it over to the Russians. Russia's intervention was rather due to Alexander's personal ambition, to his impetuosity, and to his keenly-felt desire — one may almost say, sense of mission — to liberate all Europe from the domination of France. In this he was encouraged by his closest associates of the time, the members of the so-called Unofficial Committee, who were intensely pro-British. By showing open preference for Britain and by engaging in secret negotiations with her, Alexander helped upset the delicate balance of power, and contributed greatly to the outbreak of the great cycle of wars, whose ultimate outcome was the assertion of Napoleonic hegemony over the entire European continent.

Between 1801 and 1803 the Russian legation in Paris was headed by Count A. I. MARKOV. Napoleon felt a strong aversion to Markov, because he thought him to be the head of an anti-French party at the Russian court, and the man personally responsible for the rapid deterioration of Franco-Russian relations. At first all went well in Paris, and Markov, completed with France negotiations concerning the revision of the boundaries of the SOUTHERN GERMAN principalities, which had been provided for by the Treaty of Lunéville in 1801 (the so-called "Enactment of the delegates of the Empire," formally signed in February 1803). But before long the growing estrangement between Russia and France, for which Napoleon blamed the Russian ambassador but whose real origins lay in the British sympathies of the tsar and his entourage, made itself felt in Paris, leading, as is usual in such cases, to a series of incidents. The worst of these occurred in the Summer of 1803. In July of that year Napoleon ordered the arrest of one Christin, a Frenchman in the Russian service, to whom Karamzin refers as the GENEVAN TRAMP, on charges of participation in royalist plots. Markov protested this action, and in consequence was exposed to a humiliating public reprimand by Napoleon, who, within the hearing of numerous officials and diplomats, accused the Russian government and its French ambassador of aiding the enemies of the French state. Shortly after this incident, Markov was permitted to resign his embassy, but not before receiving from St. Petersburg the Order of St. Andrew as reward for his services. After Markov's departure, in the Fall of 1803, Russia was represented in Paris only by a *chargé d'affaires,* OUBRIL, who also left the following year.

The Third Coalition, in whose formation Russia played a leading part, came into being between November 1804 and April 1805 in consequence of a series of bilateral treaties, including alliances between Russia and Austria, Sweden, and England. Prussia resisted pressures to join the Coalition, and at the outbreak of hostilities, in the Summer of 1805, professed neutrality.

The campaign went badly for the allies from the start. Napoleon, rapidly transferring his troops from the Channel ports to the valley of the Danube, defeated at ULM an Austrian army led by Marshal MACK, and captured Vienna, compelling the Austrian Emperor FRANCIS to seek refuge in Bohemia. In the meanwhile, Russian troops, commanded by Benningsen, KUTUZOV, and Tolstoy, entered Austrian Galicia, and concentrated on the Prussian frontier. The Russians wanted to traverse Prussian territory in order to get most rapidly at the main forces of Napoleon. But the Prussians claiming neutral status, refused them passage, and it was in an effort to cajole or pressure them that Alexander dispatched to Potsdam his aide-de-camp, Prince P. P. DOLGORUKOV (October, 1805). Karamzin, of course, had no way of knowing in 1810–11 what had transpired at Potsdam between the Prussian king and the Russian officer; it is, therefore, quite remarkable that he should have been able to depict so accurately the reaction of the Prussian monarch, which is known to us from later sources. Karamzin was not aware that the Prussian king had at first rejected the Russian demand, and had done so in words very much like those which he suggests. Metternich, who was present in Potsdam at this time, wrote in his Memoirs that after Frederick William had read Alexander's letter which Dolgorukov had delivered he

declared without waiting a moment that he had offered the neutrality of Prussia to the belligerent powers, and that the moment one of these powers by violating his territory broke that neutrality, he considered himself at war with them. "Return to the Emperor, gentlemen," continued the king, "and inform him of my unalterable decision." [1]

Alexander, however, was determined to cross Prussian territory with or without permission, and the Prussian reply might well have led to a war between the two countries, had it not been for the fact that the French commander, Bernadotte, marching his troops from the Netherlands toward Ulm, cut across a stretch of Prussian soil near Ansbach. News of this incident reached Potsdam at the very instant when Dolgorukov was making preparations to return to the Russian headquarters.

[1] *Memoirs of Prince Metternich, 1773–1815*, I (London, 1880), 54–55.

He was immediately recalled to the royal residence and told that, in consequence of the French violation of Prussian neutrality, Alexander's request would be granted. Dolgorukov thus returned with the "more pleasant reply" which was made public and to which Karamzin refers. Prussia was at the point of joining the Coalition, but the debacle of the allies which followed shortly caused her to remain neutral.

After the capture of Vienna, Napoleon sought peace: winter was at hand, and he preferred not to engage fresh Russian, Austrian, and possibly Prussian armies. After he had arrived at this headquarters near AUSTERLITZ, where the two opposing forces faced each other, he twice dispatched his aide-de-camp to Alexander (who in the meantime had also joined the armies), suggesting a meeting to discuss terms of peace. But Alexander, confident of victory, was unreceptive to these advances. Persuaded that Napoleon's peace feelers were signs of weakness, he ordered an attack, even before the Italian army of the Austrians, led by Archduke CHARLES, had time to arrive. The battle ended in a resounding defeat of the allies.

After the Austerlitz debacle, Alexander, anxious to avoid diplomatic isolation as a result of defections of his allies, sent OUBRIL to Paris to open peace negotiations with the French. On July 6, 1806, Oubril signed a treaty calling for the evacuation of all Russian and French troops from the Balkans and Germany, a joint undertaking to guarantee the integrity of the Ottoman Empire, and the settlement of Franco-Russian disputes in Italy and the Adriatic. The Russian government decided that this agreement was too advantageous to France, and refused to ratify it, claiming that Oubril had exceeded his competence.

While negotiating half-heartedly with France, Alexander tried to reactivate the Russo-Prussian alliance. His efforts were successful, and in the Fall of 1806 the war was resumed (the "LATEST WAR WITH THE FRENCH"). Napoleon quickly defeated the Prussians at Jena and Auerstädt (October, 1806), and then engaged the Russians in the battles of PULTUSK (December, 1806) and PREUSSISCH-EYLAU (February, 1807), both of

which ended inconclusively. He then began to make preparations for an attack on Russia proper, and sent Talleyrand
to Warsaw (then a Prussian city) to organize a Polish insurrection. Alexander made an appeal to the Russian nation
to brace itself for a forthcoming invasion, and issued a number of decrees to prepare the defenses of the country, among
them an order establishing in Russia a national militia. In
April 1807 he rejoined his armies. Ignoring the advice of his
military counselors, including that of his commander in chief,
BENNINGSEN, he decided once more to engage Napoleon in
battle. The encounter at FRIEDLAND (June, 1807) ended in
a crushing defeat of the Russo-Prussian forces. Alexander now
had no alternative but to seek peace in earnest: his army, while
not destroyed, was greatly weakened, his Prussian ally was
subjugated, and the road to Russia lay open. THE PEACE OF
TILSIT (July, 1807) reversed entirely Russia's foreign policy
of the preceding four years. While military defeats had made it
imperative for Russia to come to terms with Napoleon, it is
difficult to find any compelling reason for the far-reaching
concessions which she made at Tilsit; the latter must be
ascribed to the immaturity and vacillations of Alexander,
rather than to political or strategic exigency. The provisions
of the treaty to which Karamzin refers are: Russia's adherence
to the Continental Blockade; Russia joining France in an ulti-
matum to Portugal, Denmark, and Sweden to do likewise
under the threat of war; and the establishment of the Grand
Duchy of Warsaw from the Polish provinces previously belonging to Prussia.

One of the by-products of the Tilsit Treaty was a war between Russia and Sweden (1808–1809), in the course of which
Russia acquired FINLAND.

In April 1809 Austria again took up arms against France,
only to taste defeat once more (Battle of WAGRAM, July,
1809). The Russians — this time on the side of the French —
provided their allies with only nominal assistance, and failed
to take part in the decisive battle. One of the factors contribut-
ing to the defeat of the Austrians at Wagram was the delay in

the arrival of reinforcements, led by ARCHDUKE JEAN, who was in charge of Austria's Italian Army.

The ITALIAN HERO was Suvorov, who commanded Russian troops in the Italian and Swiss campaigns against the French in 1799–1800. TREBBIA (June, 1799) and NOVI (August, 1799) were two battles of that campaign lost by the French. I. I. HERMAN was a German officer in the Russian service who led an ill-fated Anglo-Russian expeditionary unit dispatched to the Netherlands in 1799; he was defeated in the battle of Bergen, taken prisoner, and later cashiered from the service. KORSAKOV commanded a Russian corps in Switzerland at the same time. He lost the battle of Zürich (September 1799), thus greatly neutralizing the effects of Suvorov's successes in Northern Italy.

Bibliography

The literature on the diplomatic history of the Napoleonic period is vast and readily available. For the background of the events described by Karamzin, S. S. Tatishchev's *Alexandre I-er et Napoléon d'après leur correspondance inédite, 1801–1812* (Paris, 1891), and A. Vandal, *Napoléon et Alexandre I-er: l'alliance russe sous le premier empire* (3 vols., Paris, 1893–96) are especially valuable.

3. Political Institutions

In considering Karamzin's criticism of Alexander's constitutional reforms, one must keep in mind two facts: 1) that the reforms of the period 1809–1811 were merely preliminary phases of a far-reaching constitutional project, whose ultimate aim was the transformation of Russia into a constitutional monarchy; and, 2) that the government did not make this program public, for fear of alarming society and antagonizing further the already disaffected gentry. In writing this section of the *Memoir,* therefore, Karamzin was not in possession of the vital facts; consequently, much of his criticism rests on misunderstanding of the government's motives and aims.

However, with all due allowance for these circumstances, it is still not possible to agree with Karamzin's thesis that Alexander's political reforms were superfluous, and that at the time of his accession Russia could have reverted to its eighteenth-century system of government. Political reforms were, in fact, unavoidable. They were made necessary by the gradual disintegration of Russia's administrative machinery in the second half of the eighteenth century, the very period which Karamzin praises for its alleged stability and respect for tradition, and they followed logically from the policies of Alexander's immediate predecessors.

In the political system which Russia received from Peter I, the highest administrative responsibility was vested in the SENATE and its chief, the PROCURATOR-GENERAL, which, between them, disposed of considerable legislative and judicial authority, and among other things, controlled the COLLEGES, the government's principal executive organs. The colleges (which replaced the traditional Muscovite PRIKAZY) were, as their name indicates, organized on the collegiate principle, that is, they were directed not by individuals but by committees. Responsibility for local government was entrusted partly to the Senate and partly to the colleges. This system was somewhat changed by the immediate successors of Peter I, who deprived the Senate of some of its power by the transfer of its functions first to the SUPREME COUNCIL (or, more correctly, Supreme Privy Council — *Verkhovnyi Tainyi Sovet*) (1726–30), and then to the CABINET (1731–41), but Elizabeth reverted to the Petrine model. Being little interested in politics, she ceded the reins of government to the Senate, restoring to it its previous position and prestige; the so-called CONFERENCE, which she set up at the Court as a consultative body did not impinge upon the authority of the Senate.

This Petrine system was thoroughly and irretrievably destroyed by Catherine II. Catherine was a strong monarch who wanted to rule as well as reign. She considered the power of the Senate, which had been particularly extensive in the reign of her predecessor, Elizabeth, to be incompatible with this aspiration, and soon after her accession to the throne took steps to curtail it. She divided the Senate into six separate departments, each empowered to function without reference to the others, and deprived the Senate as a whole of all administrative responsibility. The Senate was thus transformed into a primarily judiciary institution, the highest tribunal in the land, which served the monarchy as the "repository of laws" (a term which Montesquieu used in his *Spirit of Laws,* and which Catherine borrowed from him in her *Instruction*). The decentralization of government was pushed a step further in 1775 with the DECREE FOR THE ESTABLISHMENT OF THE GUBERNII. The main responsibility for the administration of the provinces was now removed from the central government, and entrusted to Governors-General, who served directly under the Crown, by-passing the Senate as well as the colleges. The colleges, useless in the new arrangement, were gradually shut down. As a result of all these changes, the center of administration now shifted to the cabinet of the empress (assisted, after 1769, by a small advisory COUNCIL), to the Procurator-General, now endowed with the authority of a full-fledged Prime Minister and entirely independent of the Senate, and to the Governors-General.

In the light of these facts it is impossible to agree with Karamzin's statement that Alexander's predecessors continued to improve on the Petrine system of government, and that Catherine II herself was a traditionalist in matters of political institutions. By abolishing the colleges and fundamentally transforming the Senate, Catherine had really undermined the Petrine system; she stripped the post-Petrine institutions of most of their power, and established a personal regime, which concentrated all the authority in the hands of the Crown and its hand-picked viceroys.

Paul I re-established the colleges, which his mother had abolished, but in a somewhat changed form: he did away with the collegiate principle, entrusting the responsibility for the management of the colleges to individual directors. These directors supplied liaison between the monarch and the executive, and were practically indistinguishable from regular ministers; indeed, in two instances (State Properties and Commerce) they were actually called "Ministers."

When Alexander I took office, Russia's government was greatly disorganized in consequence of the haphazard reforms of his predecessors, which had destroyed the very essence of the Petrine system, and yet retained intact its institutional structure. The end of the strong, personal regime of Catherine had left a void which required new institutions. This task Alexander tackled with the help of the Unofficial Committee. In March 1801 he established a Permanent Council (*Nepremennyi Sovet*), to discuss and offer advice on legislative measures, and in September 1802, on the basis of reports submitted by Prince Czartoryski and Novosiltsev, he appointed MINISTERS.

The principal advantage of the ministerial system over the collegiate one lay in its ability to provide the Crown with direct and instantaneous contact with the organs of administration through the person of the Minister, who served at one and the same time as a trusted counselor of the monarch and a responsible head of an executive department.[2] Where previously the monarch had to draft a formal instruction to one of the colleges, and then wait while his orders filtered down through the cumbersome collegiate apparatus, he was now able to make his wish known by simply informing the appropriate minister; where previously he had no way of calling an administrative body to account without dismissing a whole college board, since all of its actions were taken collectively, he was now able to hold a minister personally responsible for any shortcomings which occurred within a given sphere of government activity.

But though Russia had minist*ers,* she still lacked minist*ries.* As a concession to the senatorial opposition, the men whom Alexander appointed to ministerial posts in 1802 took over the old collegiate machinery which Paul had resuscitated, but which no longer possessed any real authority. To facilitate contact with his ministers, Alexander established a new institu-

[2] N. M. Korkunov, *Russkoe gosudarstvennoe pravo* (2 vols.; 6th ed.; St. Petersburg, 1909), II, 348–49.

tion known as the COMMITTEE of Ministers. This Committee as such had no power, that is to say, it had no power apart from that vested in each of its members; it was merely a gathering at which the ministers could discuss common problems and new legislative projects, before submitting them to the tsar. In practice, however, at certain times, and particularly during Alexander's prolonged sojourns abroad (as during the wars of 1805–07), this Committee actually ruled Russia. According to the system of government introduced at Alexander's accession, the emperor gave his instructions directly to the ministers, and they, in turn, passed them on (together with their own orders) to their respective colleges; the colleges debated and voted upon these instructions but lacked authority to alter them, as all orders of the ministers had to be carried out. Once a year, in routine fashion, the ministers were required to submit reports of their activity to the Senate. In fact, however, they soon became fully independent of the Senate or any other institution, and acquired extremely broad legislative and administrative authority. The fiction of ministerial responsibility to the Senate was formally dispensed with in 1806, when the ministers were freed from the obligation of submitting periodic reports to the Senate.

The retention of the old collegiate apparatus side by side with the office of the minister was pointless, and gradually, beginning with the Ministry of the Interior, modern bureaucratic chanceries took over. Only three of the COLLEGES: WAR, ADMIRALTY, and Foreign Affairs were preserved, the first of them until January 1812, the remaining two for a decade longer.

Such was the situation in 1808, the year when Alexander entrusted the task of reforming Russia's political and legal institutions to Speranskii. Speranskii tackled his responsibilities not only with great energy and skill, but also with an unbounded confidence in the ability of reason to impose order on the workings of human society. Much impressed by the legislative achievements of Revolutionary and Napoleonic

France, he hoped to accomplish a thoroughgoing reform of Russia's institutions, supplanting the arbitrary authority of the tsar and his officials with firm law, and introducing a harmonious relationship among the various institutions of central and local government. Ultimately, these reforms were to transform Russia from an autocracy into a constitutional monarchy.

Speranskii's constitutional project (written, in its final form, in November 1809, but published in full only in 1905), placed great reliance on the separation of powers. It called for a distribution of legislative authority between the monarch, who was to retain the exclusive rights of legislative initiative and the final approval of laws, and a new representative body, the State *Duma* (*Gosudarstvennaia Duma*). Executive power was to be vested in ministries, functioning under close supervision of a Governing Senate (*Pravitel'stvuiushchyi Senat*). Judiciary authority was to be entrusted to an institution which Speranskii called the Judiciary Senate (*Sudebnyi Senat*). The Council was to be transformed into a State Council (*Gosudarstvennyi Sovet*), and serve as a link between the emperor and the various branches of the government. The Committee of Ministers was to be abolished altogether.

This grandiose project was only partly realized. Speranskii succeeded in reorganizing the Council and the ministries, but not in splitting the Senate or in establishing a Duma. As a result, at the time of his dismissal (1812), when all reforming activity was suspended, Russia's government was perhaps somewhat more efficient than it had been previously, but it was neither more lawful nor more consistent.

The first important phase of Speranskii's reform was the transformation of the Permanent Council of 1801 into an enlarged State COUNCIL (November-December 1809). The purpose of this reform was not to provide a means "of curbing the power of the ministers," as Karamzin suggests (this was to be done by the Governing Senate), but to provide the Crown with a supreme administrative institution, a permanent link with the apparatus running the state. The new Council consisted of thirty-five prominent statesmen, civil servants, and military commanders, appointed personally by Alexander. Because Alexander failed to follow up this reform with the establishment of a Duma and the reorganization of the Senate, the State Council soon began to play a role entirely different from that which Speranskii originally had had in mind for it, namely that of Russia's supreme legislative advisory body. Here were discussed all the important laws and decrees prior to their promulgation. Alexander occasionally attended in person the Council's meetings.

Article No. 73 of the edict establishing the State Council stated that all laws of a fundamental character would henceforth contain a statement: "Having considered the Council's opinion." [3] Contrary to the opinion of Karamzin and of many other conservatives of his time, this formula did not obligate the emperor to abide by the decision of the Council's majority, although it is true that it implied his obligation to hear its opinion. Records of the State Council meetings indicate that while Alexander usually respected the majority opinion, he did not feel bound by it, and on occasions sided with the minority. In 1842, when the State Council was once more reorganized, this formula was dropped as a concession to the conservatives, who considered it incompatible with the principle of autocracy.[4]

Speranskii next proceeded to reform the ministries. He wanted first of all to increase ministerial responsibility, and to accomplish this he attempted to define with greater precision the competence of each ministry. The final edict reforming the ministries was issued on June 25, 1811, that is, about five months after Karamzin had finished writing the *Memoir*. His critique, therefore, applies not to the decree

---

[3] *Polnoe Sobranie Zakonov*, 1st ed., vol. XXXI, no. 24,064, dated January 1, 1810.

[4] *Ibid.*, 2nd ed., vol. XVII, part 1, no. 15,518.

POLITICAL INSTITUTIONS

231

itself, but to the project which Speranskii drew up in the winter of 1810–11.[5]

One of the preliminary measures in the reform of the ministries was an edict issued on August 17, 1810, which pruned the powers of the Ministry of the Interior, transferring some of its functions to a newly-created MINISTRY OF THE POLICE. Among other things this new ministry was charged with responsibility for "guardianship of the property of minors, persons of unsound mind, and others," and measures "for the prevention of infectious and other communicable diseases, as well as the establishment of quarantine." [6]

Speranskii also tried to introduce to Russia the principle of legal ministerial responsibility, by making the ministers subject to an extraordinary judiciary body when they were guilty of gross dereliction of duty. The complete text of the pertinent section of the act reforming the ministries read as follows:

Ministers account for their actions in two instances: 1) when a Minister exceeds his authority by taking a decision which alters existing laws, statutes, or establishments, or when, by his own action and in circumvention of the procedure which had been established for him, he orders the execution of a measure demanding a new law or decree; 2) when a Minister fails to make use of the authority vested in him, and allows, through negligence an important malfeasance or injury to the state.[7]

Ministers subject to this clause were to be tried before a Supreme Criminal Court, composed of Senators, members of the State Council and State Duma, and the Ministers' colleagues. This provision was never enforced.

In the final version of the edict reforming the ministries, ministers were deprived of the right to withhold their signa-

[5] Both the original draft of the ministerial project (Obshchii Ministerskii Ustav), with Speranskii's own corrections, and the printed version (Obshchee uchrezhdenie ministerstv, Part 1 "Obshchee obrazovanie ministerstv," and Part 2 "Obshchii nakaz ministerstvam," St. Petersburg, 1811), are in the Tsentral'nyi Gosudarstvennyi Istoricheskii Arkhiv in Leningrad (TsGIAL), Fond 1409, God 1811, Opis No. 1, Delo 532/4, "Uchrezhdenie Ministerstv."
[6] Polnoe Sobranie Zakonov, 1st ed., vol. XXXI, no. 24,326.
[7] Ibid., 1st ed., vol. XXXI, no. 24,686, art. 279, dated June 25, 1811.

tures from decrees, which Karamzin found so objectionable in the project. Indeed, the edict explicitly enjoined all ministers to carry out imperial directives whether or not they agreed with them.[8]

Speranskii had intended the State Duma and the revamped Senate to provide the necessary instruments of control over the ministries. Since neither of these institutions was actually established, the power of the ministries soon increased to an inordinate degree. The broad extent of authority enjoyed by Russian ministers and their freedom from any regular institutional supervision became thenceforth one of the outstanding characteristics of the political system of the Russian *ancien régime,* and the cause of some of its worst abuses.[9]

FIELD MARSHAL MÜNNICH OBSERVED . . . Münnich wrote an essay, published after his death in Denmark, entitled *Ébauche pour donner une idée de la forme du gouvernement de l'empire de Russie* (Copenhagen, 1774), in which he urged Russia to establish a State Council in order to "fill the gap between the Sovereign and the authority of the Senate." See also G. A. von Halem's *Lebensbeschreibung des . . . B. C. Grafen von Münnich* (Oldenburg, 1803).

THE COLLEGES OF THE JUDICIARY AND FISC WERE REPLACED BY BOARDS . . . In connection with the reform of the provincial administration in 1775, the government established as organs of local administration so-called Judiciary Boards (*Ssudnye Palaty*) for both civil and criminal offences, and Fiscal Boards (*Kazennye Palaty*).

PAUL . . . ABOLISHED THE SUPERFLUOUS UPPER LAND COURTS . . .

---

[8] *Ibid.,* art. 227. In Speranskii's original draft of the Ministerial Project, this article ended with the following clause: "but the Minister assumes no responsibility for the consequences of an edict [with which he disagrees]." Speranskii himself struck this clause from the final version of the project, and it did not appear in the printed version. *Obshchii Ministerskii Ustav,* Manuscript in the Tsentral'nyi Gosudarstvennyi Istoricheskii Arkhiv in Leningrad, Fond 1409, God 1811, Opis No. 1, Delo 532/4.

[9] Materials pertaining to the discussions of Speranskii's Ministerial Project at the State Council are deposited with the Tsentral'nyi Gosudarstvennyi Istoricheskii Arkhiv in Leningrad, "O rassmotrenii predpolozhenii ob ustroistve ministerstv," Fond No. 1164, God 1810, Opis No. M XVI, Delo No. 2.

— The local government reform of 1775 established in each province Upper Land Courts, as part of the general movement to decentralize Russian government. Paul I, in an effort to centralize as well as to simplify local administration had them abolished. See M. V. Klochkov, *Ocherki pravitel'stvennoi deiatel'nosti vremeni imperatora Pavla I* (Petrograd, 1916), pp. 417, 589.

The *Raspravy* were established in 1775 as courts for peasants other than those subject to manorial jurisdiction of their landlords. They were done away with by Paul in 1796, but reinstituted in the nineteenth century.

A MONARCHY, WRITES MONTESQUIEU . . . — this citation is from the *Spirit of Laws*, book 2, chapter 4.

CHURCH STATUTES — the *Dukhovnyi Reglament*, to which Karamzin refers, was actually written by Feofan Prokopovich.

Bibliography

Polnoe Sobranie Zakonov, first edition, vols. XXIV–XXXI.

Sobranie Sochinenii A. D. Gradovskogo, vols. VII and VIII (St. Petersburg, 1901, 1903).

N. M. Korkunov, *Russkoe gosudarstvennoe pravo* (St. Petersburg, 1909).

N. I. Lazarevskii, *Lektsii po russkomu gosudarstvennomu pravu* (St. Petersburg, 1908).

M. V. Klochkov, *Ocherki pravitel'stvennoi deiatel'nosti vremeni imperatora Pavla I* (Petrograd, 1916).

M. I. Bogdanovich, *Istoriia tsarstvovaniia Aleksandra I i Rossiia v ego vremia*, vols. I and III (St. Petersburg, 1869).

N. K. Shil'der *Imperator Aleksandr I, ego zhizn' i tsarstvovanie*, vols. I and II (St. Petersburg, 1904).

Plan gosudarstvennogo preobrazovaniia gr. M. M. Speranskogo, ed. *Russkaia Mysl'* (Moscow, 1905).

M. M. Speranskii, "O gosudarstvennykh ustanovleniiakh," *Arkhiv istoricheskikh i prakticheskikh svedenii otnosiakhchikhsia do Rossii*, ed. N. Kalachov, III (St. Petersburg, 1859), 15–59.

M. N. Korf, *Zhizn' gr. Speranskogo*, vol. I (St. Petersburg, 1861).

4. Some Internal Measures and Laws

In this section Karamzin touches upon only a few of the nearly five thousand legislative acts issued in the first decade of Alexander's reign.

MANIFESTO ON THE MILITIA . . . — This Manifesto came out on November 30, 1806, at a time when Napoleon, having defeated the Russo-Prussian armies, was threatening to invade Russia. It proclaimed a state of emergency in Russia, and instructed thirty-one provinces to raise a militia, composed of peasants and burghers, and commanded by the local gentry. The government hoped in this manner to raise an additional reserve force of 612,000 men, armed and equipped at the cost of the population. The provisions of this edict were never fully carried out, for the very reasons which Karamzin adduces: Russia's lack of experience with a levy en masse, and the shortage of weapons. In all, only eighteen provinces actually formed militia units of battalion strength, with a total manpower of 10,000. The Treaty of Tilsit, signed eight months after the promulgation of the Manifesto, removed the threat of a French invasion, and on September 27, 1807, the government suspended the further formation of militia units; the militia battalions already in existence were integrated into the regular army.[10]

GOVERNMENT SCHOLARSHIPS . . . — Karamzin first proposed the use of state scholarships as a means of encouraging the progress of learning in Russia in an article published in 1803, called "O vernom sposobe imet' v Rossii dovol'no uchitelei" ("Of the true method of obtaining in Russia enough teachers"), *Sochineniia Karamzina*, III (1848), 340–47.

UNIVERSITY COUNCIL . . . — Russia's educational system was reformed by the Act of January 26, 1803,[11] which centralized the administration of the school network throughout the country, and introduced a new principle according to which the higher educational institutions were responsible for the supervision of the lower schools in their district.

The whole instructional hierarchy was headed by a newly-formed MINISTRY OF EDUCATION. This Ministry supervised all the Russian universities, whose number was increased by two

[10] *Polnoe Sobranie Zakonov*, 1st ed., vol. XXIX, nos. 22,374, 22,380ff., 22,634, 22,636.

[11] *Ibid.*, vol. XXVII, no. 20,597.

with the founding of the Universities of KHARKOV and KAZAN. The universities, through their UNIVERSITY COUNCILS, were put in charge of the secondary schools in their district, and the secondary schools, in turn, in charge of the elementary schools. Article 17 of this law read: "The university will dispatch every year one or more members of its staff to inspect personally the schools in its department, and to investigate their progress." In addition, every university was ordered to found a PEDAGOGICAL INSTITUTE for the training of prospective school teachers (Article 39).

At the time when this law was passed, it was rumored that Alexander offered the directorship of the Ministry of Education to Karamzin and that Karamzin declined. If this report is correct, then Karamzin certainly refused this proposition not because he disapproved of Alexander's educational reform, but because he did not want to be distracted from his historical studies. In 1803, in an article called "O novom obrazovanii narodnogo prosveshcheniia v Rossii" ("On the new organization of popular schooling in Russia"), (Sochineniia Karamzina, III (1848), 348–58), he could not find enough words to praise these reforms. "All our new laws are wise and humanitarian," he wrote there, "but this edict on popular education is the *strongest* proof of the Monarch's divine goodness." (p. 352).

THE EXAMINATION ACT . . . — refers to an edict of August 6, 1809, called: "On the principles of promotion in the Civil Service, and on examinations in science for promotion to the ranks of Collegiate Assessor and Counselor of State," [12] which was prepared in utmost secrecy by Speranskii and Zavadovskii, the Minister of Education. The purpose of this law was not so much to promote learning, as to raise the quality of the Russian Civil Service. The modern Russian bureaucracy was originally established by Peter I on the principles of merit and seniority; according to his Table of Ranks noblemen and commoners were to be given equal opportunities of advancement in the state service, and a commoner, by attaining a certain

[12] *Ibid.*, vol. XXX, no. 23,771.

level in the service, was automatically to receive a patent of nobility. The gentry greatly disliked this feature of the Table of Ranks, and under Peter's successors exerted pressure on the government to grant them service on terms easier than those applicable to commoners. In the reign of Catherine II (1790), the government succumbed to these pressures, and passed a law which extended to the gentry important privileges in matters of civil service promotion, reducing for them the period during which it was necessary to work in one grade before being advanced to the next, and permitting them to transfer from the civil service to the military service without the customary reduction in rank. At the same time the lower bureaucracy, noble and common alike, succeeded in establishing the primacy of seniority over merit, with the result that advancement became dependent mainly on the length of service. Both these aberrations of the Petrine system of state service lowered considerably the quality of the Russian administration. It is this situation which the government wanted to correct by the law of 1809.

The Examination Act of 1809 placed hurdles in the path of bureaucratic advancement at that point where rank bestowed automatically noble status. It stipulated that no official, regardless of length of his service, was to receive promotion to the rank of COLLEGIATE ASSESSOR (Grade 8) unless able to present documentary proof from a university testifying that he had satisfactorily pursued higher studies or passed an examination on subjects relevant to the Civil Service. Promotion from the rank of Collegiate Assessor to that of COUNSELOR OF STATE was to take place as before, except that the candidate, in addition to having served the requisite number of years, was also to present proof of his qualifications including proof of university studies. The law now made it possible to promote officials directly from Grade 8 up to the rank of Counselor of State (Grade 5) by means of an examination, without regard to their seniority. The examination subjects which had to be passed by officials who were up for promotion were as follows: Russian, and one foreign language; natural law,

Roman law, civil law; economics; Russian and general history; geography; statistics, with particular emphasis on Russia; the rudiments of mathematics (arithmetic and geometry) and physics. Strictly speaking, neither GREEK nor CHEMISTRY was required, but it is true that the examination called for knowledge of a general kind rather than for evidence of specific skills. Karamzin, however, misconstrued the intent of the law, which was to raise the standards of the civil establishment, and to reintroduce the principle of personal merit where it had been all but stifled by birthright and seniority.

This law was never enforced, partly because of the difficulties inherent in it, partly because of the opposition of the bureaucracy.

5. Serfdom and the Problem of Emancipation

Alexander was much concerned with the condition of Russia's serf population, particularly at the beginning of his reign, and although he accomplished no vital improvement of its lot, he undertook a number of measures designed to abolish some of the most pernicious features of serfdom, and to pave the way toward an eventual emancipation.

The most important of such measures was the Law of Free Agriculturalists, originally conceived by Count S. P. Rumiantsev and issued in 1803.[13] This law permitted landlords to manumit their serfs, individually or by whole villages, on the basis of contractual agreements with their inhabitants, on the condition that the peasants receive an allotment of land as their property. Although in the entire reign of Alexander I it brought freedom to no more than some one hundred thousand serfs, it evoked sharp reactions from the gentry who feared that this measure would encourage their serfs to expect general emancipation by imperial decree. Karamzin had already criticized this law indirectly when it was issued in his "Pis'mo sel'skogo zhitelia" ("Letter of a country dweller") *Vestnik Evropy*, no. 17 (1803).

Another measure designed to improve the condition of the

[13] *Ibid.*, 1st ed., vol. XXVII, no. 20,620, dated February 20, 1803.

peasantry was a law which prohibited THE SALE AND THE PURCHASE OF RECRUITS. Beginning with the middle of the eighteenth century it had become customary for members of certain social groups, such as burghers and state peasants, to evade military service by substituting for themselves serfs purchased especially for that purpose from private landowners. This practice was widely recognized as one of the worst abuses of serfdom, and, beginning with Catherine II, the government made repeated if unsuccessful efforts to stop it. In 1770 it was forbidden to sell serfs without land within three months after the publication of the annual recruitment order.[14] Alexander tried to make the law even more stringent, and in 1804 issued an edict which instructed the armed forces to turn down serfs who had been sold without land in the preceding three years.[15] To circumvent this law, landlords took to selling peasants with a token quantity of land, and in 1810 the government had to issue a supplementary edict which outlawed the use of serfs as substitutes for a period of three years after they had been purchased, even if the purchase involved a transfer of land.[16]

Bibliography

The best history of the peasantry and the peasant question for this period is V. I. Semevskii's, *Krestianskii vopros v Rossii v XVIII i pervoi polovine XIX veka* (2 vols.; St. Petersburg, 1888).

6. Financial Policies

Following the example set by several contemporary European states, Russia in the eighteenth century began to experiment with paper currency. The purpose of this venture was twofold: to increase the quantity of money in circulation, and to help balance the budget. In view of the discrepancy between Russia's growing commercial and administrative needs on the one hand, and her shortage of precious metals on the other, the idea of using paper notes was sensible; but this

[14] *Ibid.*, vol. XIX, no. 13,483.
[15] *Ibid.*, vol. XXVIII, no. 21,442, dated September 7, 1804.
[16] *Ibid.*, vol. XXXI, no. 24,220; dated May 6, 1810.

form of legal tender was only imperfectly understood at that time, with the result that its introduction led everywhere to inflation, the disappearance of specie, and the rapid depreciation of the notes.

Russian paper currency, known as ASSIGNATS, grew out of the promissory notes introduced in Russia in the reign of Elizabeth. These promissory notes, then already known by the name of "assignats," had been used in commercial and financial transactions involving sums which could not be conveniently transferred in bullion form. The success and widespread acceptance of these notes induced Peter III to issue them also for general public use. On May 25, 1762, he ordered the establishment of a State Bank and the emission of five million rubles in notes, backed fully by copper. But Catherine II rescinded this order on the day she seized the throne, and it never took effect.

The first bank notes for general circulation were issued six years later, in 1768, when Catherine founded two State Banks for the emission of assignats, one in St. Petersburg, the other in Moscow. These banks were at first empowered to issue only notes of large denominations (twenty-five rubles or more) for commercial purposes, fully backed by copper deposited in their vaults. In 1782 Catherine, encouraged by the popularity of these notes and by their commercial advantages, ordered the Assignat Banks also to issue notes in denominations of five and ten rubles. At the same time she reduced the copper backing to correspond to the anticipated demand for redemption. The total quantity of Russian paper currency in 1786 was 46 million rubles, circulating side by side with specie and on a par with it.

Up to this time, the Russian government had issued paper currency only in order to facilitate commerce and provide Russia with additional media of exchange. But now, faced with serious budgetary difficulties, brought about by lengthy wars with the Ottoman Empire, it became sorely tempted to put assignats to another use, namely to help increase state revenue. In 1786 after prolonged deliberations, the government decided to issue 100 million rubles in paper, half of this sum for the redemption of the old assignats, the remainder partly to be held in reserve, and partly to be loaned on interest to the gentry and burghers. This measure was at best a calculated risk, because the treasury did not dispose of sufficient bullion or copper to back this emission; aware of this, Catherine publicly pledged under no circumstances to exceed the sum of 100 million rubles in paper. At the same time she ordered the merger of the two banks into a single Assignat Bank. The following year, when the treasury faced new deficits, the court gave it permission to spend for its current needs the entire reserve, as well as most of the money which had been set aside for loans.

In 1790, having failed to secure foreign loans, Catherine decided to renege on her recent pledge, and instructed the Bank of Assignats to issue additional paper currency, in excess of the self-imposed 100 million limit. This measure marked the beginning of the process of depreciation of the paper notes, which was to continue without interruption for twenty years, and eventually to reduce the purchasing power of the assignat to less than one fifth of its face value. In the last seven years of Catherine's reign (1790–1796), the printing presses poured forth a steady stream of assignats; at the time of her death they amounted to 157.7 million, with a par value of 107 million in silver. By now the treasury had gotten into the habit of covering approximately three fourths of its regular annual deficit by the issue of inconvertible paper money. The historical record thus does not warrant Karamzin's praise of Russian eighteenth-century fiscal policies. Chechulin, the historian of finances in the reign of Catherine II, considers Russian state finances from 1786 to 1796 to have been in a condition of total collapse.[17]

Karamzin is also mistaken when he asserts that Paul suspended the emission of assignats. Paul's government actually issued paper currency at the same rate as did Catherine's, in-

[17] N. D. Chechulin, *Ocherki po istorii russkikh finansov v tsarstvovanie Ekateriny II* (St. Petersburg, 1906).

creasing the quantity of assignats in circulation by 55 million, for a total, in 1801, of 212 million.

Russia's experience with paper money after 1786 was thus not too encouraging, although it must be recognized that Russian assignats held up far better than their French or North American counterparts. What had originally been conceived and successfully launched as a means of facilitating trade, became a means of making good the annual state deficits. The inflation which resulted from the excessive emission of assignats did not greatly harm the economy of the country as a whole, for Russia's economy was expanding, and her financial resources fell short of her commercial requirements, but it did cause a severe dislocation of state finances. The treasury was required by law to accept the paper ruble, which circulated on the market at two thirds or less of its face value, at its full face value when it was presented in payment of taxes and other revenues; but in making purchases for the army (which in some years consumed one half of the entire Russian budget), the treasury had to pay free market prices, calculated in terms of the silver ruble. The more paper money was printed to bridge the gap between revenues and expenditures, the quicker it depreciated, and the faster and steeper rose the price of goods which the government had to purchase; consequently, the sharper was the drop in real state income. In 1810, when the purchasing power of the assignat sunk to its lowest point, the treasury's nominal income was 257 million, while its real income, calculated in silver, amounted only to 79 million.

Upon his accession to the throne, Alexander suspended all further emissions of assignats, and in this manner he succeeded for a time in stabilizing their rate. But soon he too became involved in costly wars, and like his grandmother, finding himself unable to cover mounting deficits in any other manner, he had recourse to the printing press. Beginning with the War of the Third Coalition (1805), the Assignat Bank printed paper currency in quantities sufficient to give the budget the appearance of balance, and to enable the government to feed, clothe, and arm its military establishment. In the

winter of 1810–11, when Karamzin wrote the *Memoir,* there
were in circulation 577 million rubles in assignats (365 million of which had been issued in Alexander's reign), with a
par course of approximately five rubles in paper to one ruble
in silver. Abroad, the assignat ruble fetched at this time between 9 and 11 Dutch STIVERS in Amsterdam, and between
95 and 116 centimes (or 19–23 SOUS) in Paris.

The difficulties which the Russian treasury experienced from
the depreciation of paper currency and the flight of specie,
were temporarily compounded by a shortage of COPPER, Russia's principal coinage metal. This situation was partly due
to the impact of the bank notes on the Russian money market,
and partly to a sudden rise in the price of copper ingots in
Europe. Between 1802 and 1806 the price of copper rose from
11 rubles a pood (36 lbs.) to 17 and even 18½ rubles a pood,
whereas the treasury continued to mint copper coins at the
traditional ratio of 16 rubles to a pood. As a consequence of
this discrepancy between the price of copper in ingot and coin
form, copper coins began to disappear either because they were
melted down (usually to make alcoholic stills) or because they
were exported abroad. The mint also suffered considerable
losses from this situation: in 1803, when copper prices were
at their height, it cost the mint 120 kopeks to coin 85 kopeks.
This latter consideration induced the mint to curtail the emission of copper coins; as a result, between 1807 and 1809 Russia
experienced a severe shortage of small change.

By 1809, the condition of Russian finances was so desperate
that Alexander decided on a thorough review and reorganization of fiscal policies. He entrusted this task, like so many
others, to Speranskii. The final version of the Project of Financial Reform, which Speranskii submitted at the end of the
year, was the product of many hands. Ikonnikov, the biographer of Count Mordvinov, states that the original draft was
prepared by M. A. Balugianskii, a Hungarian-born jurist and
political scientist teaching in St. Petersburg; that it was re-
viewed and emended by Speranskii; and that finally it was discussed by a circle of statesmen, who met frequently at the

residence of Count Severin Potocki to examine Speranskii's reform projects. This circle consisted, in addition to Speranskii and the host, of Balugianskii, N. S. Mordvinov, V. P. Kochubei, B. B. Kampengauzen (V. S. Ikonnikov, *Graf N. S. Mordvinov*, St. Petersburg, 1873, p. 77).

The Financial Reform Project was submitted to the newly-created State Council in January 1810, at its very first session. At the basis of the Project lay a drastic redefinition of Russian paper currency. The authors of the Project declared that every expenditure of the treasury, which was not covered by revenue or guaranteed by state property, constituted, properly speaking, either a tax or a debt. Taxes and debts could be overt or hidden. Judged by this definition, assignats did not constitute a form of currency: "Assignats are notes founded upon assumptions. They are not trustworthy, and therefore represent nothing but a concealed debt." This debt the state must recognize, otherwise it is guilty of imposing surreptitiously a highly unfair form of taxation.

Proceeding from these premises, the Project recommended that the state recognize formally all assignats then in circulation as an indebtedness of the Russian government, that it promptly redeem and withdraw them from circulation, and that it recognize the silver ruble as Russia's main legal tender.

This Project was approved by Alexander and the State Council. It resulted in the promulgation of four important edicts, which constitute the target of Karamzin's criticism.

The Manifesto of February 2, 1810,[18] stated that all assignats in circulation represented an internal indebtedness of the Russian state. It promised that no more assignats would be issued, that future deficits would be met by means of regular internal loans, and that state expenditures would at once be reduced by 20 MILLION rubles. This Manifesto also increased certain taxes, including the soul-tax and the rent of state peasants, and imposed an extraordinary levy on burghers, artisans, serf-owners, and some categories of merchandise.

The second decree in this series limited officially the quan-

[18] *Polnoe Sobranie Zakonov*, vol. XXXI, no. 24,116.

tity of assignats to 577 million, the amount then in circulation.[19]

A third decree spelled out the measures which the government was to take in order to reduce and eventually withdraw all assignats from circulation. This was to be accomplished in two operations: the sale of state properties, and a public loan. The government set aside from its domains certain landed properties which were to be sold publicly in the course of the following five years; the money raised from these sales was to be used to redeem assignats. This transaction was to be carried out by a SPECIAL COMMISSION FOR THE LIQUIDATION OF THE DEBT. In addition, the government made provisions for citizens to submit their assignats to this commission, in exchange for regular, interest-bearing State Debentures. These debentures matured in 1817, and were then redeemable for silver or gold at the rate of 2 assignat rubles for one silver ruble.[20]

The fourth, and final, decree made the silver ruble Russia's main legal tender.[21]

The government hoped to raise enough money from the sale of its lands and the loan to enable it to withdraw the bulk of the assignats, but its hopes were quickly disappointed. The land sales, which began in 1811 and continued until the outbreak of the war the following year, raised less than 3 million assignat rubles, instead of the 40 million which they were expected to bring each year for five years. The failure of these sales was due to the absence of good surveys and descriptions of the properties offered for sale, and also to the cumbersome formalities connected with the transfer of titles of ownership from the state to private citizens. The 100 million ruble loan proved much more successful, because its terms were most advantageous to the subscribers, who were assured of receiving in six years a 150 per cent return on their investment: an investment of 2 paper rubles, worth 40 silver kopeks in 1810, was to bring 100 silver kopeks in 1817.

---

[19] *Ibid.*, vol. XXXI, no. 24,197, dated April 13, 1810.
[20] *Ibid.*, no. 24,244, dated May 27, 1810.
[21] *Ibid.*, no. 24,264, dated June 20, 1810.

The government at the same time took measures to alleviate the shortage of copper coins. In a Manifesto of August 29, 1810, it reformed the copper coinage, decreeing that henceforth a pood of copper would be minted into 24 rubles, instead of the customary 16.[22] While this reform was in progress, the international price of copper ingots fell sharply, enabling the mint to reduce further its losses in the manufacture of copper coins, although it was only in the 1830's that these losses were entirely wiped out.

It does not seem possible to ascertain the source of Karamzin's statement that in his time a pood of copper cost 40 rubles. Contemporary statistics indicate that copper in 1810 fetched $13\frac{1}{3}$ silver rubles a pood. It is possible that Karamzin had here in mind not silver but paper rubles; if so, he was inconsistent in applying, for the purpose of comparison, a silver standard to copper in coinage, and an assignat standard to copper in bulk. It is more likely that he was simply misinformed.

The fiscal reforms of 1810 did not greatly improve the condition of Russian finances, but they did put a temporary stop to the inflation, stabilize the exchange rate of assignats, and furnish the country with the requisite quantity of small change. Russia's gradual withdrawal from the Continental System, leading to a revival of her maritime trade, further improved the standing of the ruble. But in 1812, with the resumption of war, the government found itself compelled to revoke the 1810 reforms, and to resort once more to printing assignats. By 1818 the quantity of assignats in circulation reached an all-time high of 836 million rubles. Their emission was again suspended in 1821, and they were finally withdrawn from circulation in the reign of Nicholas I.

BÜSCH — Johann Georg (1728–1800), German mercantilist, author of numerous works, including *Abhandlung von dem Geldsumlauf in anhaltender Rücksicht auf die Staatswirtschaft und Handlung* (2 vols., Hamburg-Kiel, 1780), and *Sämtliche*

[22] *Ibid.*, no. 24,334.

Schriften über Banken und Münzwesen (Hamburg, 1801).

IUGRA (UGRA) — an area located in northeastern Russia, near the lower course of the River Ob. The term also applies to a Finnic tribe, now extinct, which had once lived there.

SPIRIT OF THE MANIFESTO — In the reign of Alexander I imperial manifestoes were often accompanied by commentaries, called *dukh zakona* (from the French *l'esprit du manifeste*).

THE MANIFESTO ON TARIFFS — issued on December 19, 1810,[23] ordered drastic cuts in the importation of foreign luxuries, especially textiles and foodstuffs, forbidding the importation of some, and imposing heavy duties on others. It remained in force until 1816. Article 26 of this Tariff exempted from confiscation all merchandise which had been imported before the Tariff went into effect, but it SET NO TIME LIMIT on the disposal of such goods.

KORENNOI USTAV — Karamzin apparently refers to a Manifesto issued on January 1, 1807[24] called "O darovannykh kupechestvu novykh vygodakh, otlichiiakh, preimushchestvakh i novykh sposobakh k rasprostraneniiu i usileniiu torgovykh predpriatii" ("On the granting of new benefits, distinctions, and privileges to merchants, and on the new means for the spread and strengthening of commercial undertakings").

Bibliography

R. Gonnard, *Histoire des doctrines monétaires* (Paris, 1936).

Ministerstvo Finansov, 1802–1902, vol. I (St. Petersburg, 1902).

I. S. Bliokh, *Finansy Rossii XIX stoletiia*, vol. I (St. Petersburg, 1882). Unreliable.

N. Brzheskii, *Gosudarstvennye dolgi Rossii* (St. Petersburg, 1884).

N. D. Chechulin, *Ocherki po istorii russkikh finansov v tsarstvovanie Ekateriny II* (St. Petersburg, 1906). Also publishe . serially in the *Zhurnal Ministerstva Narodnogo Prosveshcheniia* for 1904–06.

M. M. Speranskii, "Plan Finansov," *Sbornik Imperatorskogo Russkogo Istoricheskogo Obshchestva*, XLV (1885), 1–72.

Arkhiv Gosudarstvennogo Soveta, vol. I, part 2 (St. Petersburg, 1870).

P. A. Shtorkh, "Materialy dlia istorii gosudarstvennykh denezhnykh

[23] *Ibid.*, no. 24,464.
[24] *Ibid.*, XXIX, no. 22,418.

znakov v Rossii s 1653 po 1840 god," *Zhurnal Ministerstva Narodnogo Prosveshcheniia*, March 1868, pp. 772–847.

7. Codification of Russian Law

In 1810 Russia was, for all practical purposes, without a legal code. The most recent code, the *Ulozhenie* of Tsar Alexis, had been compiled in 1649, and by the time of Alexander was of purely academic interest. What effect this fact had on Russian administration and justice can be easily imagined. Neither officials nor judges possessed authoritative legal texts to guide them in the execution of their duties — a deficiency which encouraged even further the tendencies toward the arbitrary use of power which were inherent in the Russian political system of the time. Imperial manifestoes, as well as instructions issued by the Senate and the Synod, administrative measures, tariff acts, criminal statutes of various reigns, and many other kinds of legislative and judiciary acts, often contradictory, were all indiscriminately lumped together as "law." Even the Senate, the highest tribunal and the official repository of laws, was frequently unable to determine which laws applied to a given situation, while the lower courts lacked the basic means of rendering justice. This hindered the functioning of the Russian judiciary system, and violated the basic canon of the monarchic ideal of the time, which held that true royal authority rested on law.

All during the eighteenth century attempts were made to remedy this situation, and no less than nine separate commissions were appointed to compile a new code (1700, 1714, 1720, 1728, 1730, 1754, 1760, 1767, and 1797), but all of them failed to accomplish their task. One of the principal reasons for their failure was the absence in Russia of a clear distinction between general law (*jus*) and particular edicts (*leges*), since all legal acts were issued in the name of the Autocrat and possessed therefore equal legal status.[25] Codification, therefore, entailed

[25] This distinction was formally established only in 1906. *Cf.* G. F. Shershenevich, *Uchebnik russkogo grazhdanskogo prava* (7th ed.; St. Petersburg, 1909), p. 48.

considerably more than a compilation of existing laws: it entailed much positive lawmaking, for which the commissions lacked authority as well as qualified personnel.

Shortly after his accession to the throne, Alexander reorganized the ninth codificatory commission, originally appointed by his father; he put it under his own patronage, and entrusted the directorship over it to Count Zavadovskii. This arrangement also produced no positive results, and at the end of 1803 Alexander decided to vest the responsibility for codification in a NEW COMMISSION, which he now subordinated to the Ministry of Justice, and put in charge of Novosiltsev, a member of the Unofficial Committee and Deputy Minister of Justice. The actual work on the code was placed in the hands of the new commission's First Secretary, Baron G. A. Rozenkampf, a Livonian who had the requisite legal background, having studied law at Leipzig, but who unfortunately was severely handicapped in his work by his ignorance of the Russian language. Rozenkampf submitted a general plan of work, which Alexander approved, and spent the next five years assembling and sifting an enormous quantity of documents.

In August 1808 Alexander brought Speranskii into this work. He appointed him a member of the Codificatory Commission (which consisted of the Minister of Justice, Lopukhin, and his deputy, Novosiltsev) and gave him wide authority to deal with the problem. The following month, Alexander took Speranskii to the Erfurt Conference, and there introduced him to Talleyrand. Alexander also discussed the problem of codification with Napoleon. Talleyrand suggested that Speranskii contact Dupont de Nemours, and Napoleon further offered the services of two French jurisconsults, Jean-Guillaume Locré, who had prepared a project of the French Civil Code, and Philippe Legras, who had done similar work on the Commercial Code. These Frenchmen were later appointed corresponding members of the Russian Codificatory Commission, but their contribution did not go beyond a few letters of advice.

Upon his return from Erfurt, Speranskii was promoted to

the post of Deputy Minister of Justice, replacing Novosiltsev. Speranskii lacked formal training, but he possessed an inherent genius for law, as well as an uncommon capacity for work. In addition, he enjoyed at this time the unbounded confidence of the tsar, and felt free to tamper with laws to an extent which would have been inconceivable to his predecessors. With the help of assistants (among whom Rozenkampf was most active), Speranskii produced in two years the Project of a Civil Code.

In preparing this draft, Speranskii adopted a method entirely different from that followed by his predecessors. Instead of assembling first all the laws issued since 1649 in chronological order, then revising and classifying them, and last of all writing a systematic code, he began with the end-product, that is with the systematic code. In so doing, he seems to have been inspired by two motives: a general feeling of contempt for Russian law, which he considered barbarian, and a desire to avoid the fate of his predecessors who had drowned in a sea of legal documents. For his model he took the *Code Napoléon*.

The first part of the Civil Code, treating of persons, and written by Rozenkampf under Speranskii's supervision, was ready at the end of 1809, and soon afterwards came before the State Council. At this time the status of the Codificatory Commission was once more changed: the Commission was withdrawn from the jurisdiction of the Ministry of Justice, and placed under that of the Council of State. Speranskii was now made its Director in Chief. In the course of its deliberations, the Council submitted the Project to some gentle criticism. A year later Speranskii presented the Project of the Second Part of the Civil Code, dealing with property laws. On December 14, 1810, both parts of the Project were printed.[26]

Karamzin was in an advantageous position to secure data on the work of the Codificatory Commission because at the time when he was working on the *Memoir* the Ministry of Justice was headed by one of his oldest and closest friends, the poet

---

[26] *Proekt grazhdanskogo ulozheniia Rossiiskoi Imperii* (2 vols.; St. Petersburg, 1810).

I. I. Dmitriev. In a letter which he wrote in December 1810 he asked Dmitriev, without telling him the reason for his request:

Send me as soon as possible all that your office publishes by New Year's and after on the subject of legislation, public education, and so forth. Of course, I am only asking for what is printed, public, and nothing else.[27]

Dmitriev apparently sent Karamzin the printed texts of both parts of the Civil Code Project, which had appeared eleven days earlier, and perhaps also some additional documents. With these materials in his possession, Karamzin had little difficulty in subjecting the Project to a devastating critique.

The first part of the Project begins with a chapter on the CIVIL RIGHTS of Russian subjects, and corresponds to the opening chapters of the *Code Napoléon*. The only sections of this part which Karamzin cites have to do with the loss of civil rights. The complete text of the French reads: "Les condamnations à des peines dont l'effet est de priver celui qui est condamné de toute PARTICIPATION AUX DROITS CIVILS CI-APRÈS exprimés, emporteront la mort civile" ("The imposition of a penalty the effect of which is to deprive the condemned of all participation in the civil rights enumerated below, implies civil death"). (Article 22 of the *Code Napoléon*.) The passage which Karamzin cites from the Russian Project reads in full: "A person deprived of civil rights cannot appear in court either as plaintiff or as defendant." (Civil Code Project of 1810, Article 12, Paragraph 6). This corresponds to a clause of Article 25 of the *Code Napoléon*, which reads in full: "Il ne peut procéder en justice, ni en défendant, ni en demandant, que sous le nom et par le ministère d'un curateur spécial qui lui est nommé par le tribunal où l'action est portée." ("He cannot undertake legal action, either as defendant or as plaintiff, except in the name and through the agency of a special curator nominated for him by the tribunal concerned with the action.")

[27] *Pis'ma N. M. Karamzina k I. I. Dmitrievu* (St. Petersburg, 1866), p. 136. Letter dated December 21, 1810.

The remainder of Karamzin's critique applies to Part 2 of the Project.[28]

The passage dealing with the distinctions between movable and immovable property beginning with the words LES GLACES, quoted by Karamzin, is from Article 525 of the *Code Napoléon*. It reads, in translation: "The mirrors of an apartment are considered immovable when the floor to which they are attached is joined to the woodwork. . . . As far as statues are concerned, they constitute immovable property when placed in niches executed specifically for that purpose, even when they can be removed without either breakage or wear." The corresponding passage in the Russian Project was apparently removed as a result of discussions in the Council of State, for it is not to be found in the revised 1814 edition.

ALLUVION is a legal term which denotes the extension of land, such as riverbanks or seashores, by the gradual accretion of matter; according to the *Code Napoléon*, Article 556, it belongs to the proprietor of the land which borders on the water. This item corresponds to Article 45, Part 2, of the 1810 project: "The extension of shores resulting from the accumulation of land, or the gradual recession or ebbing of waters, accrues to the owners of the adjoining land, with the exception of the towpaths mentioned previously."

CONSEIL DE FAMILLE — this institution was introduced under the name *semeistvennyi sovet* in the section dealing with guardianship (Articles 425 ff.). In the *Code Napoléon* it is treated in Articles 389 ff.

"A STILLBORN CHILD DOES NOT INHERIT," is in Article 103, Part 2, of the 1810 Project. Karamzin quotes from Article 725 of the French Code.

The expression LOZHE REKI (river bed) appears in Article

---

[28] Part 2 of the Civil Law Project of 1810 in its original version is available at the *Tsentral'nyi Gosudarstvennyi Istoricheskii Arkhiv* in Leningrad, and at the Lenin Library in Moscow. The *Arkhiv Gosudarstvennogo Soveta, Zhurnaly po delam Departamenta Zakonov*, vol. IV, part 1 (St. Petersburg, 1874), contains this part only in its second edition, that of 1814; this was the only edition at my disposal.

51. It is considered today acceptable, if archaic. (A thorough critique of the language, used in the 1810 Project was made, from his own linguistic viewpoint, by Shishkov in the State Council.)[29]

KORMCHAIA KNIGA — (*Nomokanon*), a collection of church and state laws, together with amendments and additions, originally adopted by the Orthodox Slavs from Byzantium.

THE LAW DEALING WITH THE DIVISION OF LANDED PROPERTY. — The second part of the Code Project contained elaborate provisions dealing with inheritance. It specified, among other things, that sons were to receive four times the share of daughters, and twice the share of the surviving parent (Articles 158 ff.).

Speranskii went into exile before the Code Project was formally approved, but the Commission which he had directed survived and continued to function. In 1814 and 1815 the various projects which it had prepared both during and since Speranskii's tenure of office were submitted to the State Council. This time they came under detailed and rather severe criticism. By now it became obvious that no progress could be made along the lines charted by Speranskii in 1809–10, and his projects were shelved.

Efforts at codification were resumed upon the accession of Nicholas I in 1826, and this time at long last brought to a successful conclusion. The direction of this task was once more entrusted to Speranskii, rehabilitated from his disgrace, and working as a member of the Imperial Chancery. This time, Speranskii followed an entirely different plan. In fact, he now adhered to a schedule virtually identical with that which, unknown to him, Karamzin had suggested in the *Memoir*. He first assembled all the laws in chronological order, in the *Polnoe Sobranie Zakonov;* he then proceeded to arrange them systematically in the *Svod Zakonov;* and he intended to crown the undertaking with a complete systematic code, which would have eliminated all anachronistic laws and filled the existing

[29] *Arkhiv Gosudarstvennogo Soveta, Zhurnaly po delam Departamenta Zakonov,* vol. IV, part 1, 100–19.

gaps with new laws, but Nicholas vetoed this final step. The successful completion of this enormous undertaking was the greatest achievement of Speranskii's long career of state service.

UNIFORM LAWS — In the Russian Empire in the eighteenth and first half of the nineteenth century, certain territories and nations continued to enforce all or parts of their native legal systems. In the reign of Alexander I, they were: Poland (French Civil Code), Finland (Swedish Code of 1734), the Baltic provinces, Georgia (the Code of Vakhtang), and the Little Russian provinces of Poltava and Chernigov, where certain disputes over property rights were settled according to the Lithuanian statute. The report of the Codificatory Commission of 1803 recognized the desirability of retaining a certain diversity of laws, and urged a careful review of the advantages and disadvantages of local laws in every area of the empire, but this issue was ignored in the Projects of 1810.

Bibliography

Arkhiv Gosudarstvennogo Soveta, vol. IV, *Zhurnaly-po delam Departamenta Zakonov,* part 1 (St. Petersburg, 1874). Contains texts of Speranskii's Code Projects, and accounts of discussions in the State Council.

S. V. Pakhman, *Istoriia kodifikatsii grazhdanskogo prava,* vol. I, (St. Petersburg, 1876).

V. N. Latkin, *Uchebnik istorii russkogo prava perioda Imperii (XVIII–XIX st.)* (2nd ed.; St. Petersburg, 1909).

L. A. Kasso, "K istorii svoda zakonov grazhdanskikh," *Zhurnal Ministerstva Iustitsii,* X (March 1904), part 2, pp. 53–89.

N. V. Kalachov, "O znachenii Karamzina v istorii russkogo zakonodatel'stva," *Besedy v obshchestve liubitelei rossiiskoi slovesnosti pri Imperatorskom Moskovskom Universitete,* Vypusk 1 (Moscow, 1867), Prilozhenie 1, pp. 1–23.

SELECTED BIBLIOGRAPHY

The bibliography which follows is supplemented by the specialized bibliographies appended to the Notes and Comments section. The first part deals with Karamzin, the second with the general historical literature on the subject matter of this book. The system of transliteration is based on that of the Library of Congress, with the ligatures and diacritical marks omitted.

Part One: KARAMZIN

Primary Sources

The handiest edition of Karamzin's works is the fifth, issued by A. Smirdin as part of a standard series of Russian authors: *Sochineniia Karamzina* (3 vols.; St. Petersburg, 1848); it contains the poetry, short stories and essays, as well as the *Letters of a Russian Traveler*. This edition is far from complete, and suffers, in addition to incompleteness, from many imperfections caused either by censorship or by faulty editing, but until a better one is issued it will have to do. Smirdin's edition is implemented by L. Polivanov's *Izbrannye sochineniia N. M. Karamzina*, vol. I (Moscow, 1884), which contains Karamzin's early writings (1783–1801), some of which are extremely scarce. During World War I the Russian Academy of Sciences undertook to publish a definitive edition of Karamzin's works, but the Revolution interrupted this effort, and only the first volume, edited by V. V. Sipovskii and containing the poetry, ever came out: *Sochineniia Karamzina*, vol. I (Petrograd, 1917); it is greatly to be preferred to the corresponding volume in the Smirdin set.

The *History of the Russian State* went through numerous editions, of which the fifth is generally considered the best: *Istoriia Gosudarstva Rossiiskogo*, ed. P. Einerling (3 vols.; St. Petersburg, 1842–43). This edition has an index prepared by P. Stroev, *Kliuch . . . k Istorii Gosudarstva Rossiiskogo N. M. Karamzina* (St. Petersburg, 1844).

The different versions of the *Memoir on Ancient and Modern Russia* are listed in the section dealing with the history of the text.

Of other editions of Karamzin's writings the following are of the greatest importance: *Neizdannye sochineniia i perepiska Nikolaia Mikhailovicha Karamzina*, vol. I (St. Petersburg, 1862) (no more volumes published), and his letters to his life long friend Dmitriev, *Pis'ma N. M. Karamzina k I. I. Dmitrievu* (St. Petersburg, 1866), superbly edited by Ia. Grot and P. Pekarskii. The *Moskovskoi Zhurnal* (Moscow, 1791–92) and the *Vestnik Evropy* (Moscow, 1802–03) contain writings from the pen of Karamzin, many of them not included in his collected works. Of the other correspondence, one may mention the letters to A. I. Turgenev (*Russkaia Starina*, vol. XCVII, 1899, pp. 211–38, 463–80, 707–16), P. A. Viazemskii (*Starina i Novizna*, Moscow, 1897, book 1, part 2, pp. 1–204), and Malinovskii: *Pis'ma Karamzina k A. F. Malinovskomu*, N. M. Longinov, ed. (Moscow, 1860).

Finally, one should note the original version of Karamzin's eulogy of Catherine II, rich in political opinions, *Istoricheskoe pokhval'noe slovo Ekaterine vtoroi* (Moscow, 1802) as well as a condensed translation of the *Letters of a Russian Traveler, 1789–90*, by F. Jonas (New York, 1957).

Secondary Sources

Bibliographies

The most complete bibliographies of Karamziniana are by S. I. Ponomarev, "Materialy dlia bibliografii literatury o N. M. Karamzine," *Sbornik otdeleniia Russkogo iazyka i slovesnosti Imperatorskoi Akademii Nauk*, vol. XXXII, no. 8 (1883), and by S. A. Vengerov, *Istochniki slovaria russkikh pisatelei*, II (St. Petersburg, 1910), 586–98.

Biographies

There is no definite biography of Karamzin. The closest approximation is M. Pogodin's *Nikolai Mikhailovich Karamzin* (2 vols.; Moscow, 1866), but this book is a collection of raw materials (*nota bene* often unreliably edited) rather than a proper biographical study. V. V. Sipovskii's *N. M. Karamzin — avtor 'Pisem russkogo puteshestvennika'* (St. Petersburg, 1899), contains in addition to a thorough study of the literary sources of the *Letters of a Russian Traveler* also a wealth of information on the life and thoughts of Karamzin in the first thirty years of his life. But in the case of Sipovskii, ás in that of Pogodin, the biographer's diligence exceeds his powers of analysis, and the end-product is unsatisfactory. There is a good brief account of Karamzin's life by K. Bestuzhev-Riumin in the *Russkii biograficheskii slovar'*, Volume "Ibak — Kliucharev" (St. Petersburg, 1897), pp. 500–14.

Of the other biographical and critical studies of Karamzin, the following are worthy of mention (listed in chronological order of appearance):

A. [V] Starchevskii, *Nikolai Mikhailovich Karamzin* (St. Petersburg, 1849).

P. A. Viazemskii, *Polnoe sobranie sochinenii*, VII (St. Petersburg, 1882), 133–57, and *passim*.

Simbirskii iubilei N. M. Karamzina (Simbirsk, 1867); contains among other things, an inferior biographical essay by N. N. Bulich.

E. A. Solov'ev, *N. M. Karamzin* (St. Petersburg, 1894).

N. S. Tikhonravov, "Chetyre goda iz zhizni Karamzina," *Sochineniia*, III, part 1 (Moscow, 1898), 258–75; deals with the years 1785–1789.

Ia. K. Grot, "Ocherk deiatel'nosti i lichnosti Karamzina," *Trudy Ia. K. Grota*, III (St. Petersburg, 1901), 120–66.

V. I. Pokrovskii, ed., *Nikolai Mikhailovich Karamzin, ego zhizn' i sochineniia* (Moscow, 1908).

A. A. Kizevetter, "N. M. Karamzin," *Russkii Istoricheskii Zhurnal*, books 1–2 (1917), pp. 9–26.

Some Special Studies

The most thorough analysis of Karamzin's political ideas comes from the pen of W. Mitter, "Die Entwicklung der politischen Anschaungen Karamzins," *Forschungen zur Osteuropäischen Geschichte*, II (Berlin, 1955), 165–285. There is a critical account, from a liberal viewpoint, by A. N. Pypin, *Obshchestvennoe dvizhenie v Rossii pri Aleksandre I* (St. Petersburg, 1908), pp. 183–260, and by I. A. Linnichenko, "Politicheskie vozzreniia N. M. Karamzina," *Golos minuvshego*, No. 1 (Moscow, 1917), pp. 116–34. *Cf.* also R. Pipes, "Karamzin's conception of the Monarchy," *Russian Thought and Politics — Harvard Slavic Studies*, IV (Cambridge, Mass., 1957), 35–58.

Karamzin's historical views and contributions were first treated in a thorough manner by S. M. Solov'ev, "N. M. Karamzin i ego 'Istoriia Gosudarstva Rossiiskogo,'" *Sobranie sochinenii S. M. Solov'eva* (St. Petersburg, n.d.), pp. 1389–1540. There is a highly critical analysis by P. Miliukov in his *Glavnye techeniia russkoi istoricheskoi mysli* (St. Petersburg, 1913), pp. 128–224. The most recent study is by R. Bächtold, *Karamzins Weg zur Geschichte*, published in *Basler Beiträge zur Geschichtswissenschaft*, vol. 23 (Basel, 1946).

On Karamzin's linguistics and the controversy with Shishkov the best study is still by Ia. K. Grot, "Karamzin v istorii russkogo literaturnogo iazyka," *Trudy Ia. K. Grota*, II (St. Petersburg, 1899), 46–98.

Part Two: GENERAL WORKS

General Histories of the Reign of Alexander I

The standard histories of the period of Alexander I are: M. I. Bogdanovich, *Istoriia tsarstvovaniia Imperatora Aleksandra I i Rossii v ego vremia* (6 vols.; St. Petersburg, 1869–71), outdated but still useful, and N. K. Shil'der, *Imperator Aleksandr I, ego zhizn' i tsarstvovanie* (4 vols.; St. Petersburg, 1904–05); *cf.* also Velikii kniaz' Nikolai Mikhailovich, *Imperator Aleksandr I, opyt istoricheskogo issledovaniia* (2 vols.; St. Petersburg, 1912).

Political Ideas and Institutions

On the eighteenth-century antecedents of conservative thought the most useful books are biographies of leading proponents of autocratic ideas: G. Gurvich, *"Pravda voli monarshei" Feofana Prokopovicha i ee zapadnoevropeiskie istochniki* (Iurev, 1915); N. I. Popov, *V. N. Tatishchev i ego vremia* (Moscow, 1861); and the works of D. A. Korsakov: *Iz zhizni russkikh deiatelei XVIII veka* (Kazan, 1891), "A. P. Volynskii," *Drevniaia i novaia Rossiia*, book I (1876) and books I and III (1877), and, above all, his masterly *Votsarenie Imperatritsy Anny Ivannovny* (Kazan, 1880).

On the so-called senatorial opposition in Alexander's time, see G. G. Tel'berg, *Pravitel'stvuiushchii Senat i samoderzhavnaia vlast' v nachale XIX veka* (Moscow, 1914), and A. N. Fateev, "Politicheskie napravleniia pervogo desiatiletiia XIX veka v bor'be za Senat," *Sbornik Russkogo Instituta v Prage*, I (Prague, 1929), 205–60.

On institutions, one may consult the standard studies of Russian constitutional law by Gradovskii, Korkunov, and Lazarevskii (*cf.* above, p. 233).

The Gentry

The best history of the Russian gentry is by A. Romanovich-Slavatinskii, *Dvorianstvo v Rossii ot nachala XVIII v. do otmeny krepostnogo prava* (2nd ed.; Kiev, 1912). The following works are also useful:

M. Iablochkov, *Istoriia dvorianskogo sosloviia v Rossii* (St. Petersburg, 1876).

S. A. Korf, *Dvorianstvo i ego soslovnoe upravlenie* (St. Petersburg, 1906).

V. Kliuchevskii, *Istoriia soslovii v Rossii* (Moscow, 1914).

Cultural Life

There is an excellent history of Russian literature in the eighteenth century by G. A. Gukovskii, *Russkaia literatura XVIII veka* (Moscow, 1939). On cultural currents in the reign of Alexander, including a discussion of Karamzin, see A. N. Pypin, *Obshchestvennoe dvizhenie v Rossii pri Aleksandre I* (St. Petersburg, 1908).

On the Masonic circles, there is the brilliant monograph of M. N. Longinov, *Novikov i moskovskie Martinisty* (Moscow, 1867), and two more general histories, A. N. Pypin's *Russkoe Masonstvo XVIII i pervaia chetvert' XIX veka* (Petrograd, 1916), and G. Vernadskii's *Russkoe Masonstvo v tsarstvovanie Ekateriny II* (Petrograd, 1917); see also Ia. L. Barskov, *Perepiska moskovskikh masonov XVIII veka, 1780–1792*

(Petrograd, 1915) and V. Bogoliubov, *N. I. Novikov i ego vremiia* (Moscow, 1916).

Memoirs, Biographies, Correspondence

I. N. Bozherianov, *Velikaia kniaginia Ekaterina Pavlovna* (St. Petersburg, 1888).

I. I. Dmitriev, *Vzgliad na moiu zhizn'*, in *Sochineniia*, vol. II (St. Petersburg, 1895).

M. A. Korf, *Zhizn' grafa Speranskogo* (2 vols.; St. Petersburg, 1861).

M. Raeff, *Michael Speransky, statesman of imperial Russia, 1772–1839* (The Hague, 1957).

E. Kovalevskii, *Graf Bludov i ego vremia* (St. Petersburg, 1866).

Grand Duke Nikolai Mikhailovich, ed., *Correspondance de l'Empereur Alexandre Ier avec sa soeur la Grande-Duchesse Catherine* (St. Petersburg, 1910).

P. Pekarskii, ed., *Istoricheskie bumagi sobrannye Konstantinom Ivanovichem Arsen'evym* (St. Petersburg, 1872).

INDEX

References to the text of Karamzin's *Memoir* are in italics; indirect references are in brackets.

RICHARD PIPES was born in Poland, where he lived until 1939. He has taught at Harvard since 1946 in the field of Russian History. Among his books are SOCIAL DEMOCRACY AND THE ST. PETERSBURG LABOR MOVEMENT and FORMATION OF THE SOVIET UNION.

Atheneum Paperbacks

HISTORY

HISTORY—ASIA

Atheneum Paperbacks

HISTORY—AMERICAN—BEFORE 1900

Atheneum Paperbacks

HISTORY–AMERICAN–1900 TO THE PRESENT

Atheneum Paperbacks

STUDIES IN AMERICAN NEGRO LIFE

Atheneum Paperbacks

TEMPLE BOOKS—*The Jewish Publication Society*

PHILOSOPHY AND RELIGION

Atheneum Paperbacks

THE NEW YORK TIMES BYLINE BOOKS

THE ADAMS PAPERS

ECONOMICS AND BUSINESS

PHYSICAL SCIENCES AND MATHEMATICS

Atheneum Paperbacks

LITERATURE AND THE ARTS